HOW TO PAINT DABBLING DUCKS

A Guide to Materials, Tools, and Technique

David Mohrhardt

Stackpole Books

Published by
STACKPOLE BOOKS
Cameron and Kelker Streets
P.O. Box 1831
Harrisburg, PA 17105

First Edition

10 9 8 7 6 5 4 3 2 1

Cover and series design by Tracy Patterson

Mohrhardt, David.
How to paint dabbling ducks: a guide to materials, tools, and technique / David Mohrhardt.—1st ed.
p. cm.
Includes bibliographical references.
ISBN 0-8117-3010-7
1. Ducks in art. 2. Artists' materials. 3. Artists' tools.
4. Painting—Technique. I. Title.
ND1380.M58 1991
751.4'2—dc20 90-38135
CIP

Printed in Hong Kong

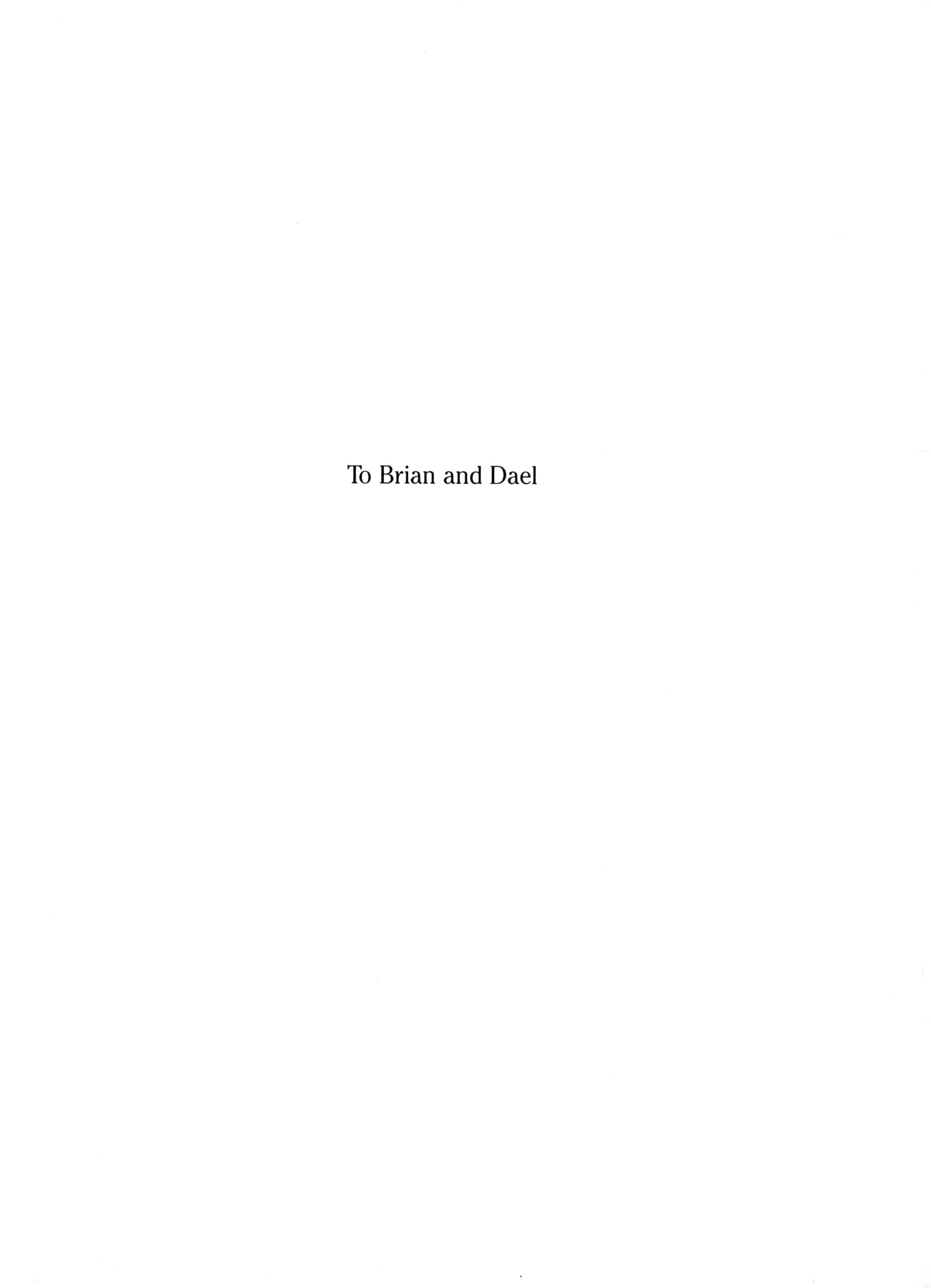

To Brian and Dael

Contents

Introduction

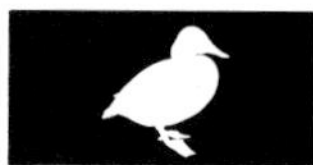

The sight of a duck with its head submerged and its tail pointed upward, or of a duck swimming with its head held low so its bill dabbles in the water instantly identifies a duck as a dabbler. Their methods of feeding and their preference for ponds or rivers has earned dabbling ducks a variety of nicknames: tip-up ducks, puddle ducks, river ducks, and dipping ducks are only a few. The head-down tail-up position enables dabblers to feed on shallow, submerged plants, while the bill strains large amounts of water and captures small plants and organisms. Dabblers not only congregate in large flocks to feed in water, they also gather on land where they prefer to eat waste grain. Dabblers normally do not dive beneath the surface; when extremely frightened, however, especially during the molt, they are capable of diving for short periods of time.

Dabblers can land on small bodies of water and then use their powerful wings to rise almost vertically from land or water. Thus, they are able to feed and nest in and around almost any size body of fresh water—from weedy roadside ponds to flowing rivers. A common spring and summer sight is a female dabbler out for a stroll or swim with her young in tow.

The migration brings groups of dabblers together and, in flight, they may form a loose V or fly in a disorganized group. Whichever form they take, they are strong fliers crossing great distances from summer nesting grounds to wintering areas.

Dabbling ducks are similar in basic body and wing shapes but have diverse colorations and head and tail configurations. Males exhibit most of the color variations while females have a much more consistent appearance. Females are more muted in color and their initial impression is one of brown or gray with no distinguishing patterns. It would be misleading, however, to simplify the coloration of females in this way because individual feather patterns and subtle color changes are beautiful and complex.

In the painting examples, this book will concentrate on males because of their striking patterns, coloration, and ease of recognition. The sections on anatomical features and study drawings apply to females as well as males, and the information in these sections will lead to a greater understanding of dabbling ducks.

The discussions of paints, brushes, and tools will help you choose the materials needed to begin painting. The color painting examples use techniques that, when mastered, will enable you to successfully paint any dabbling duck.

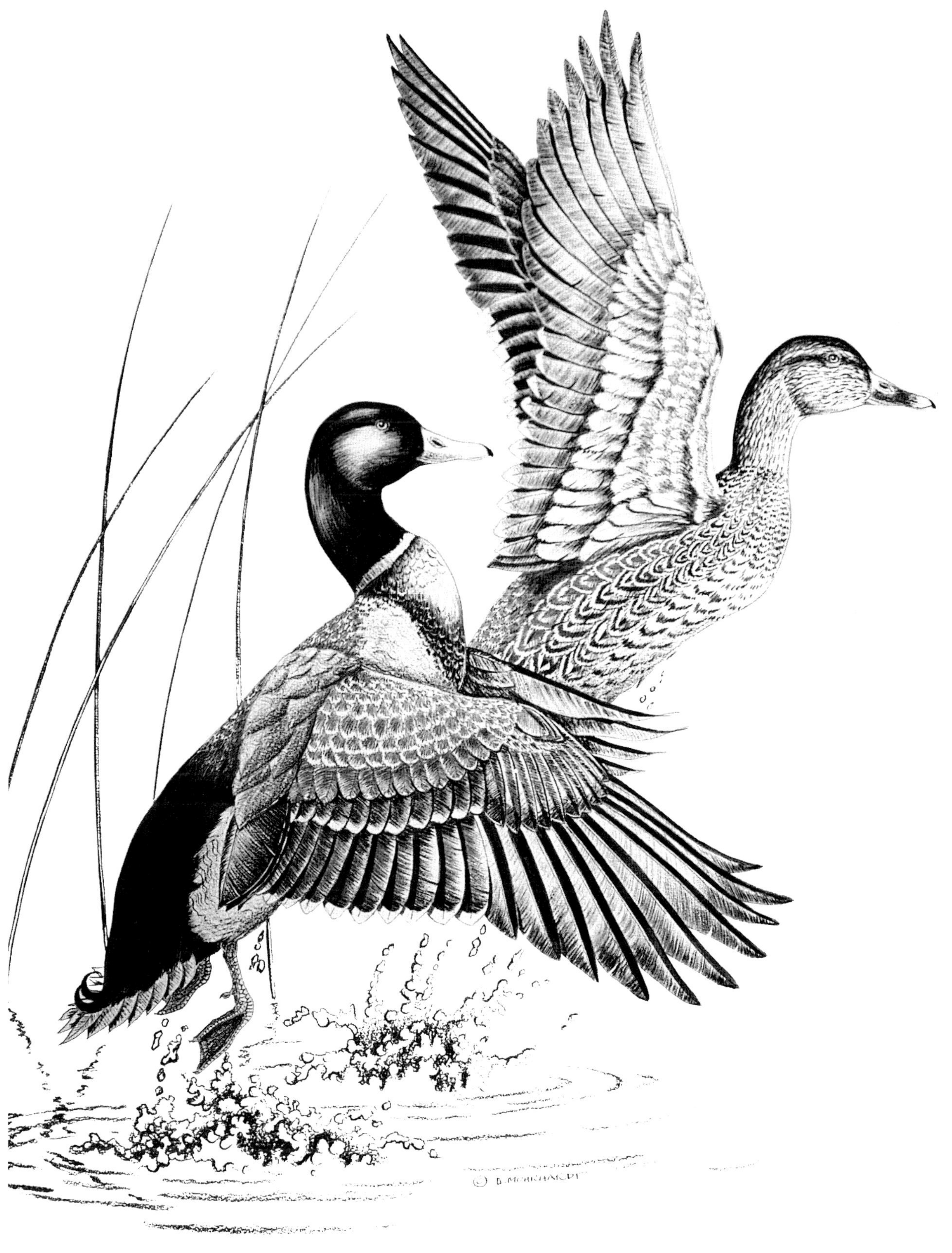

1
Painting Mediums

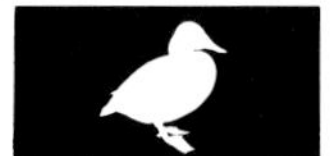

Many mediums may be used in bird painting; however, two in particular—gouache (opaque watercolor, designers colors) and acrylics—are used more frequently and with greater success by most wildlife artists. These two mediums, although dissimilar in some respects, are alike in others. They are both water-soluble, have good covering ability, dry rapidly, and may be used opaquely or transparently.

Oil paints and transparent watercolors are beautiful mediums, but they do not lend themselves easily to bird painting. Oils require oil solvents as a thinner, are rather thick to work with, and dry quite slowly. They may be used thinly, but this technique requires a great deal of experience. The newer water-based "oil" paints are thinned by water but work in a manner similar to traditional oils. Conversely, transparent watercolors are applied very thinly and dry quickly. Their great disadvantage is their inherent transparency, which means that it is hard to cover one color with another, and mistakes are difficult to correct.

A word of caution here: whichever medium you choose, keep in mind that many of the pigments used are toxic or carcinogenic in one degree or another. This does not mean that under normal conditions painting is hazardous to your health; it means that you should use common sense. After painting, wash your hands before eating or smoking, or any time there is excess paint on your hands, because some toxic materials may be absorbed through the skin. And *never* point your brush by putting it in your mouth.

You can purchase a wide variety of premixed colors, but it is wise to buy only a few basic ones (red, yellow, blue, green, black, white, raw umber, burnt sienna), work with them, and then buy additional colors as needed. Whether you are a beginner or an expert, painting is easier with a limited palette.

Color mixing in any medium is almost an art in itself. It is best to familiarize yourself with the basics of colors and color mixing by getting a beginner's book on color theory and then experimenting, blending colors to obtain the best results. When you obtain a desired color, either while experimenting or while painting, make a note of which colors were mixed to obtain that color. Never trust your memory; later you may try to duplicate a particular color and be unsuccessful. Making color notes is tedious but worthwhile.

Gouache

Gouache is the easiest medium to work with because of its forgiving qualities; its opaqueness allows mistakes and corrections to be made and the paint remains workable even when dry, permitting you to blend and scrub out colors.

Gouache may be used thinly to give a very transparent color, layers of color may be built up, or it may be used in a completely opaque manner with darks over lights, or vice versa. Whichever effect you choose, it's all done by adding water to the concentrated pigment. Gouache should not be used too thickly, however, or it will crack.

Dry gouache paint has a matte, nonglossy finish and great visual weight. It is available in a wide variety of colors but, as with most pigments, the degree of *light-fastness* (permanence) can vary widely. Most color charts have a key that indicates the light-fastness of the various colors. The ratings are: Excellent (E); Very Good (V); Good (G); and Fugitive (F). For art that is to last, never use any colors below the Very Good rating.

Not only does the permanence of colors vary, but colors with the same name from different manufacturers can have very different color values, particularly in the earth tones. Familiarize yourself with the color differences between the brands by looking at color charts. These are available free or at a nominal cost from the manufacturers or art-supply stores. Then choose the colors and brands with which you are most comfortable. When you look at the color charts you will notice the great variety among the basic colors (reds, yellows, blues, and so on), but don't ignore the blacks—they have their own color characteristics. *Ivory* (bone) *black* has a brownish tone, *lamp black* has a bluish tone, and *mars* (jet) *black* is a deep velvet black. When mixed with other colors or white they can give very different results.

Gouache may be purchased in tubes, cakes, or jars. Tube gouache is the most readily available. Paints in tubes and jars remain workable for a long period of time as long as the caps are kept securely in place. The key is to keep air away from the paint, especially in tubes where the paint is more viscous than in jars or cakes. After squeezing paint from a tube, whether transparent watercolor, oil, acrylic, or gouache, never squeeze the sides of the tube to suck the paint back in—this only invites excess air into the tube and accelerates drying in the tube. With gouache and acrylics, it is advisable to put the colors on the palette only as you need them because they will dry out on the palette. Gouache may be worked when dry, but acrylic will dry completely, rendering it useless.

A shortcoming of gouache is that because it remains water-soluble even when dry, it is possible for one color already painted to bleed into a second color applied over it, if the second color is worked too much with the brush. Even when dry, the surface of gouache will rub off slightly with vigorous movement, so it is advisable to place a small piece of paper under that part of your hand that is touching the art so that traces of color already applied are not picked up and dragged around.

Despite the minor disadvantages of gouache, it is still the most versatile and easiest medium to use in bird painting on flat surfaces and is the choice of beginners and experts alike.

Gouache Mediums

Gum arabic is the basic binder used in the manufacture of gouache. It is also used, in small quantities, to increase the transparency of gouache and impart a slight gloss to the normally matte finish. It is most commonly available in small jars.

Ox gall is made from the bladder of oxen. This natural wetting agent is the best material to increase the uniform flow of gouache, particularly in washes. Only small amounts are used, and it is available in small jars.

Acrylics

As mentioned previously, gouache and acrylics have much in common: rapid drying time, water solubility, and opaque or transparent use. But there the major similarities end. Although acrylics and gouache are both suitable for painting on flat surfaces, acrylics are best for painting birds in the round, whether wood or clay. The basic color selection of acrylic colors is not as broad as that for gouache, and acrylics are only available in tubes and jars.

Again, color charts should be consulted to familiarize yourself with the colors available. The consistency of paint between tubes and jars is quite different; the paint in jars is less viscous and easier to thin to a flowing or brushing consistency.

One of the difficulties that a beginner encounters is achieving the proper working consistency for acrylics. Whereas gouache cannot be used thickly, acrylics may be used from a transparent wash to a thick impasto; obviously, the working consistencies can vary widely. A rather disconcerting quality of acrylics, especially for beginners, is that even though they may appear opaque and dense on the palette, they work very thinly on the painting surface so it may take two or three applications of paint to achieve a solid color, if indeed that is your intent.

The short drying time of acrylics cannot be overemphasized. When acrylics dry, they are *dry;* they become extremely hard and are not water-soluble. This means that wet-in-wet blending between colors must be done while the paints are still workable. A blended or shaded effect may be achieved, however, if a graded wash is put on over an already dry color (see Techniques). The hard nonsoluble surface is a distinct advantage when applying glazes (thin washes of other colors) or other solid colors over an already painted surface because the paints will not bleed into one another. The surface of dry acrylics will not rub off, thus your painting hand won't drag colors around.

Acrylics have excellent permanence and may be used on virtually any surface. A ground coat of gesso is necessary on many surfaces, especially canvas, wood, and clay. The colors have great visual weight and look juicier and brighter than gouache; the surface of the dry paint has a slight sheen.

The big cautionary note for acrylics is that because of their rapid and hard-drying qualities, care must be taken to clean brushes and other tools immediately after use; dry acrylic is virtually impossible to remove from many surfaces, including clothing and floors.

Initially, acrylics seem difficult to control, but don't be dismayed by first attempts—work with them until you've mastered their use. They are a valuable and versatile medium, whatever the painting surface.

Acrylic Mediums

Acrylic retarder is a gel that retards the drying time of acrylic paint. It is usually available in tubes. Care must be taken to add the proper amount of retardant to the paint; follow the instructions on the container.

Acrylic flow release is added to acrylics in small amounts to reduce surface tension, thus increasing the flowability and permitting more even washes on paper or paperboard.

Acrylic gel medium is a thickening material that allows an impasto effect to be achieved and makes the paint more transparent. It has very limited uses in bird painting.

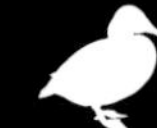

2
Brushes

Almost any hair, bristle, or fiber may be used in the manufacture of paint brushes and all have different characteristics. The brush is painting's most important tool. There is nothing more frustrating or self-defeating than trying to work with a poor brush. Buy the highest quality brush(es) you can afford. Don't be dismayed at the array of shapes and sizes; only a few brushes are necessary for successful bird painting.

What determines a good brush is a combination of abilities: to carry an adequate load of paint, to hold a sharp edge in a flat brush, to hold a sharp point in a round brush, and to spring back into shape after use. Emphasis here will be on the materials and shapes used most frequently in bird painting with gouache and acrylic paints.

Types of Hair and Filament

Kolinsky Sable. The finest and most expensive brushes made are from Kolinsky sable, but even these will vary in quality depending on the manufacturer. Kolinskys are typically in a round shape and usually display all of the desirable qualities of a good brush. Although there are many brands, the two I recommend for availability and consistent quality are the Strathmore series 585 and the Winsor & Newton series 7.

Red Sable. Sable hairs that are of a lesser quality than Kolinsky. Usually not as springy, and in rounds do not point up as well as Kolinskys. In other shapes—flats and filberts—they are fine brushes.

Sableline. A fancy name for dyed ox hair. They do not point up well in the rounds, but they hold a good load of paint and are fine flat and large wash brushes.

Nylon. Sometimes described as synthetic sables, nylons have great spring but little ability to point or hold paint. The development of synthetic filaments has not yet reached the quality found in natural hair.

Blends. The most common blend is nylon–sable, and although it's a better brush than pure nylon, it is still lacking in paint retention and the ability to hold a fine point.

Shapes of Brushes

Standard Round. Usually called a "round," this is the most popular and versatile brush shape. It is found in a variety of sizes. Although this is called a *standard* round, various characteristics, such as hair length, may vary between manufacturers. The two most popular brands are Winsor & Newton and Strathmore. The brush I recommend in this style is the Strathmore Kolinsky Sable #585. It is an all-round good brush that holds a very fine point.

Designer Round. These have a longer and thinner shape than do standard rounds and come to a narrow sharp point that can pull a very fine line. This is a good style but not quite as versatile as the standard round.

Flats. There are two categories to be considered in this style: watercolor and oil flats.

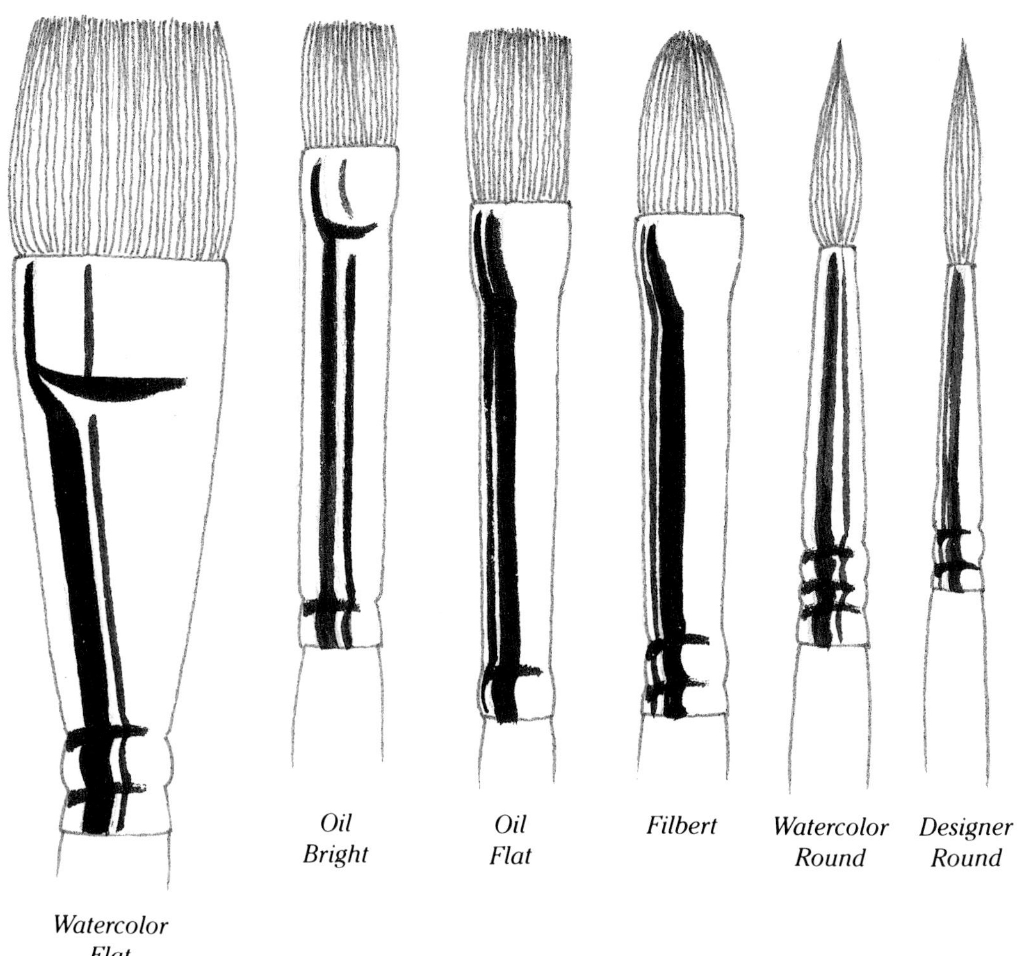

Brush Shapes

Watercolor Flats. Initially, this brush category may seem confusing because watercolor flats may also be called *aquarelles,* which are large, thick flats, or one-stroke brushes that usually have slightly longer hairs than do normal flats. Regardless, they are all watercolor flats and are used primarily for washes or filling in large areas. They are generally not available in very small sizes, and the most common sizes are 1/4, 3/8, 1/2, 3/4 and 1 inch. Red sable and sableline are the preferred hairs in this shape; lesser-quality brushes in this shape have a ragged edge, don't hold much paint, and have the annoying habit of losing hairs when painting. Another brush to be considered here is a large flat called a *wash brush,* used, as the name implies, for putting washes on large flat surfaces. A good large wash brush is the 1 1/2- or 2-inch Oxhair by Strathmore.

Oil Flats. These come in a much greater variety of sizes, have shorter hairs, and are more stout than watercolor flats. Oil flats are used for oils and acrylics on canvas or wood. The *bright* is another flat but with slightly shorter hairs than the oil flat.

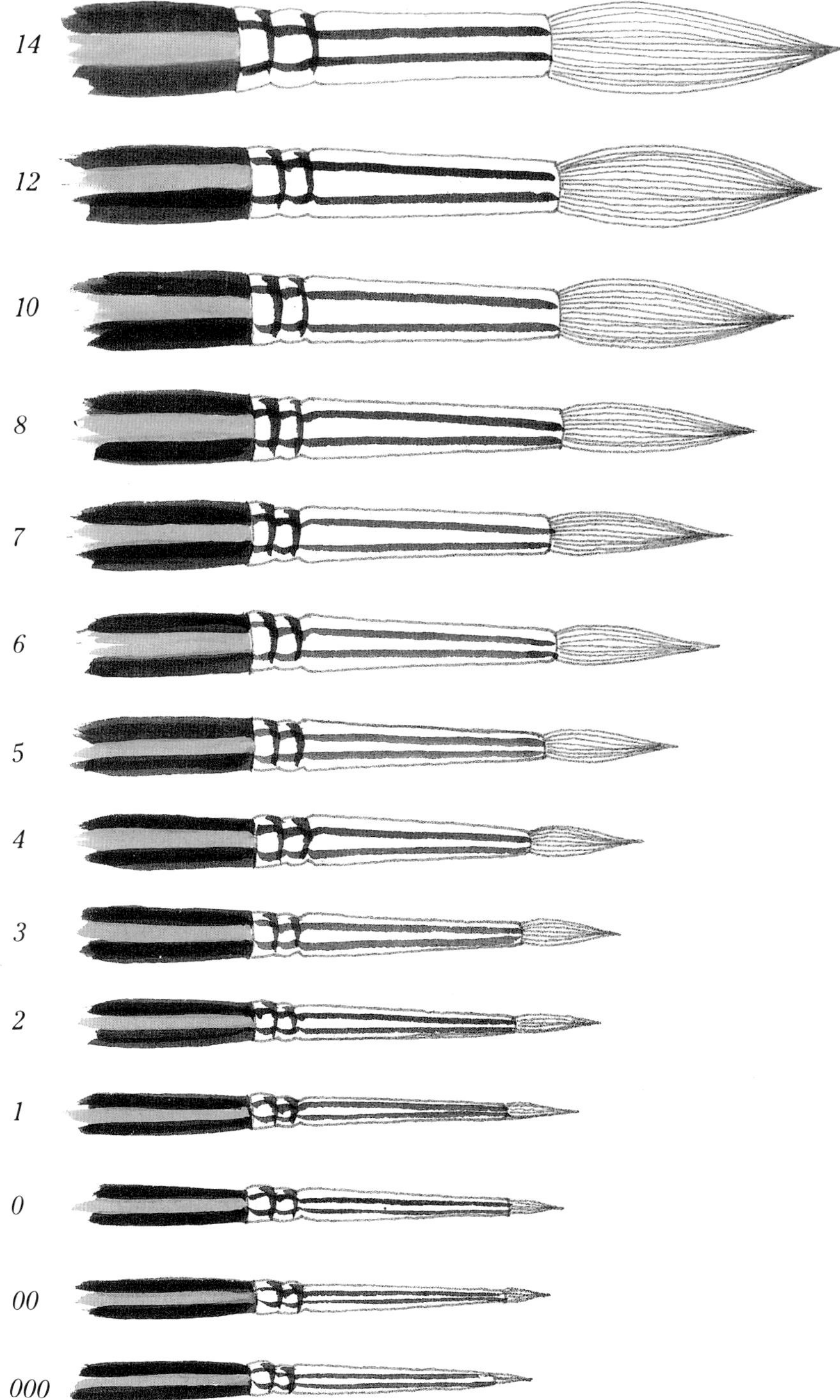

Watercolor Rounds (Actual Size)

Filbert. This is a flat with a rounded rather than a square tip. Traditionally regarded as an oil-painting brush, it is now an important shape for painting birds in both gouache and acrylic. Used in an unconventional manner it produces unique featherlike marks (see Techniques). The various sizes of this brush make different sizes of feather marks, so the size you will need will be determined by the size of the bird being painted. The various types of hair used in this style make different types of marks. Red sable would be the best hair choice with which to start, but be sure to experiment with other types of hair and bristle.

Care of Brushes

Several good brushes may represent a considerable investment, so it is wise to care for this investment with the small amount of time it takes to keep brushes in good condition. Cleaning water-based paints from brushes only requires thorough rinsing in body-temperature water, then gently scrubbing them with a pure soap, such as Ivory bar soap. After rinsing all the soap out, reshape the tip of the brush and hang it hair- or bristle-down to dry. When you are using several brushes it is difficult to stop painting and clean them. In such cases, you can use a brush washer or brush holder: a container of water with a coiled metal holder mounted above the water level. When the brush handle is put in the coil, the hairs are suspended in the water, keeping the paint in the brush moist until it can be thoroughly washed.

If you have extra brushes or some that are used infrequently, store them in a closed—but not airtight—container along with some moth crystals. (Moth larvae love to munch on hairs and bristles.) With proper care some brushes may last a lifetime, but even if the ends wear off they are still useful (see Techniques).

Buying Brushes

The ideal way to buy a brush is to go to an art-supply store where you can test the brush before buying; it is especially wise to test the quality of sable rounds. To test, wet the brush in water to remove the starch (used to protect the brushes), then, when it is thoroughly wet, flick the brush quickly to see if it points well. After that, press the damp hairs sideways on a hard surface, then release them to see if the brush snaps back into shape. If the brush behaves well, buy it; if not, repeat the performance with another brush. It is often necessary to order brushes from a mail-order company. Stick with reliable brands and you will usually be pleased. If not, most firms have a complete return policy.

The recommendations given here are intended only as a guide. All artists have individual preferences; the best way to satisfy your artistic needs is to experiment until you find the brushes that are best for you.

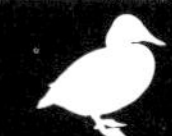

3
Painting Surfaces

Although any surface may be painted, only those widely used with gouache and acrylics will be covered here.

Watercolor papers are available in a wide variety of weights, finishes, and shades of white and gray. The following is an overview of the terms used to describe watercolor paper and its characteristics.

Watercolor paper is commonly available in three finishes, or surface textures, although the degrees of texture on same-named finishes can vary among manufacturers. These papers are available in rolls, pads, and individual sheets. Although watercolor paper is intended for use with transparent watercolors, gouache may be used on it with great success; however, it is not recommended for the inexperienced acrylic painter.

Hot press is the smoothest surface and will take very fine-line detail. It is used mainly for hard-edged paintings. The surface has very little "tooth" (roughness to the fiber) to hold paint, which has a tendency to lift off the paper at inopportune times.

Cold press is the intermediate finish between hot press and rough. With a moderate surface and tooth, it is the finish of choice for the beginning artist.

Rough, as the name implies, is a very rough finish, and because of this is a very difficult surface on which to work. It is an attractive board but it does not lend itself to detailed paintings.

Watercolor paper is listed by weight as well as finish and, if the paper dimensions are the same, the higher weight will be the thicker paper. Size is

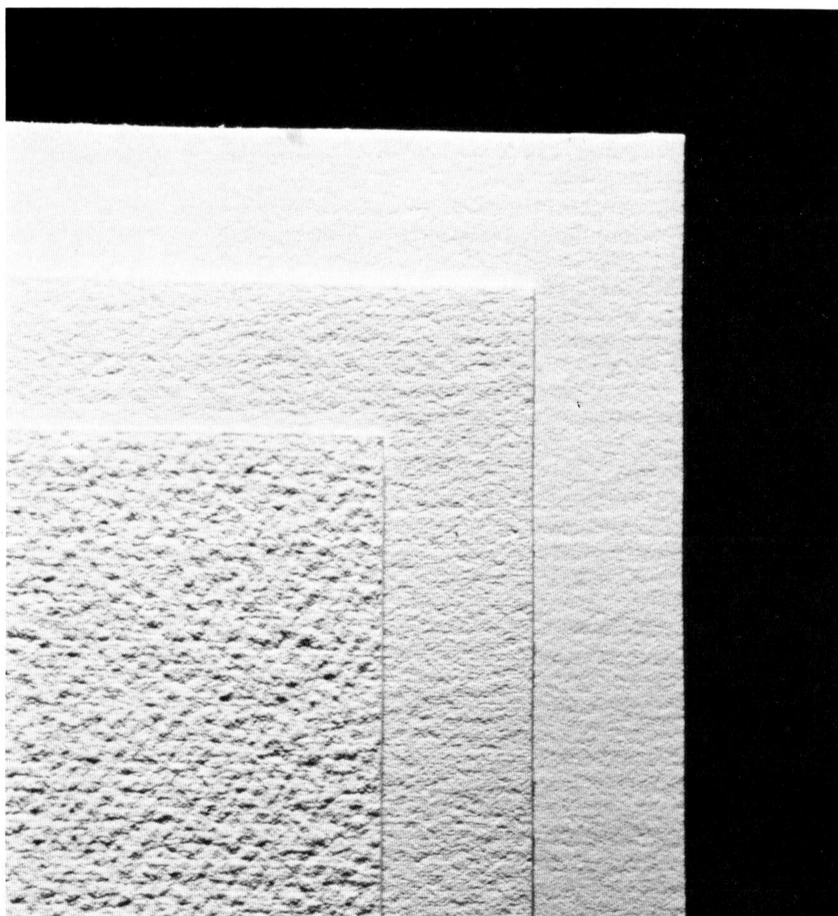

Watercolor paper surfaces. From the left: *rough, cold press, hot press*

important because the standard is based on how much a ream (500 sheets) weighs, no matter the size. Thus, a larger sheet of the same thickness will be listed at a greater weight.

Most lighter-weight watercolor papers must be stretched prior to use to avoid buckling. This is a simple process. Soak the paper in a pan or tub of water, remove the paper when thoroughly wet, and drain off excess surface water. Then place the wet paper on a flat surface, such as a drawing board, and tape all the edges using a gummed paper tape. Tack the corners through the tape and let dry. The paper will dry very tight and may be used taped to the board or cut free. Stretching is not necessary with heavy-weight watercolor papers.

Illustration and watercolor boards are stiff boards with either illustration or watercolor paper adhered to one side. Because of their stiffness, these boards can stand rougher treatment than papers and do not require any prepainting preparation.

Illustration board is lighter in weight than watercolor board and has a slight tendency to warp when large areas are painted. To remedy this problem, brush a thin coat of gesso or paint on the reverse side to equalize the pull of the paint, thus flattening the board. Illustration boards are available in two surfaces: *hot press* and *cold press*. Hot press is the smoother and less desirable of the two. Cold press provides good surface for both gouache and acrylics.

The difference in thickness between illustration board (left) *and watercolor board* (right).

Watercolor boards are made with a heavier backing than are illustration boards and thus are more resistant to warping. Because the surface is watercolor paper, it responds well to paint. The three surface finishes available are the same as those described for watercolor paper. The watercolor board I prefer is Crescent #112 cold press, a very heavy board with Strathmore watercolor paper adhered to it. Gouache and acrylics may be used with great success on this fine board.

Matboards are made of tinted papers adhered to stiff backing. There is a temptation to use this board for painting and it can be done; just be aware that the tinted paper will fade badly.

Hardboard, commonly known under the trade name Masonite, is made of compressed wood fibers and is found in tempered and untempered forms. Only the untempered board should be used for painting because the tempered board is impregnated with oil. Before painting, the board must be coated with acrylic gesso to provide a suitable ground (surface) for the paint. Preparation with gesso requires rolling or brushing a base coat of thinned gesso, then sanding with fine sandpaper, dusting, and applying more gesso. Repeat the process until at least three coats of gesso are on the surface. The reverse side of the board also must be coated, but it need not be sanded. This offsets the board's tendency to bow by creating surface tension on the reverse side. Gouache may be used on hardboard panels but only with limited success. Acrylics work well on hardboard, but exercise patience because paints initially go on the slick gesso surface rather irregularly. After additional applications of color, however, the paint goes on smoothly. A finished acrylic painting on hardboard is very crisp and bright.

Primed linen canvas

Canvas is available in both linen and cotton and both are sold in different grades and weaves; the tighter weaves are more expensive. Gouache may be used on canvas, but acrylics are used with much greater success. Because of the inherent texture of the fabric, canvas does not easily lend itself to fine-line paintings—except for portrait linen canvases.

Cotton canvas is available in several forms: rolls, panels, pads, and prestretched; the form most suitable for acrylics is the prestretched, acrylic-primed canvas. Found in a wide assortment of sizes, these canvases are ready to use and easy to store. The surface of cotton canvas can be rather coarse, with irregularities in the weave.

Linen canvas is more tightly woven, stronger, smoother, and more expensive than cotton canvas and is available only in rolls or prestretched and primed. The latter is preferable for our purposes. Because of the weave and stability, linen canvas is the choice of many artists because its fine surface permits detailed paintings.

Wood has also been traditionally used as a painting surface. Especially relevant here is the carved wood used by bird carvers. Finished carvings must be primed to accept the paint and to provide a white ground that enables the colors to be crisp and clear. Wood must first be sealed with clear lacquer or sanding sealer, then one or two coats of acrylic gesso, thinned to the point where it will not fill in carved detail, is brushed onto the surface. When dry, this provides an excellent ground for acrylics. Gouache is not suitable for carvings because of its soft surface.

Primed cotton canvas

Additional Mediums, Tools, and Accessories

Just a peek inside an art-supply store or catalog is enough to bewilder any artist. Besides the array of brushes, paints, and paper, there are myriad accessories and gadgets, some useful, some not. Listed here are only those additional art items that are necessary for successful bird painting.

Liquid masking fluid (liquid frisket) is a thin rubber-cementlike fluid that is painted over an area to be left white after painting washes or specific areas. Use a worn or inexpensive brush to apply the frisket because it quickly dries and balls up in the brush. Immediately after use, wash the brush in water. When the background color is completely dry, remove the frisket by gently rubbing it off with your finger(s) or with the help of a rubber cement pickup. Liquid frisket is used extensively in bird painting (see Techniques).

Palettes may be made of metal, plastic, paper, china, wood, or glass. Available in any shape or size, some have wells to hold the color, and some have lids to keep the paint moist. Despite the variety available, the best palette is usually the simplest one and almost anything that will hold paint can be used. Most acrylic painters prefer something that is peelable or disposable, such as an old plate, pizza pan, or hardboard scrap. A pan with a shallow lip or an enameled tray is ideal for gouache.

Transfer paper is a thin paper coated on one side with graphite, and it is used to transfer a drawing to another surface. Available commercially, you also can easily make it by rubbing a thin coat of graphite from a soft pencil or graphite stick on one side of a piece of tracing paper or on the reverse side of a drawing, then smearing the graphite around with a tissue to get a more even coating. To transfer a finished drawing to the painting surface, prepare the back of the drawing as described or place a piece of transfer paper between the drawing and surface, trace over the lines of the drawing, remove the drawing, and the traced lines are transferred to the painting surface. This acts the same as carbon paper, which, incidentally, should not be used for drawing transfers because carbon paper smears badly and is difficult to erase. If the transfer is to be made onto a dark surface that will not show graphite, instead smear the back of the drawing with silver- or white-colored pencil, and white lines will be transferred.

Brush washers or *holders,* as mentioned previously, are a handy and inexpensive piece of equipment.

Water jars hold water used for diluting paints and washing brushes while painting. From hand-thrown pots to a canning jar, you can use anything that will hold water.

Spray bottles are used to evenly prewet surfaces. Trigger types are superior to pump types; they may be purchased empty at nurseries, hardware stores, and beauty shops.

Sponges, both natural and artificial, have a variety of surface textures and are used for special effects as well as controlling water and washes.

Hobby knives (X-acto types) are used in painting to scratch white lines on painted surfaces and to carefully remove unwanted hairs, paint flakes, and so on, that may suddenly appear on a painting.

Tissues, paper towels, and *rags* are always handy for removing excess paint or water and for blotting paint from brushes.

Q-tips are a ready-made tool for blotting small areas of paint, as in lifting off (see Techniques).

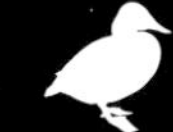

4
Techniques

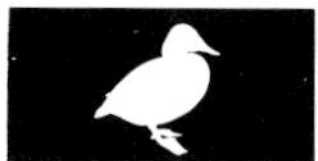

All the basic techniques discussed here apply to gouache. Not all, however, apply to acrylics because they cannot be reworked when dry; alternate techniques are described for them. Though every effort is made to indicate how the techniques are executed, it is difficult, if not impossible, to describe the proper consistency of a paint, the wetness of a wash, or the amount of pressure on a brush. These are variables that can be learned only through doing. Even experienced artists keep a board scrap handy while painting to continually check for consistency, color, load of paint in the brush, or to practice line shapes. Don't be discouraged—these techniques are easy to master through practice.

Flat Opaque Colors. Dilute the paint to a creamy consistency and, using the appropriate brush size for the area being filled, use broad strokes to fill in with opaque color. Acrylics may require two coats to cover completely.

Wet-in-Wet Wash. This method is used for backgrounds or on the bird itself wherever a continuous, even, transparent color is desired. For a large background wash have a puddle of thinned paint ready to go, then place the board on a slight angle so that the water, and then the paint, will flow slowly and evenly down the board. Thoroughly wet the board surface so it shines; then, starting at the top of the board and working downward, brush on the thinned paint from side to side, adding paint and brushing until an even wash is obtained. If the first wash is too thin, wait until completely dry and repeat the process. When working a small area on a bird, wet only the area to be colored and brush carefully. The paint will brush evenly into the premoistened area, giving a beautiful, thin, even coat.

Graded Wet Wash. The preparation is the same as that for a wet-in-wet wash; the difference is that the brush is charged with paint only once and, as the brush works down the board, there is a decreasing amount of pigment so that the final effect is a graded tone. After the first color to be graded is applied, it is often washed down the surface with a clean damp brush. This is very useful in bird painting, especially for achieving a shaded effect in acrylics by grading a wash over a base color (glazing).

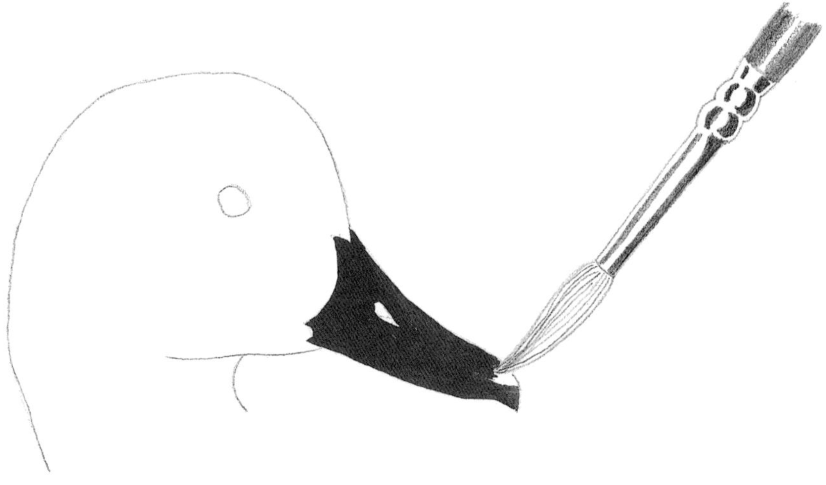

flat opaque colors

wet-in-wet wash

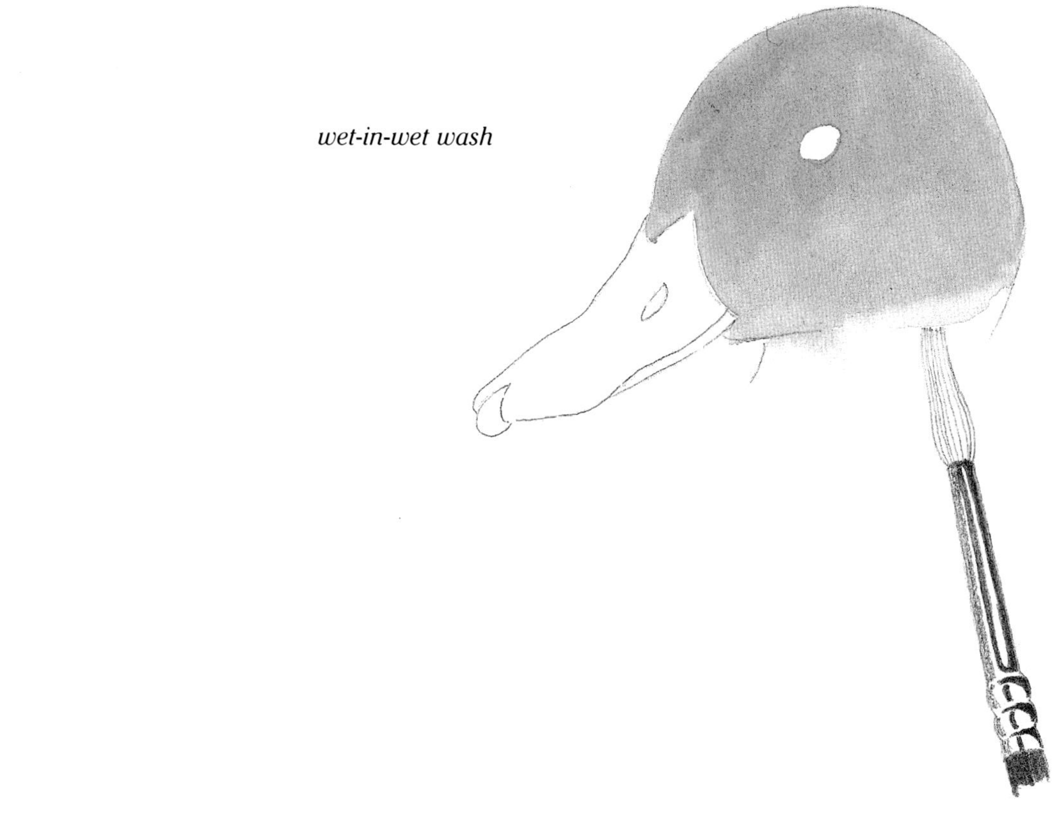

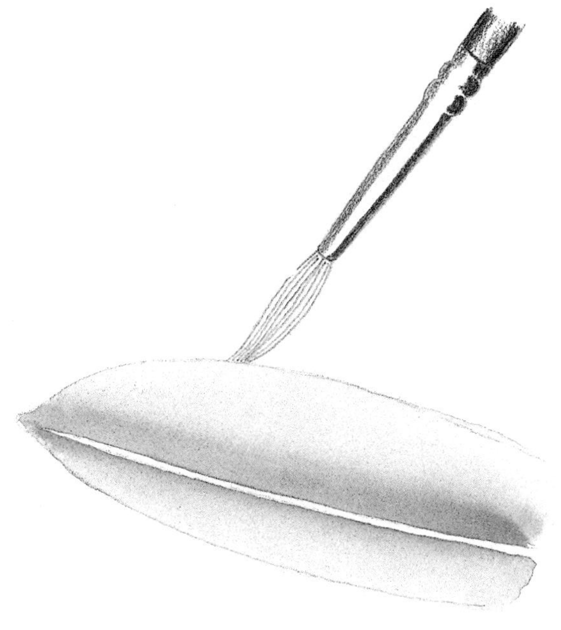

graded wet wash

Wet Blending. Paint two areas of color close to each other on a damp surface and work the edges of each color into the other while still wet until a blended effect is achieved. This technique may be used with acrylics, but you must plan ahead and quickly work the colors toward each other and blend them while still wet. To soften the edges of highlights, such as on bills, claws, or with splitbrushing, the softening must be done while the highlights or splitbrushing is still wet. Each color stroke must be blended (softened) with a clean damp brush as the color is applied.

Dry Blending. This technique is easily done with gouache, but is impossible with acrylics. This is, quite simply, blending two adjacent dry colors with a clean, damp brush. Use a light touch on the brush and move it back and forth across the colors' edges until they are coarsely blended, then brush along the edge to achieve a smooth blend. This is very handy for softening the edges of thin lines, as on wing edges, and for highlighting on claws and bills.

Glazing. This is an application of a thin wash of color over an already dry one, allowing the colors to mix visually. A graded wash painted over a base color is an example of glazing. Acrylics lend themselves beautifully to this technique, but care must be taken with gouache not to overwork the second color on the surface or the colors will bleed together.

Drybrush. Although this technique is rarely used on the image of the bird, it is frequently used on the supports (twigs, logs, and so on). The brush is charged with color, blotted until almost dry, then dragged across the surface creating an unpredictable broken, shaded effect. The tip or side of the brush may be used.

Splitbrush. Also known as *heeling* or *feathering,* this technique is versatile and fun—and one that may be overused. A round brush is charged with paint and severely pinched or pressed down at the heel (where the hairs and ferrule meet) until the hairs spread apart. Then the tips of the spread hairs are brushed lightly across the surface to make a series of tiny lines. The brush may be blotted to produce drybrush broken lines. A graded or blended effect may be achieved by using a series of light, short strokes on the edge of a color. Short, light splitbrush strokes are a very effective way to soften the

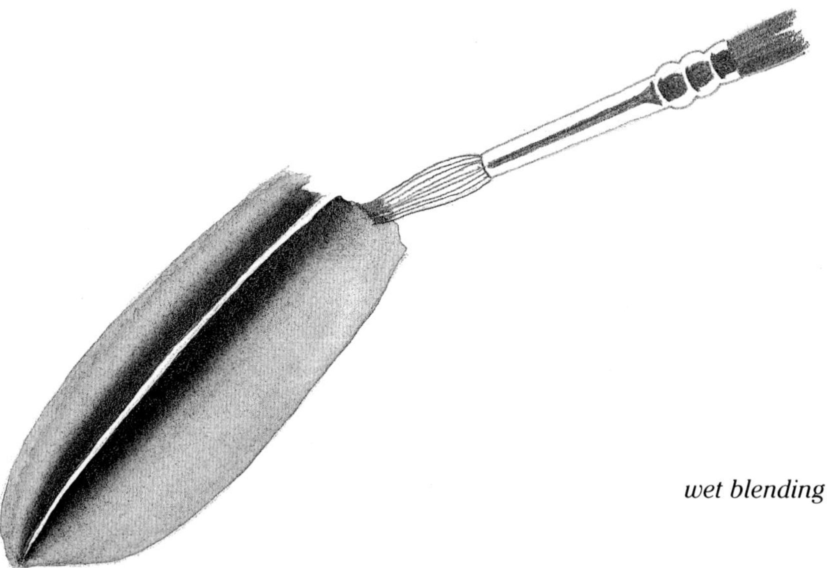

wet blending

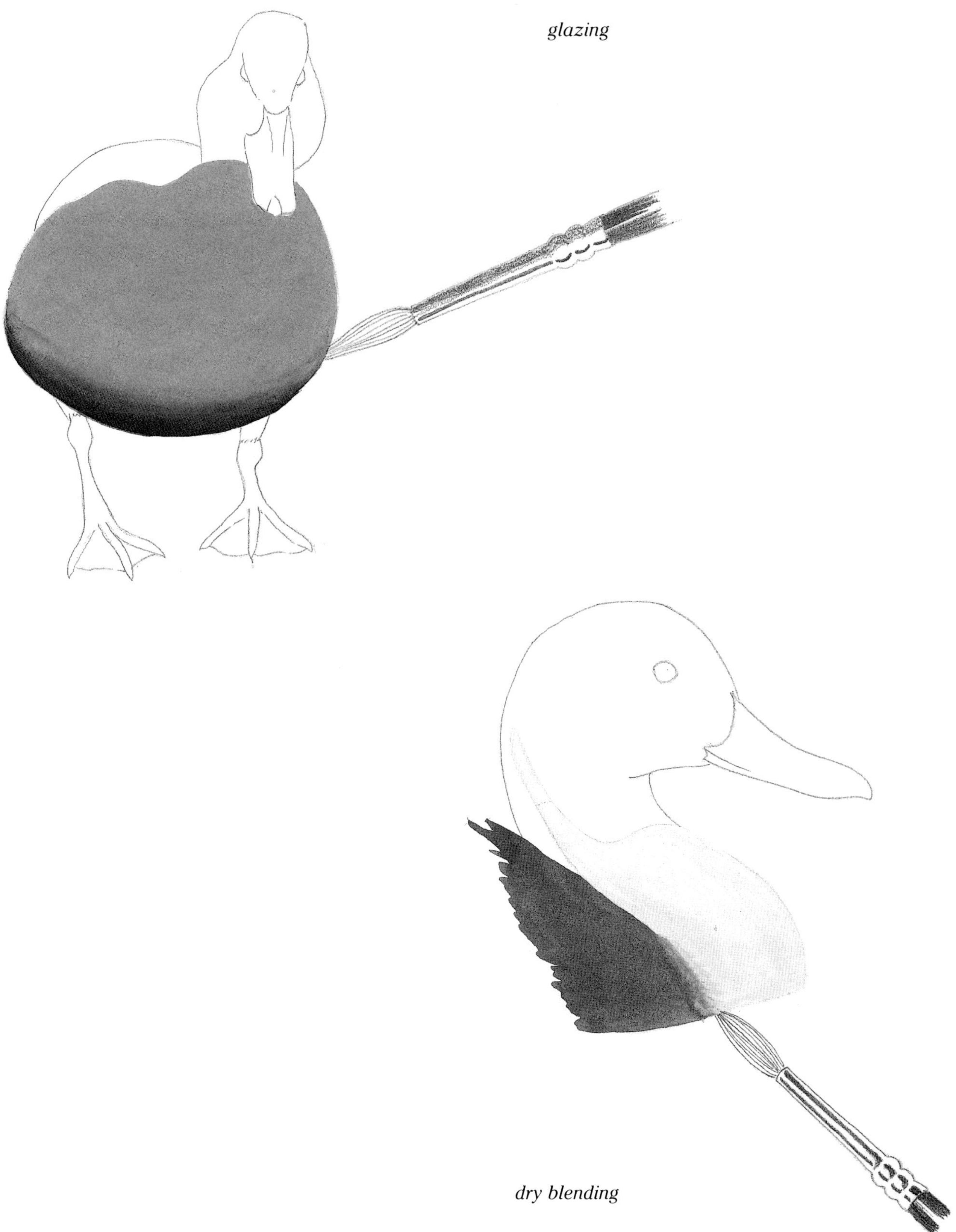

glazing

dry blending

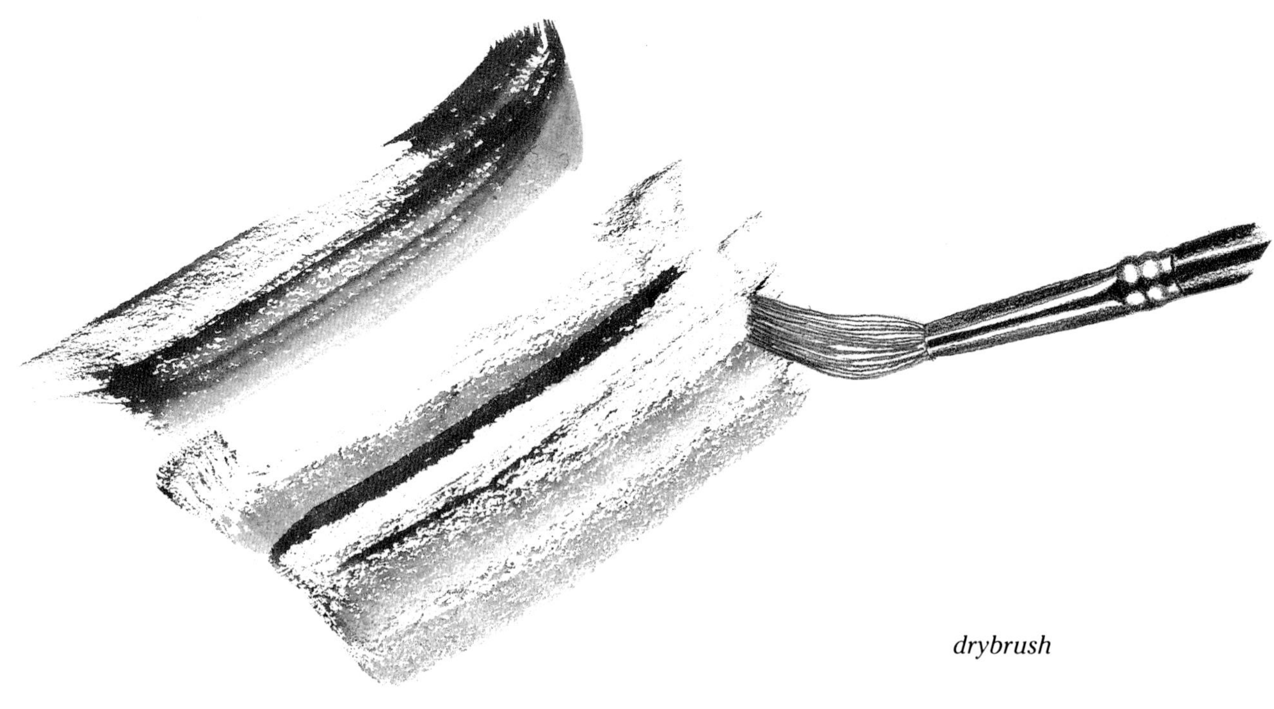

drybrush

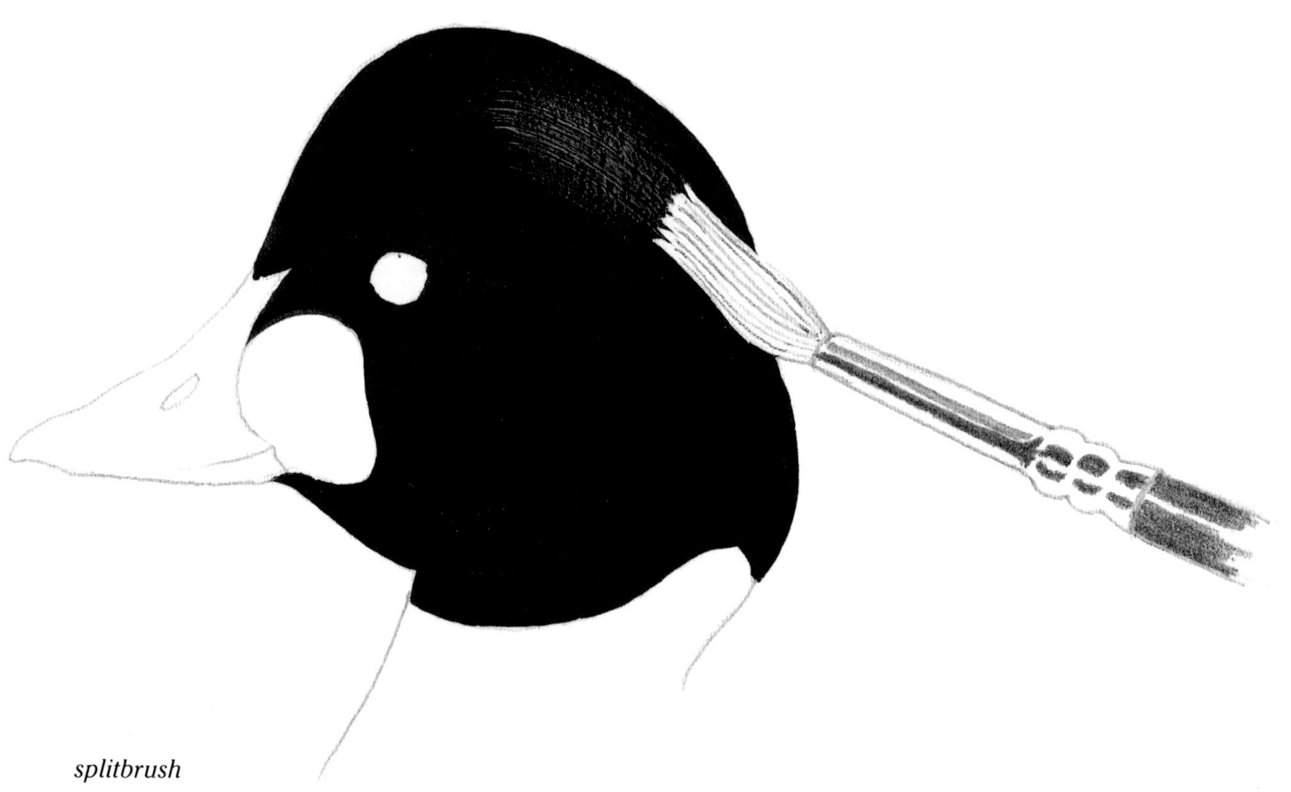

splitbrush

edge of wet acrylic paint, producing a blended effect. This is very hard on brushes; thus old, worn brushes are recommended.

Tipping. The filbert-shaped brush is most effective for tipping, and care should be taken not to overuse this technique. The brush is not held in the conventional manner, like a pencil, but instead is held almost parallel to the surface at a slight angle. The brush is charged with paint, then the tip is lightly pressed and lifted from the surface. Varying amounts of paint, degree of pressure, or pressing then pulling the brush, all produce a wide variety of featherlike marks.

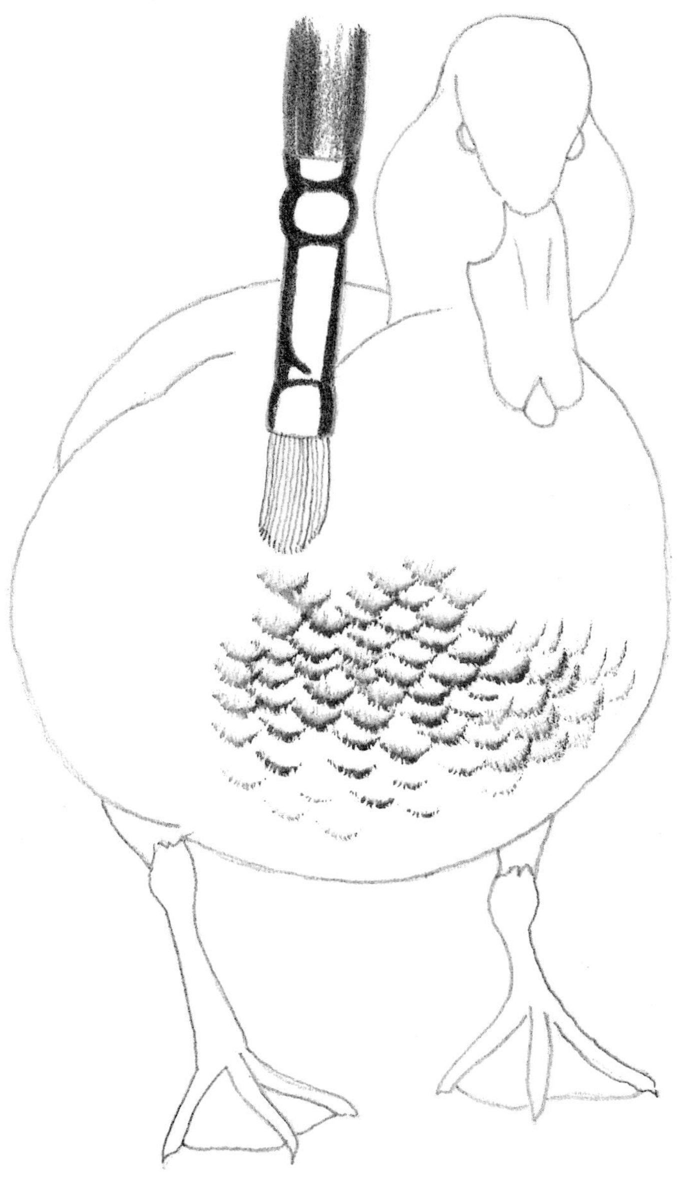

tipping

Lifting Off. Rather than adding color to the surface, this subtracts color (it cannot be done with dry acrylics). A brush filled with clean water is lightly scrubbed over a selected area of dry paint. While the area is still wet, a Q-tip or clean, dry brush is used to lift the loosened pigment from the scrubbed area. This leaves a subtle highlighted area, the shape and size of which is determined by the motion of the wetted brush.

Detailing. Usually the last technique used on a painting, this adds the finishing detail. It is usually executed with a small, fine-point round brush. In bird painting, the wing edges, highlights, and other finishing touches are described as detailing.

Spatter. This technique is not used on the bird but rather on the background to suggest an irregular sandylike surface. It is accomplished by dipping an old toothbrush in very thin color then lightly rubbing the bristles of the toothbrush with a stick or finger. As the bristles snap back and forth, random-sized dots of color appear on the surface. Both light and dark colors may be spattered. To control the area being spattered, frame it with a piece of torn paper; this will give a varied and more interesting edge to the spattered area.

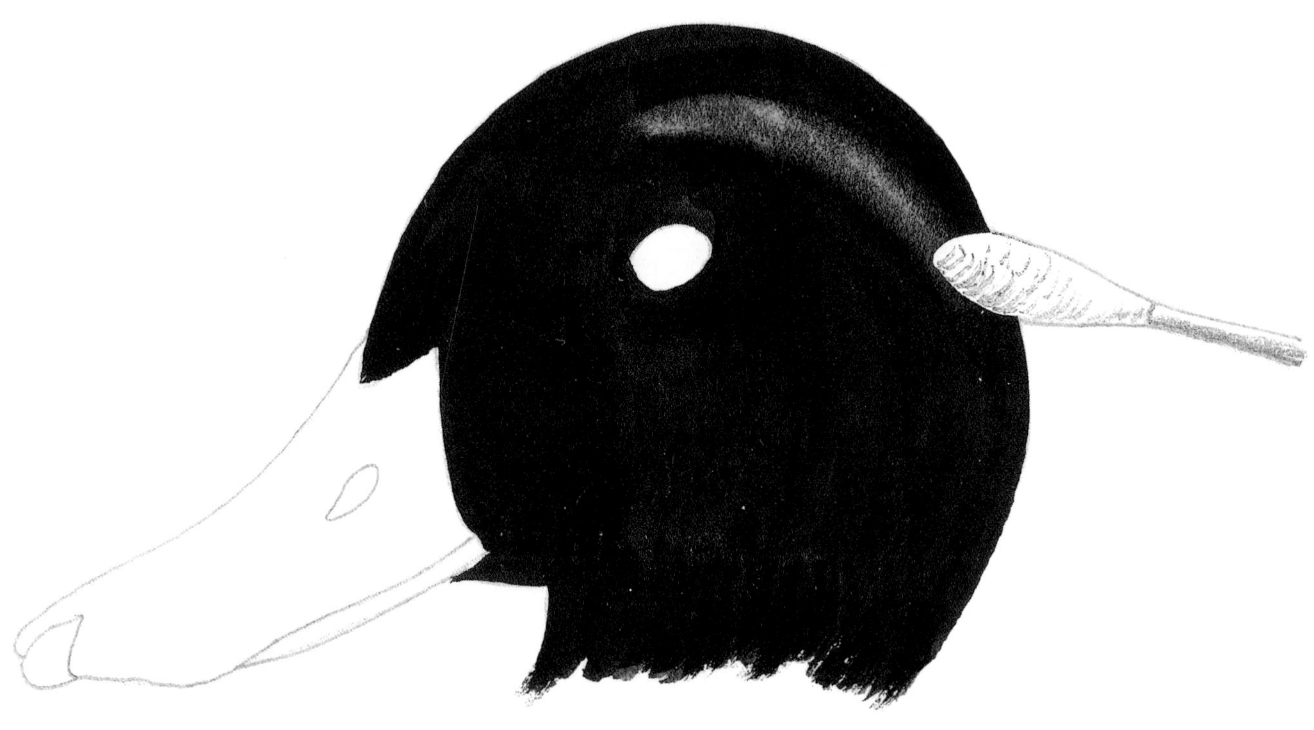

lifting off

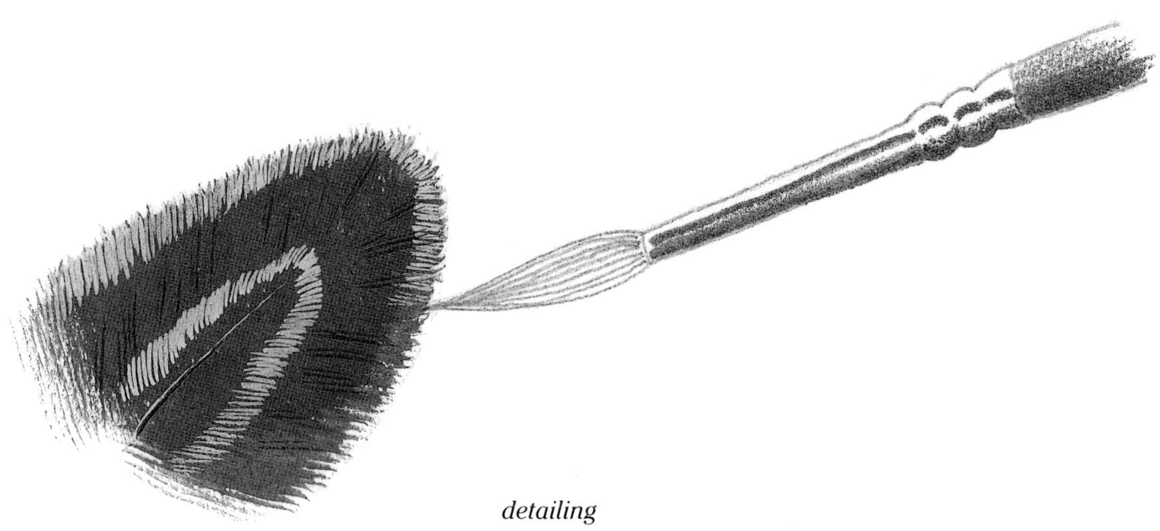

detailing

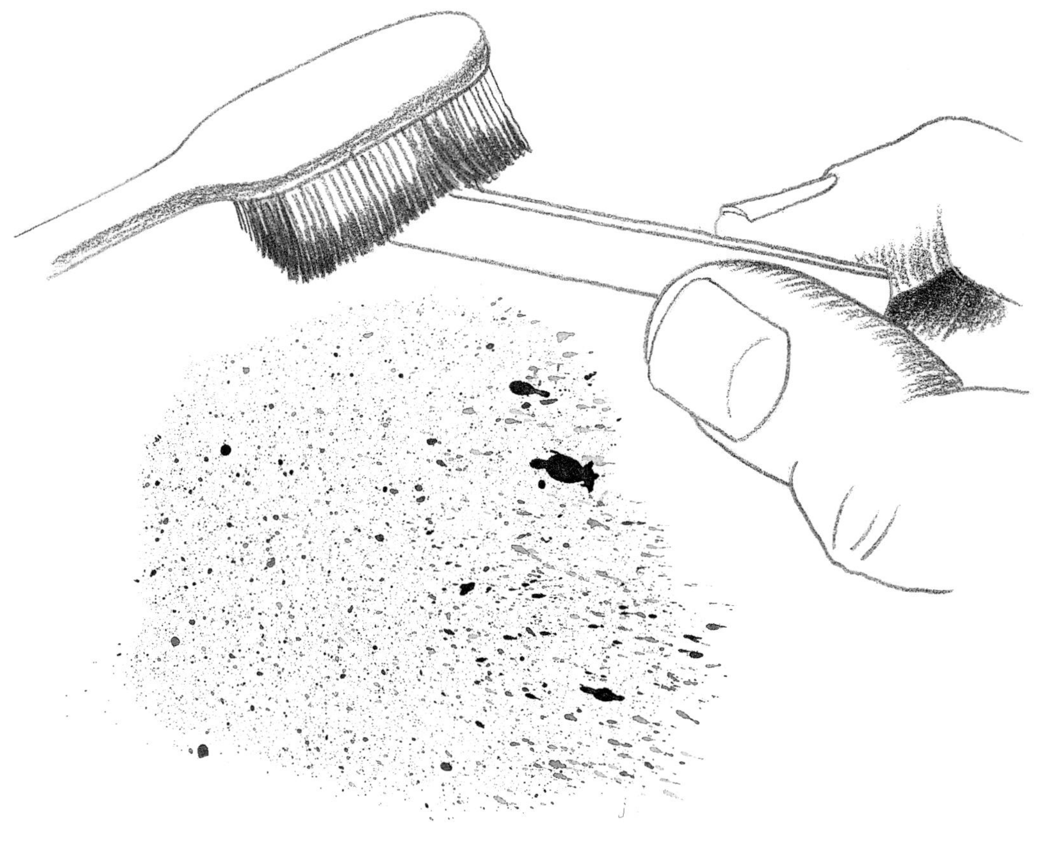

spatter

5
Putting the Techniques Together

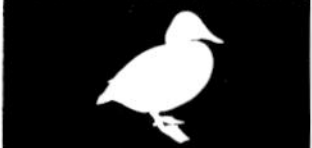

You have read descriptions of the various techniques used to paint birds, now it is time to see how they are applied. Naturally, the complexity of the bird being painted will determine how many techniques are used in the painting. The mallard example employs a wide variety of these techniques, including tipping, splitbrush, spatter, and blending. It also demonstrates the use of transferring and liquid masking. The painting was done on cold press watercolor board with #1 and #3 Kolinsky rounds and a #4 filbert, except for the background wash where a 1½-inch sableline brush was used. A toothbrush was used for the spatter. Unless otherwise noted, the #3 round will be the brush used.

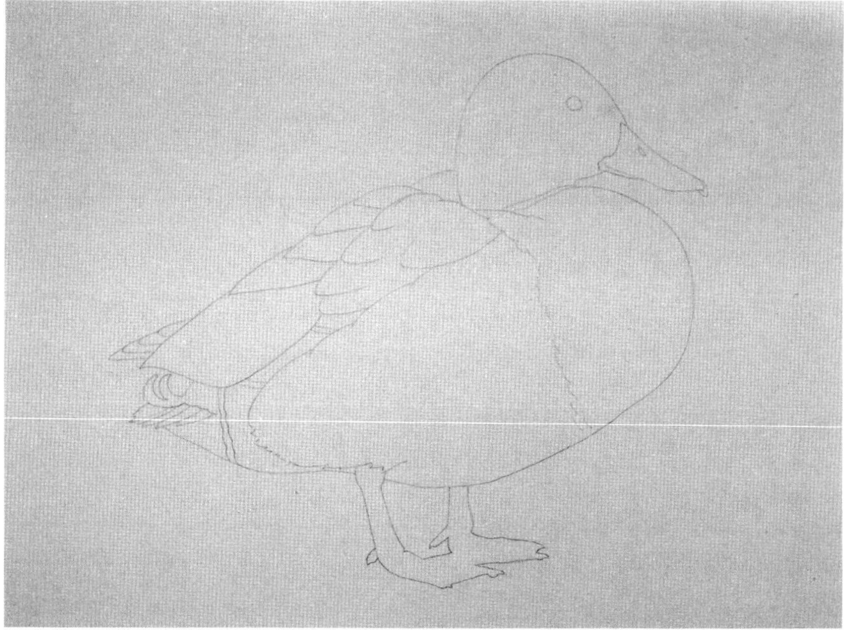

The drawing is prepared for transfer by rubbing the reverse side with graphite, then it is transferred to the painting surface in the manner described on page 22. Only the outline of the legs and feet are transferred.

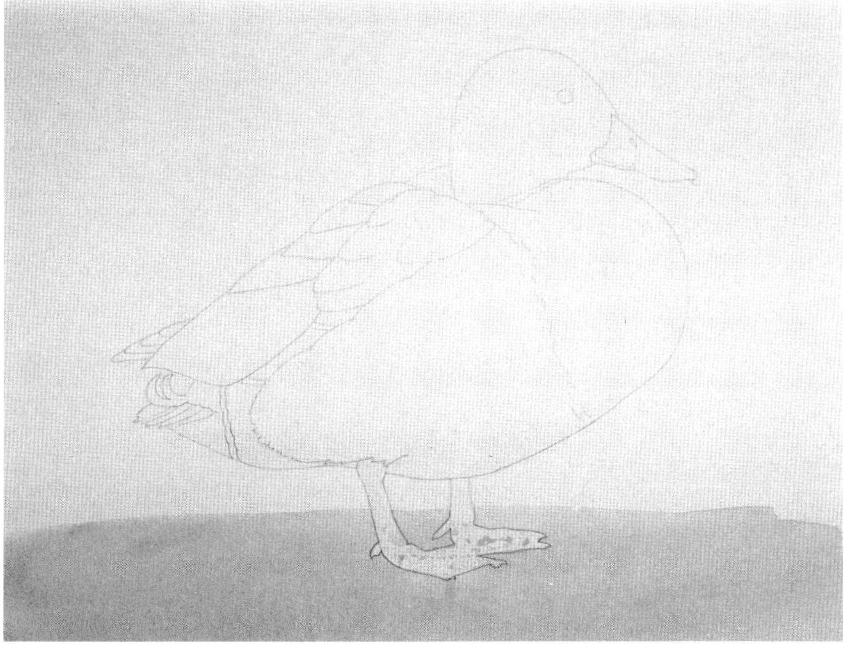

Liquid masking is painted over the feet and legs so they won't be colored by the wash (refer to page 22). When it is dry, a thin wet-in-wet wash using the 1½-inch wash brush is painted over them to indicate ground.

When the ground wash is dry, a piece of torn paper is placed over the bird and a dark color is spattered with the toothbrush to show texture on the ground.

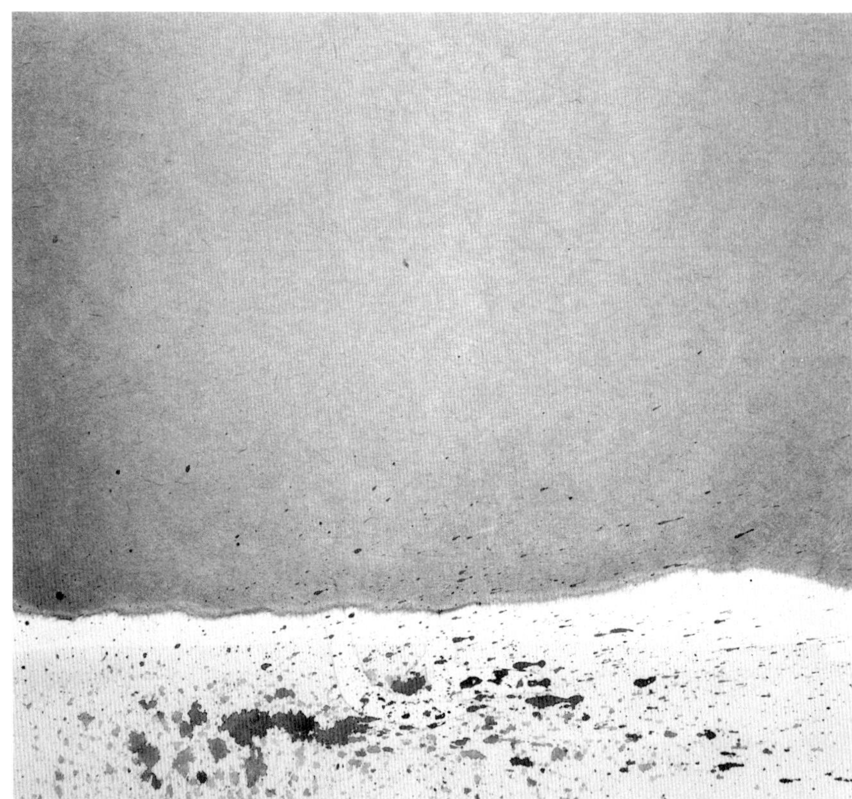

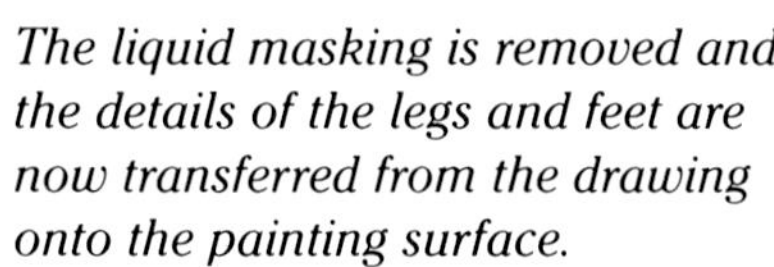

The liquid masking is removed and the details of the legs and feet are now transferred from the drawing onto the painting surface.

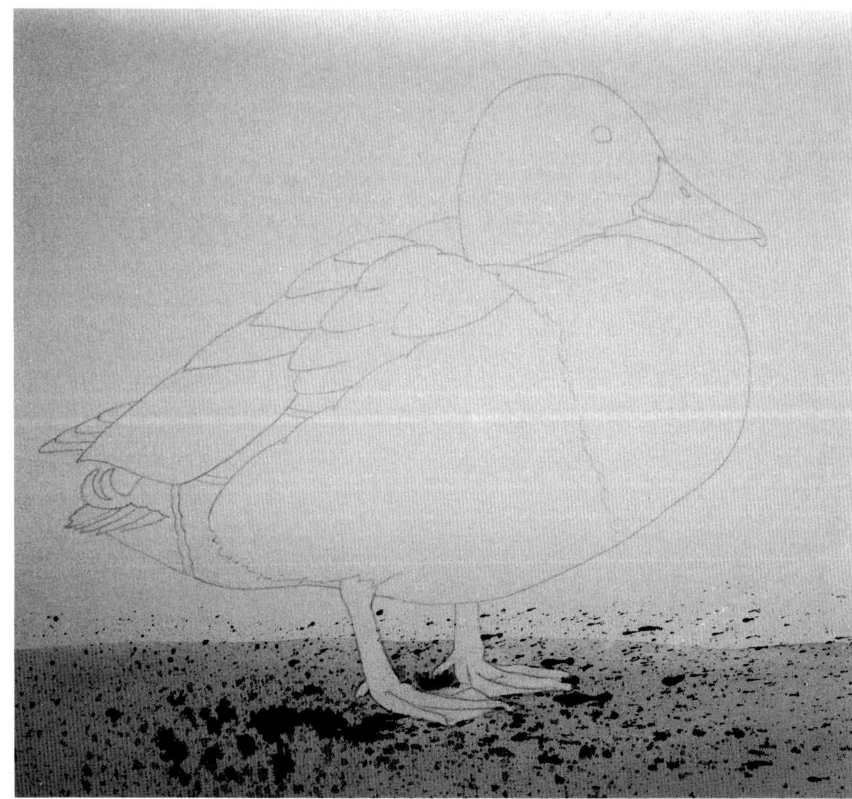

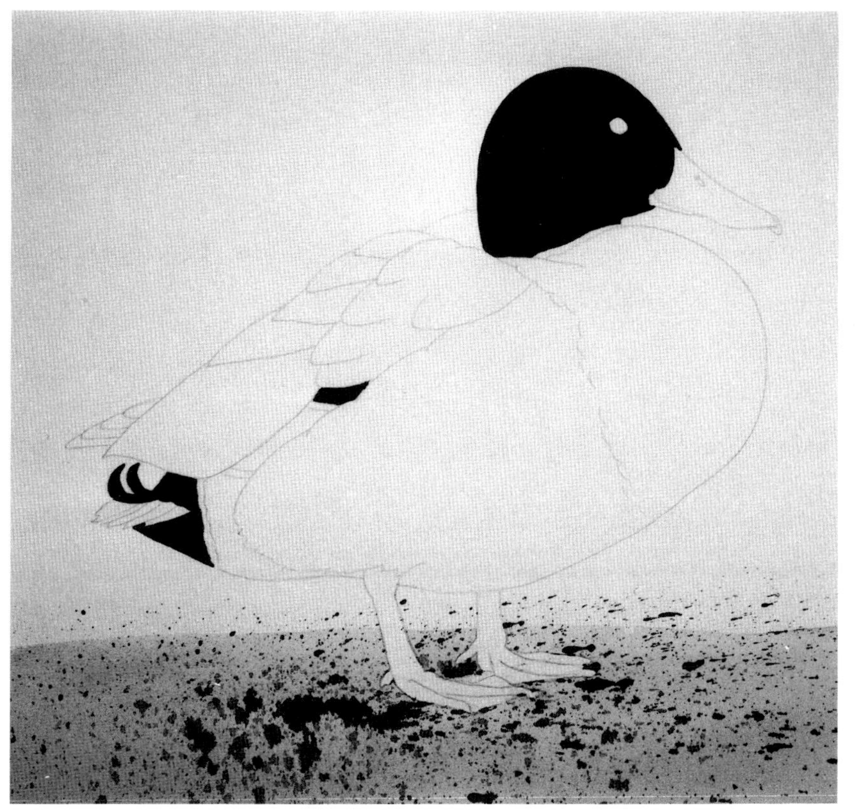

A dark flat opaque color is applied to the head, coverts, and tail area. This color completely covers the white of the board.

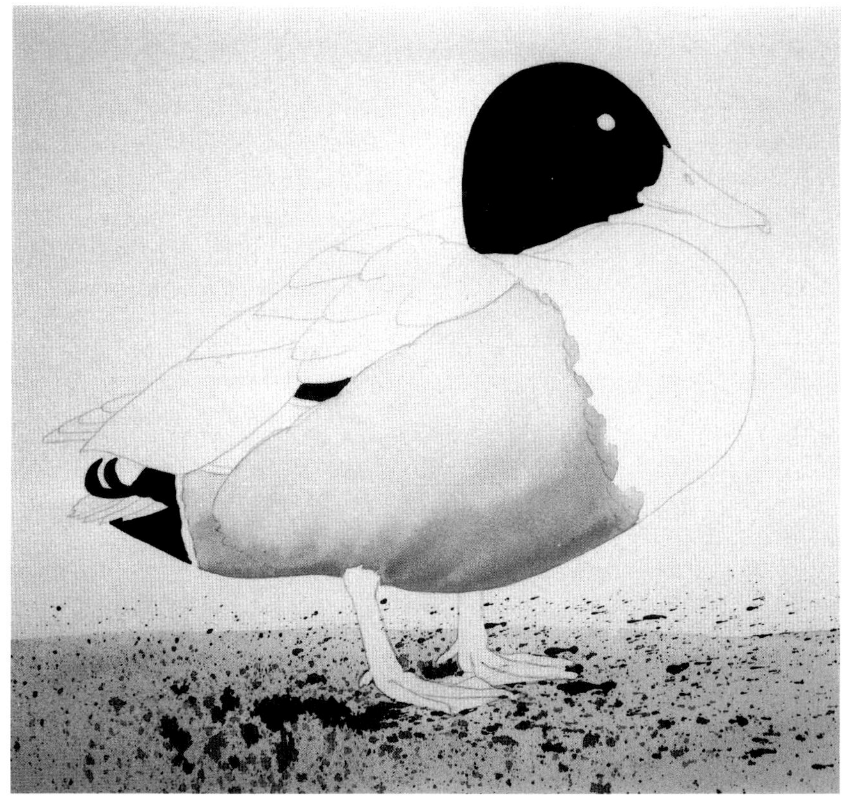

The first in a series of graded washes, which give shading and form to the mallard, is begun. The initial wash is from the belly up to the flanks. Turn the picture upside down and coat the entire area to be washed with clean clear water, then paint color on the area to be darkest and pull it into the wet area without adding any more pigment to the brush.

The next graded wash is painted on the scapulars and executed in the same manner as on the belly. Notice how the traced lines show through the wash.

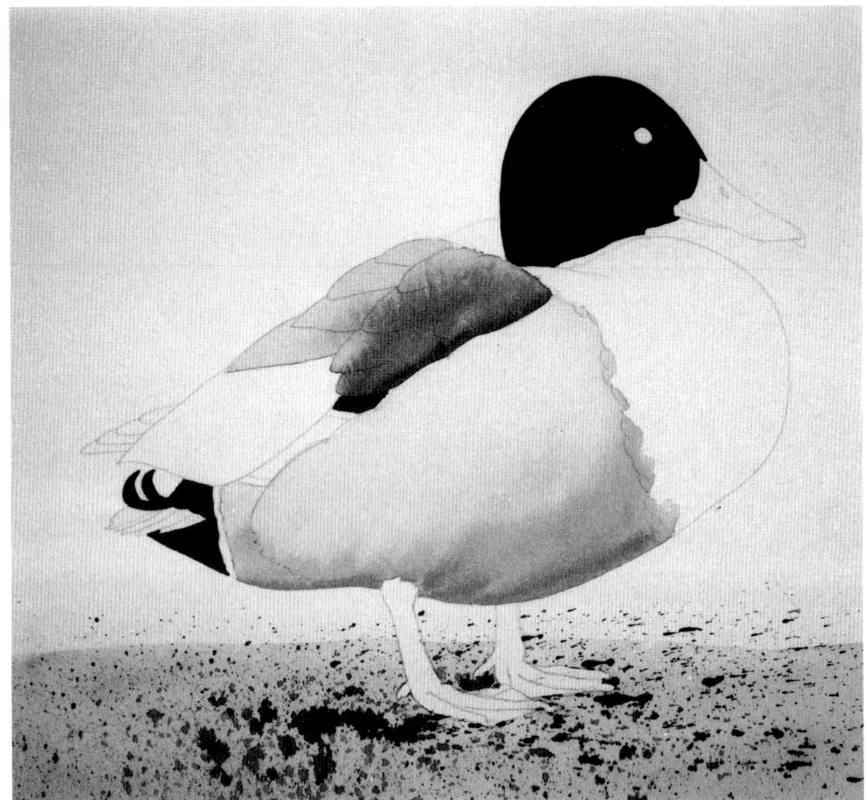

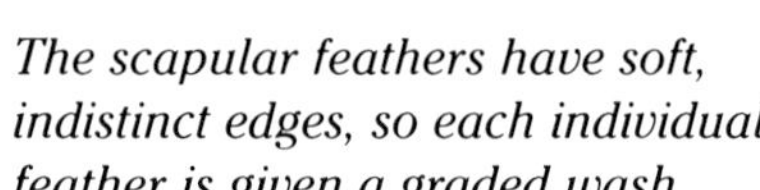

The scapular feathers have soft, indistinct edges, so each individual feather is given a graded wash.

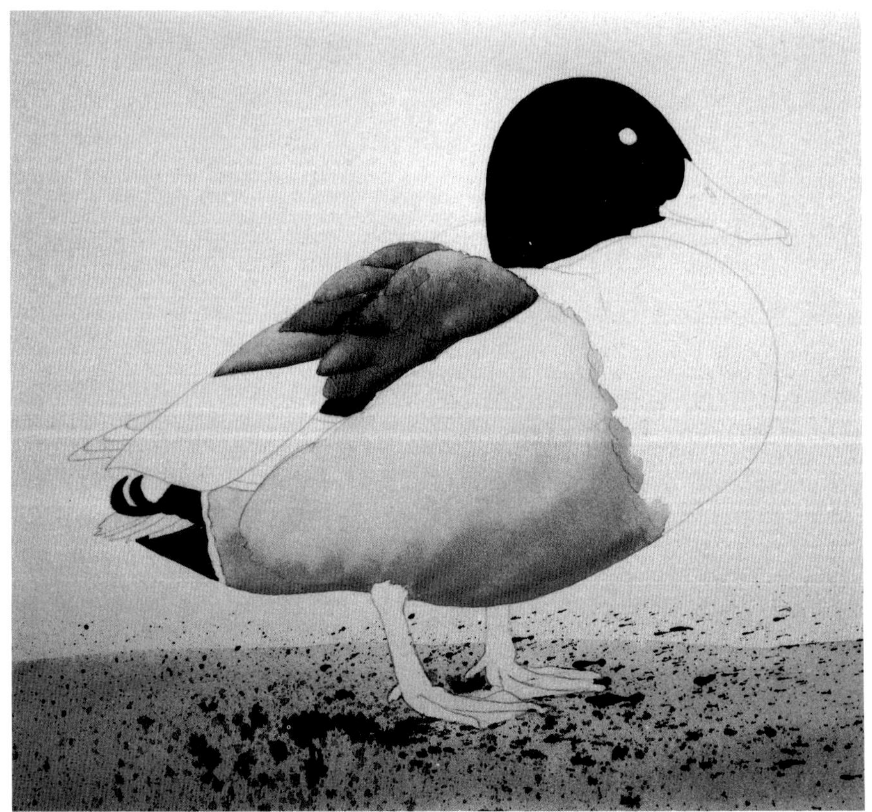

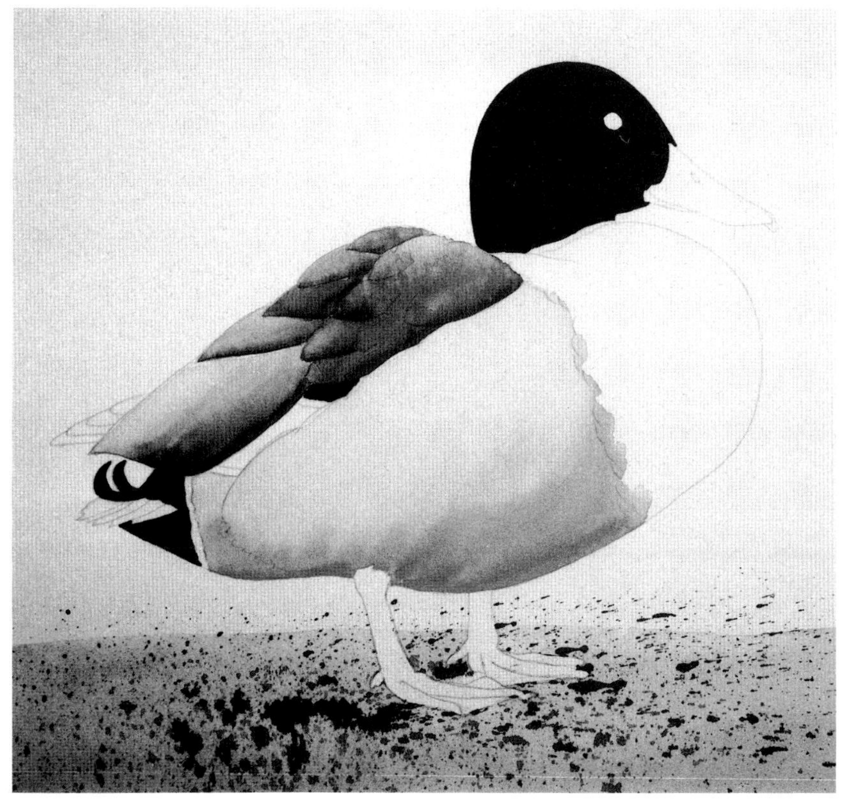

The final graded wash is painted on the single large exposed tertial.

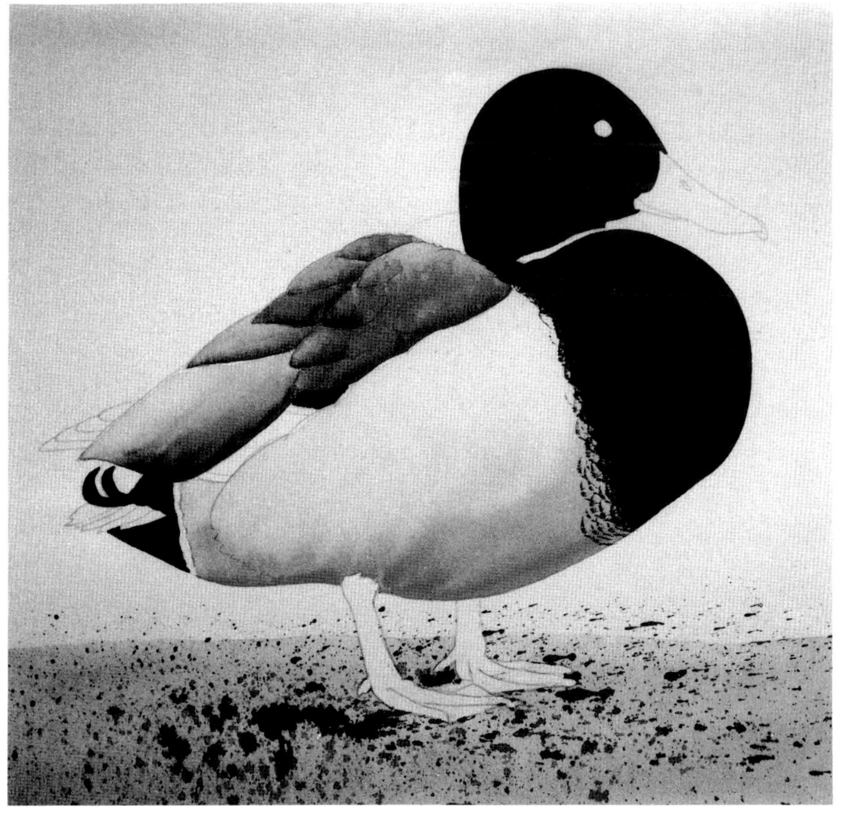

Flat opaque color is painted on the breast. Where the breast meets the belly, some of the breast feathers extend into the belly area; this is shown by tipping in opaque breast color with the filbert.

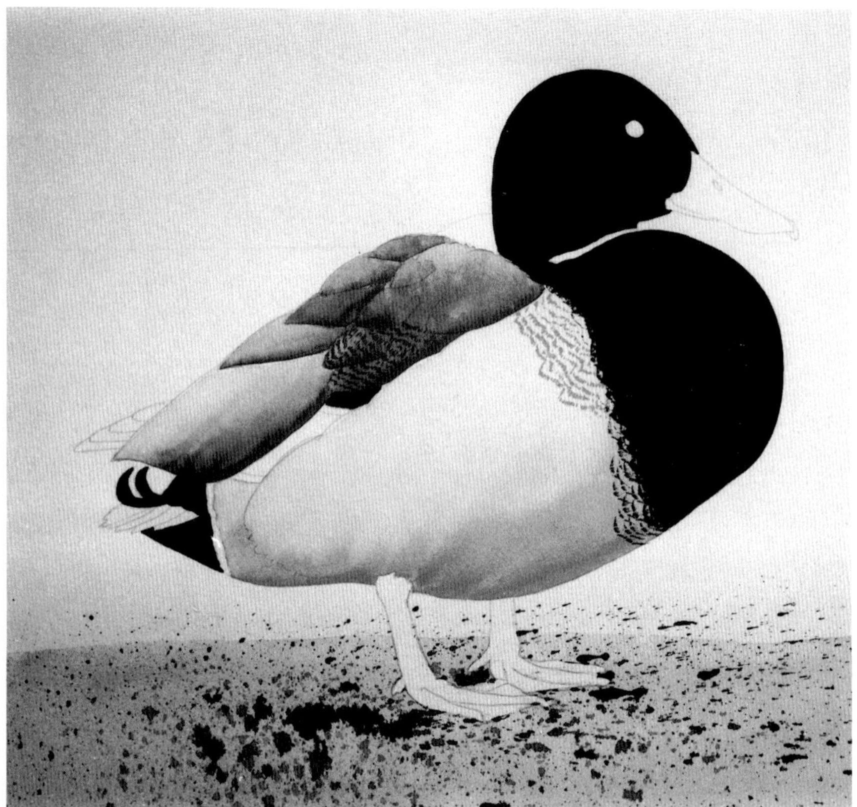

The tiny wavy feather pattern lines called vermiculation (see the Body Feathers section in chapter 6) are started by detailing them onto the flanks, belly, and scapulars with thinned paint in the #1 round.

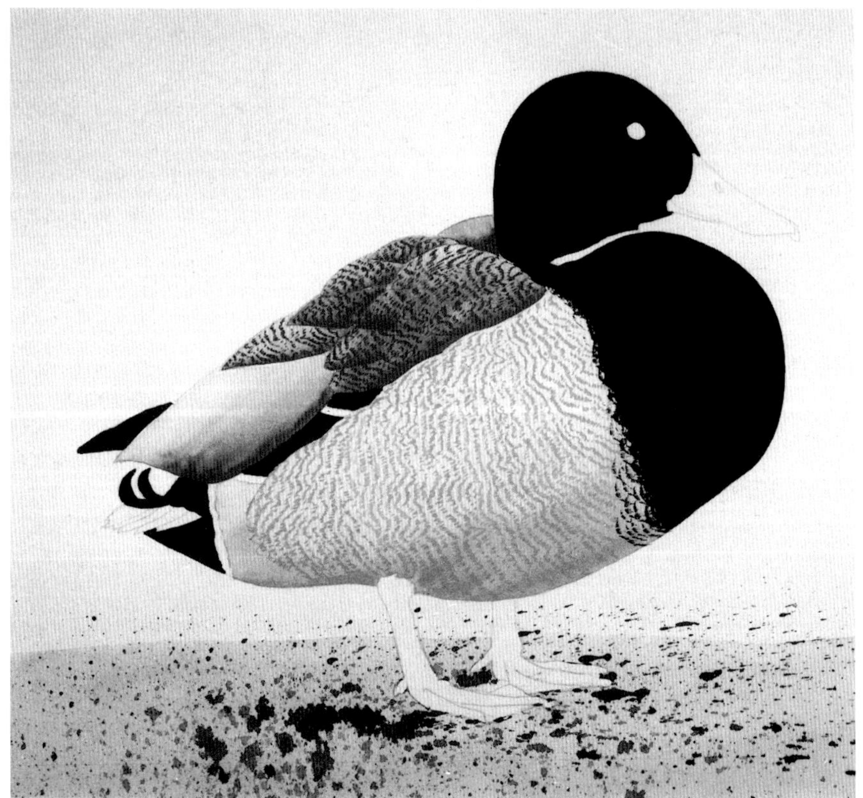

The vermiculation is completed. There is no easy way to do this because every line must be individually painted. Opaque color is painted on the speculum and primaries. A small graded wash is placed on the far side of the back.

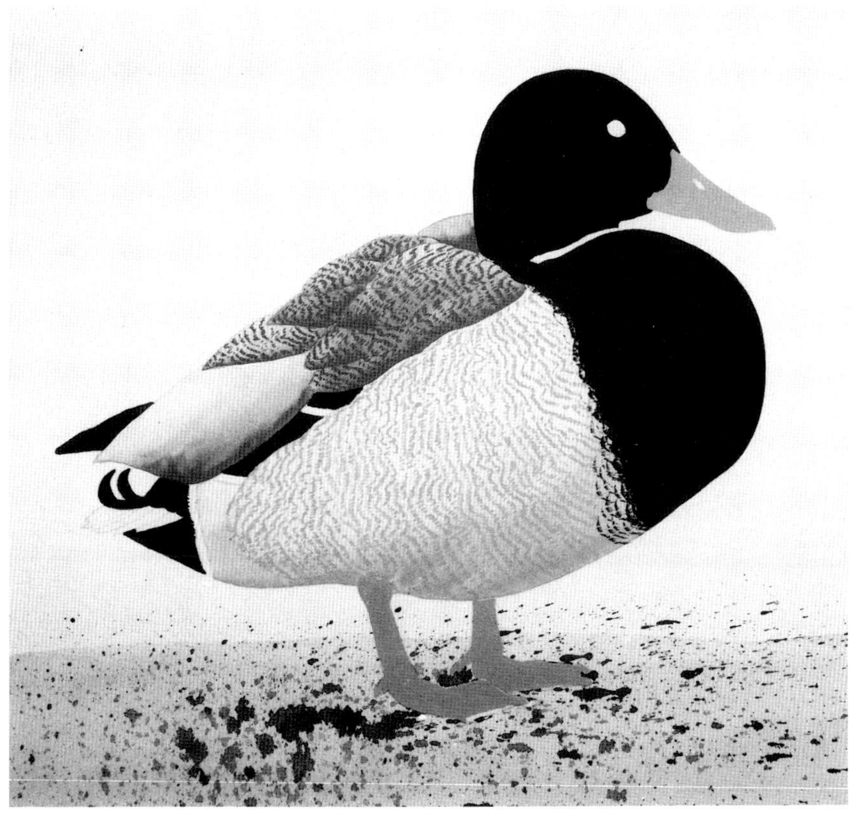

Opaque color is painted on the bill and feet. Opaque white is detailed on the tail, neck ring, and wing.

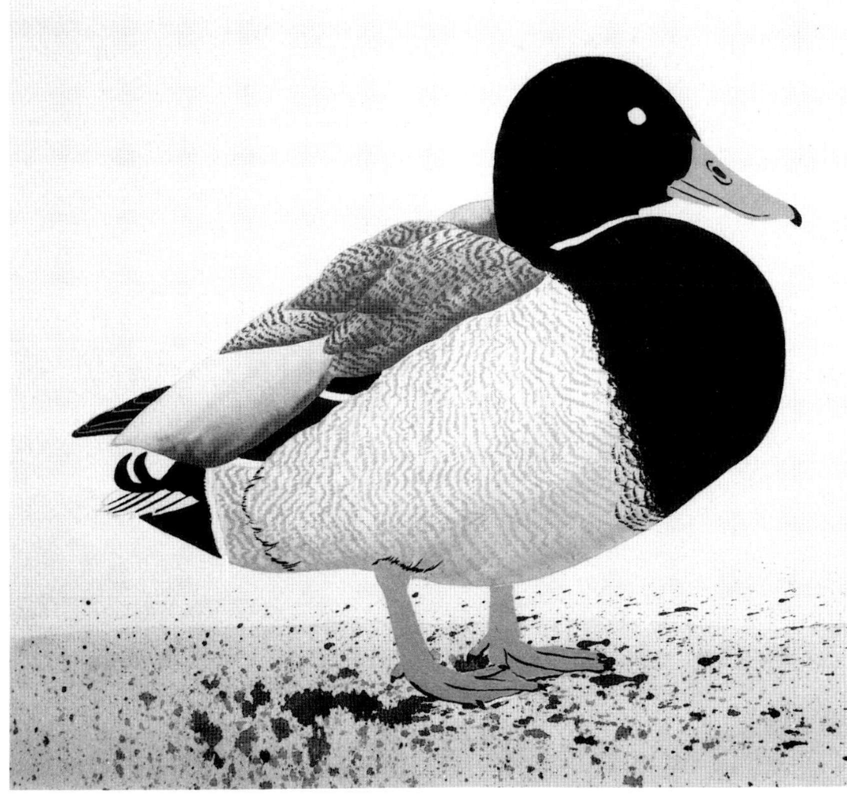

More vermiculation is painted to the rear of the sidepocket. Light color is used to detail and separate the primaries. Dark color is used to paint rough shadow areas on the tail, sidepocket, and feet; where the leg inserts into the body; the bill, the nail on the bill, and the nails on the toes.

Dark shadow areas painted in the previous step are softened and blended with a clean damp brush. Opaque white is painted on the bill and blended as it was in the dark areas. Thinned white is dabbed on the feet and legs to suggest scales. The webs of the feet are painted in with a thin dark color. Opaque black paints in the eye. White is used in the splitbrush to add highlights to the dark head.

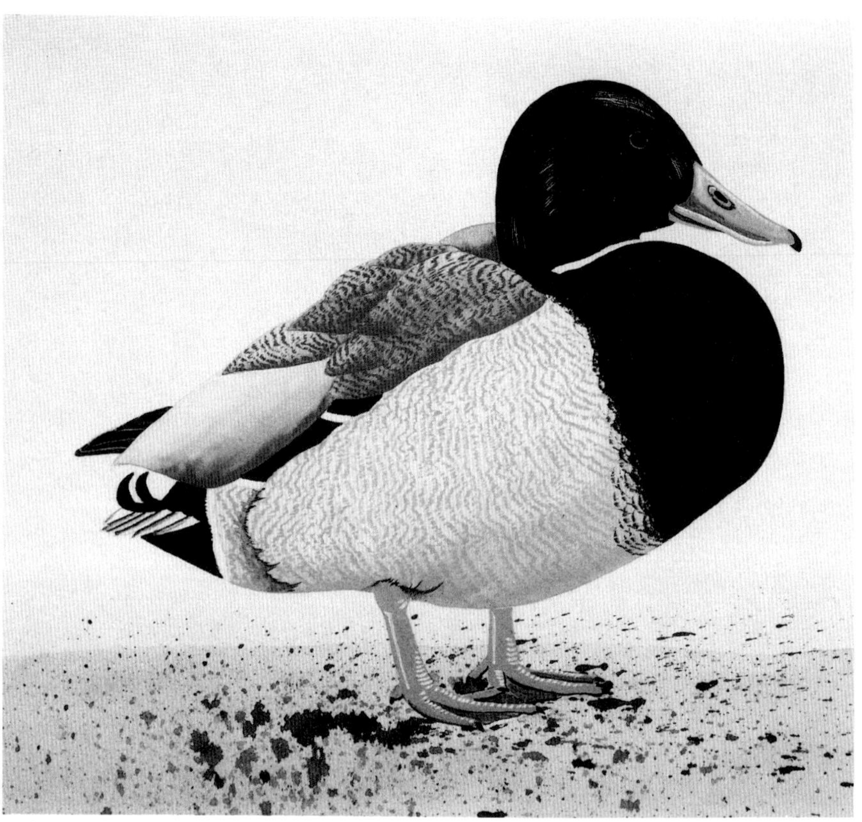

With the filbert brush, light color is tipped back into the dark breast to show lighter feather edges. The feet are defined with dark color to show shading. Opaque white is splitbrushed on the belly to impart an irregular featheration. A light eye ring is detailed in with the #1 round and an opaque white highlight is placed in the eye to give the mallard life.

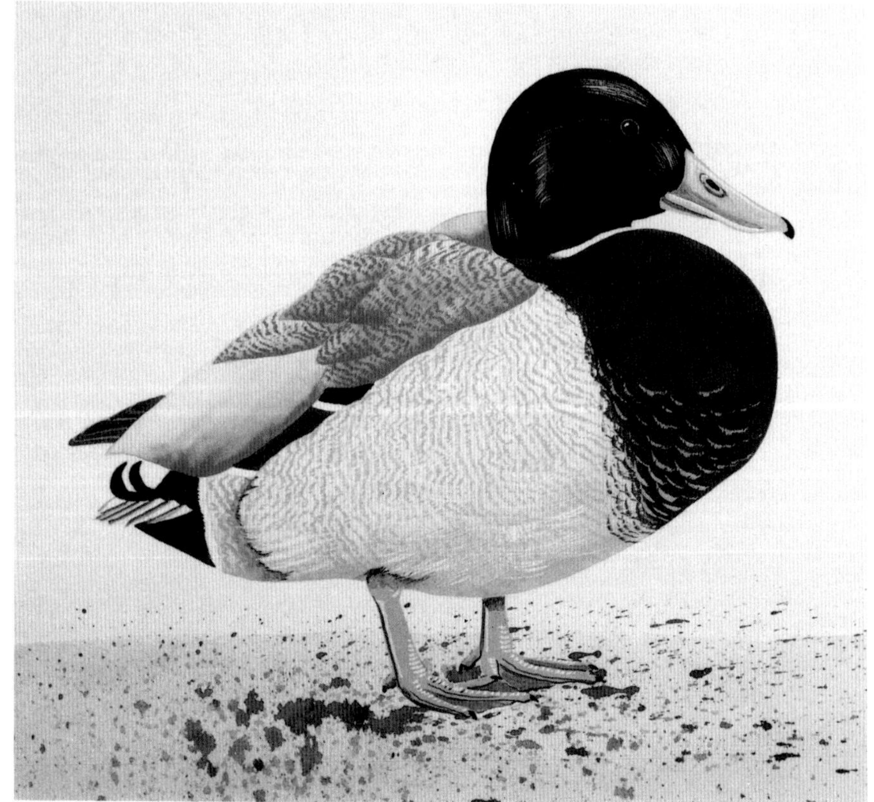

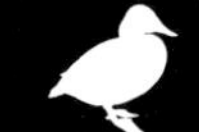

6 Describing Dabbling Ducks

Body Feathers

"Sheds moisture like water off a duck's back." Although this saying is true enough, the most commonly held belief is that this water repellancy is due to a protective oil or some other coating on the feathers. Dabbling ducks do have an oil gland and do preen their feathers with oil, but the major reason they are able to shed water is not oil, but the construction and arrangement of the feathers themselves. Their structure traps and holds air, and it is this air that repells most of the water. The wing, however, is less able to trap air and is more vulnerable to wetting. Special feather groups are arranged so that they protect the wing when puddle ducks are resting or feeding. The wing tucks into the main body feathers and is almost completely covered by the flank (sidepocket) and scapulars.

The names of feather groups on ducks correspond to those of other birds. In the case of ducks, however, two groups have been given other names: the flank feathers are known as the sidepocket, and the secondaries of the wing are called the speculum. These two names will be used throughout this book. It is important, I'd even say essential, to become familiar with the terms used to describe the feather groups. This not only will aid identification but also will facilitate following the painting examples.

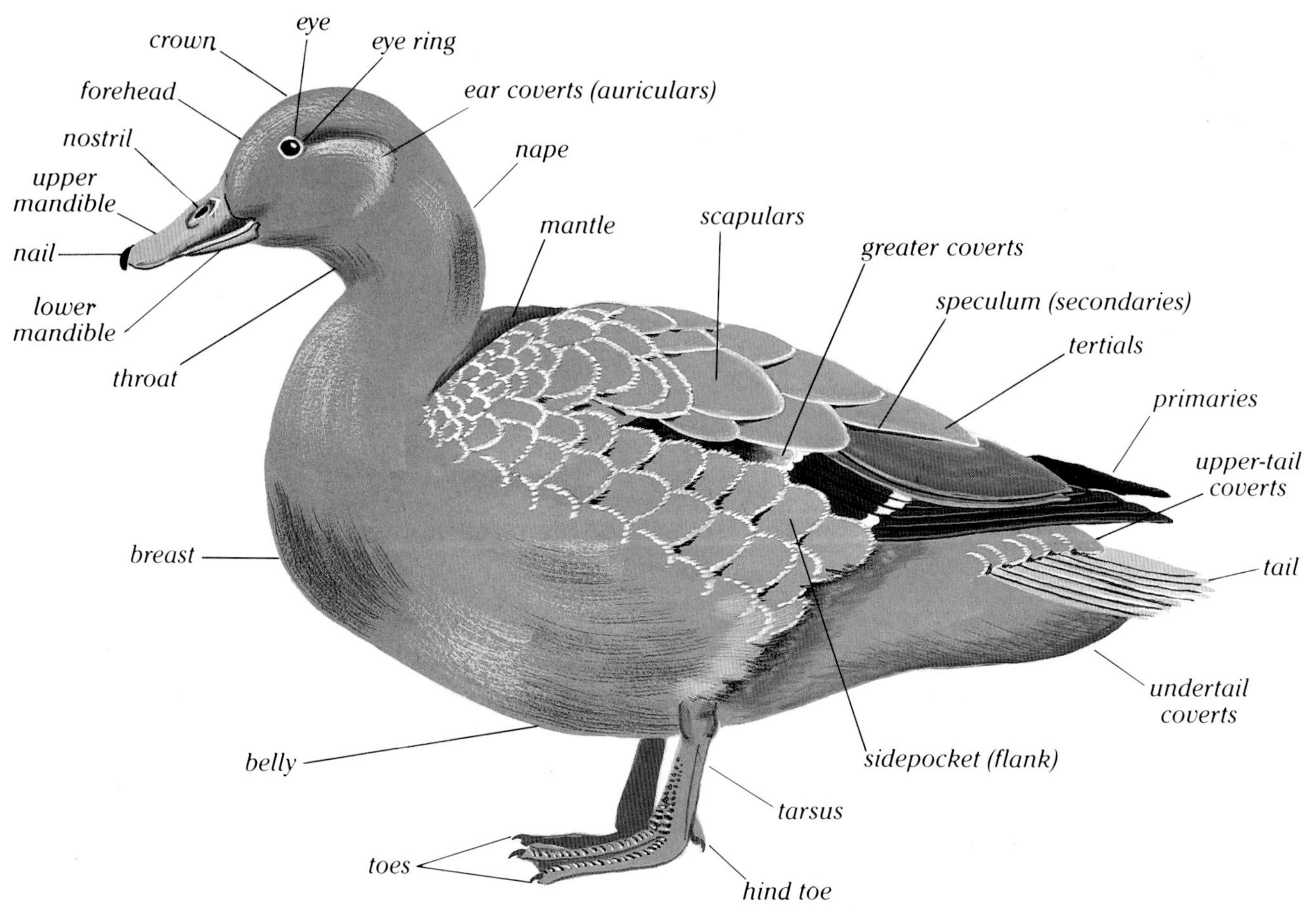

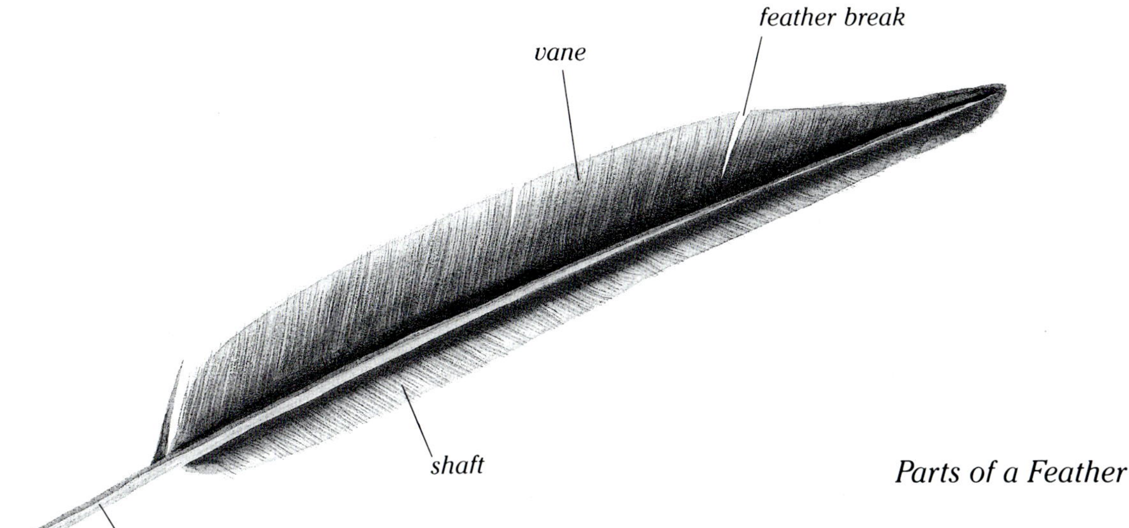

Parts of a Feather

Painting and understanding duck feathers poses distinct problems not usually found in other bird groups. These are iridescence, vermiculation, and seasonal plumage changes. To the beginner these problems may seem very difficult, but they are not. The following descriptions should help take the mystery out of understanding and dealing with them.

Iridescence. Iridescence is the characteristic of feathers to reflect brilliant colors. The structure of the feathers interferes with light rays that strike them, making the light break up and scatter, giving a changeable brilliant effect as opposed to a solid field of color. Although changeable in intensity, the color and shade usually depend on the angle and quality of light (bright or dim) striking the feathers. On overcast days or in shadow, feathers that would normally reflect a great deal just appear to be a dull gray.

The basic way to paint iridescence is to have the main color, for example a dark green, blend into black for contrast, and then paint lighter shades of green on top of the dark green until an iridescent effect is achieved.

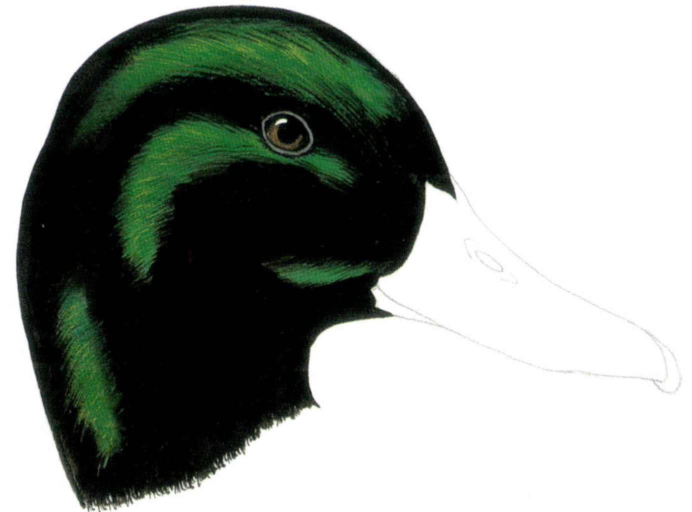

Painting iridescence. *The dark green areas of the iridescence are painted first, then black is painted opaquely over the rest of the head, using a splitbrush where it meets the dark green. Finally yellow-green highlights are lightly splitbrushed onto the dark green.*

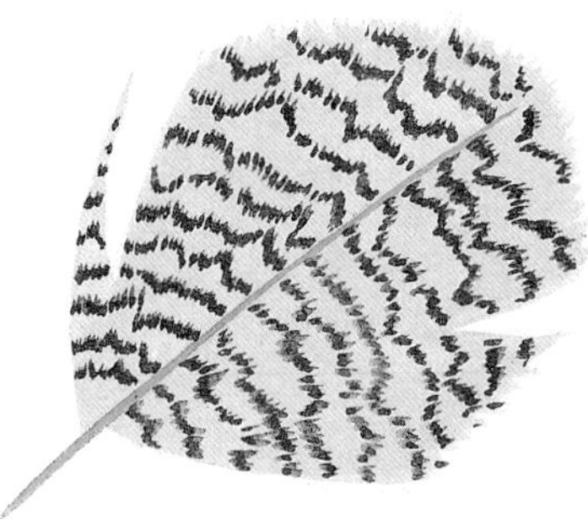

Vermiculation

Certain pearlescent paints have qualities that enable them to scatter light much like iridescence. While selected use of these paints is very effective in wood carvings, their use on flat surfaces produces a glitzy, hard look that detracts from the painting.

Vermiculation. Vermiculation literally means wormlike marks. On ducks these are the dark wiggly patterns that are usually on the sidepocket and/or scapulars. At first glance, the vermiculation appears to be a continuous pattern; a closer look, however, reveals that this is not the case. Each individual feather, whether on the sidepocket or scapular, has its own pattern; the human eye sees the overlapping of the feathers and tries to make it into a continuous pattern. In reality, the feathers create a random pattern that almost never duplicates itself. The tiny gray or gray-brown lines, which comprise the pattern, may range from spotty and light to bold and dark, depending on the species. Additionally, the wetness or dryness of the feathers may affect how dark or continuous the patterns appear.

Painting vermiculation takes observation, time, and patience—it is tedious work. When painting a very detailed close-up duck portrait, each feather vermiculation should be detailed with either a small round brush or with a

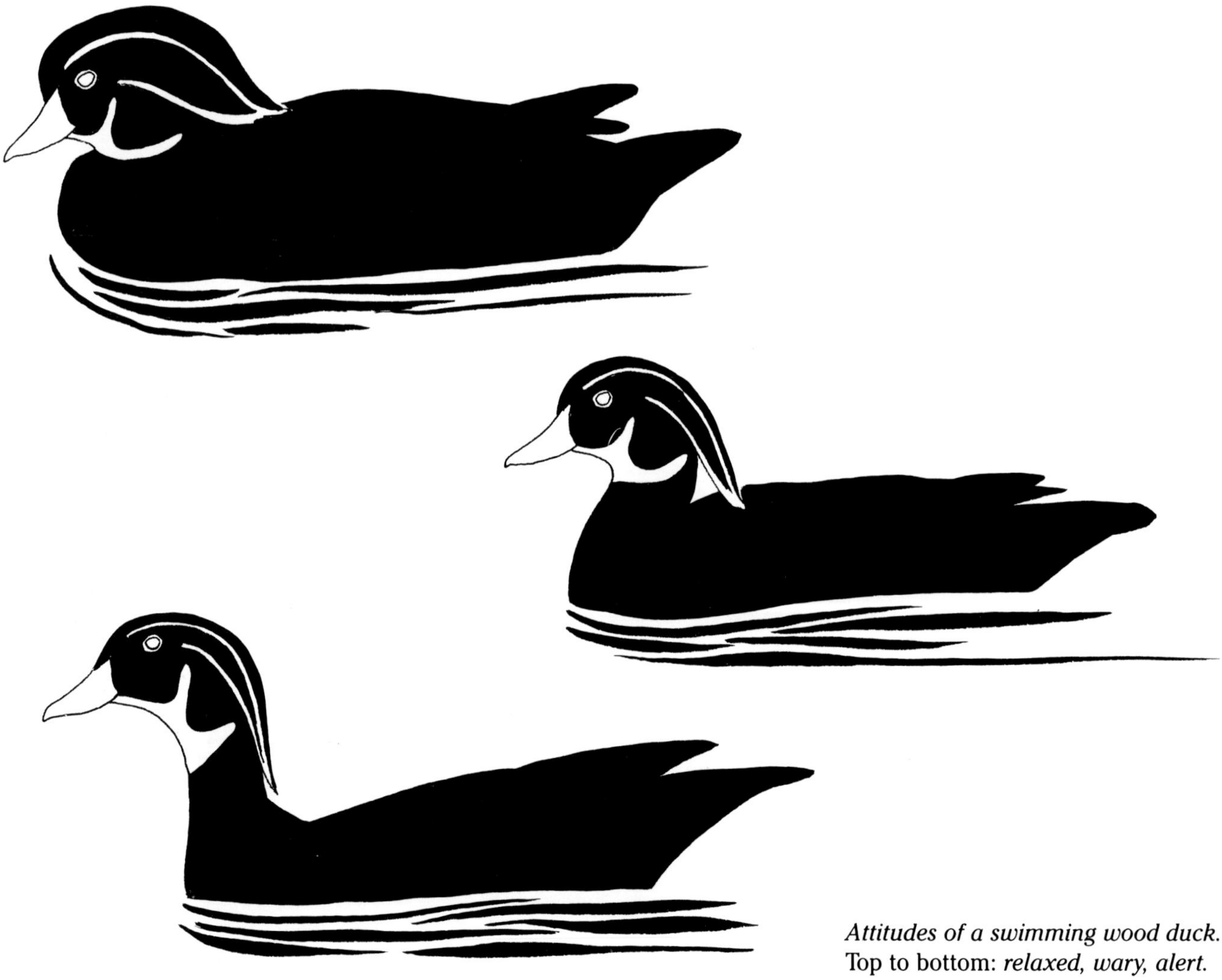

Attitudes of a swimming wood duck.
Top to bottom: *relaxed, wary, alert.*

small-tipped drafting pen loaded with thinned paint. When painting a picture where the duck is at a distance, or need not be as detailed (such as in the painting examples in this book), the vermiculation need not be as precise; groups rather than individual feathers may be painted. Unfortunately, even when painting general vermiculation there are no short cuts, each line or dot must be painted separately.

Plumage Changes. All birds go through a period of seasonal plumage change (molting), when the old feathers are replaced with new ones. What makes a duck's molt so distinctive, however, is that the change is much more apparent and occurs at certain times of the year for specific species. When painting backgrounds and vegetation, you must be sure that the color and condition of the habitat matches the duck's seasonal plumage.

Body Shape

The body shape of dabbling ducks is determined by their response to the conditions around them and to the wetness or dryness of their feathers.

It is relatively easy to judge whether a duck is excited, calm, or watchful. Body shapes and attitudes are exaggerated in response to external stimuli. A relaxed, calm, resting duck has its head tucked into its body, the body feathers are relaxed and loose, the scapulars droop; it has a rather plump look. When wary and watchful, the neck begins to extend and the feathers start to compress. When alert and greatly excited, the neck is extended fully, the feathers are compressed to the body, and, if floating, the duck rides lower in the water. The appearance is of a longer, sleeker duck.

The wetness or dryness of the feathers also affects body shape. When

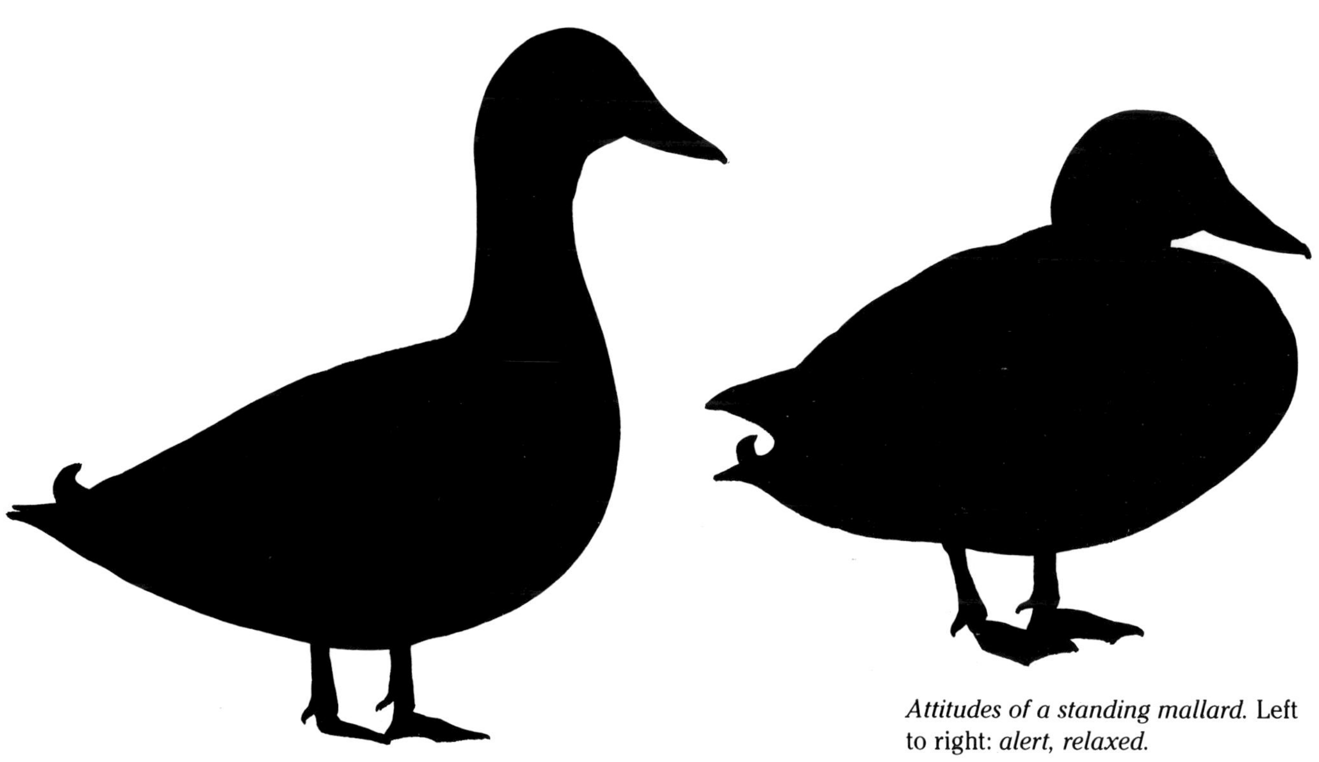

Attitudes of a standing mallard. Left to right: *alert, relaxed.*

Parts of a Green-winged Teal Wing

Upper Wing

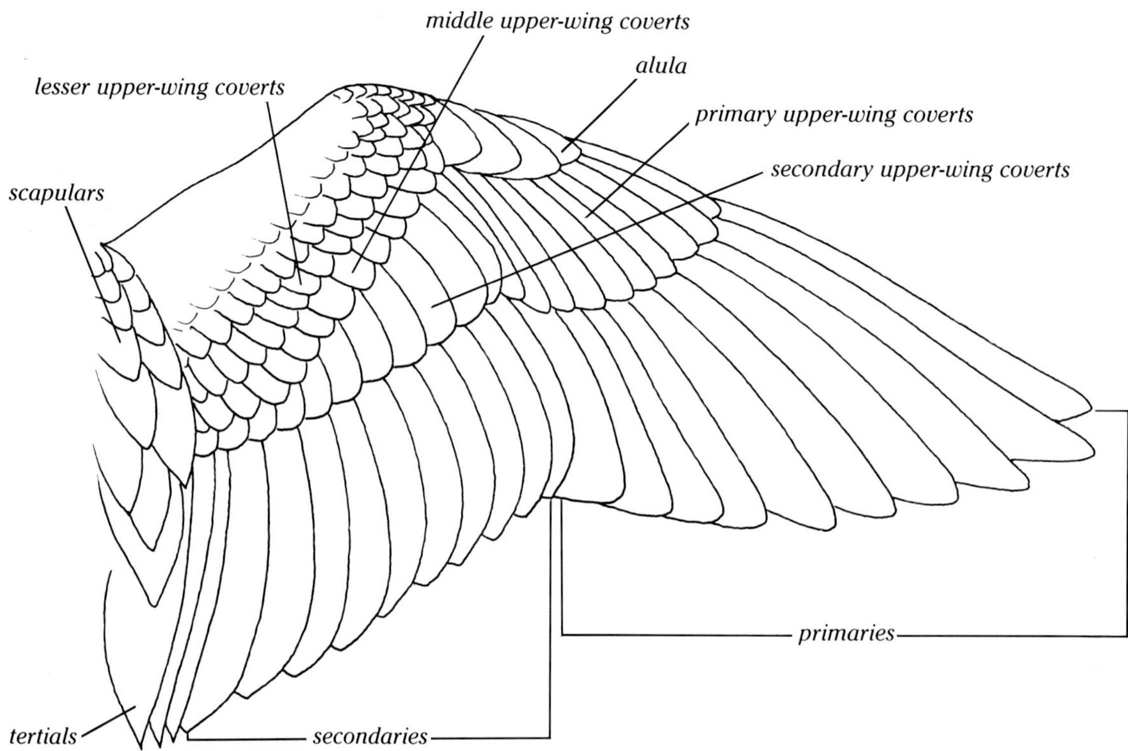

Underwing

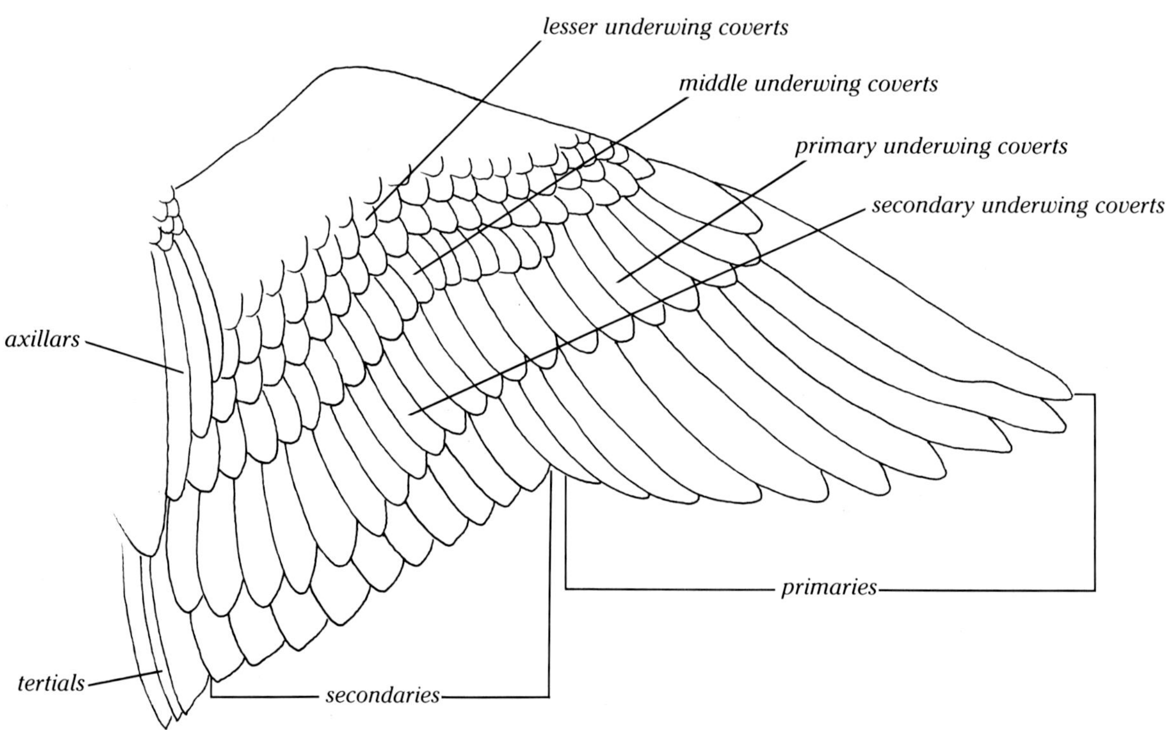

dry, dabblers have a more full-bodied look. When wet, after feeding, the head and neck feathers are slicked back and provide a very slim profile. Although most of the other body feathers will look normal, the sidepocket may be very damp and appear compressed, unlike the smooth appearance it has when dry.

Wings

The wings of dabbling ducks are suited perfectly to powerful, almost vertical take-offs and fast-maneuvering flights between trees and into small bodies of water. Strong fliers, their wings are large in proportion to their bodies and are much longer and broader than those of diving ducks. The individual feather groups of the outer part of the wing are quite easy to identify, but the feather groups of the inner part of the wing, the scapulars and tertials, often blend together and are more difficult to separate.

For painting accuracy, it is necessary to know how the feathers overlap one another. It is also essential to know the correct number of larger (flight) feathers in the wing: there are always ten primaries and ten secondaries (the speculum). Notice how the size and profiles of the tips of these feathers vary and how the speculum shows iridescence. There are usually five tertials, though this varies between species. The tertials are actually part of the secondary feather group, but because they differ in size and shape they are given a name of their own. The tertials show variation in shape and size not only between species but also between males and females of the same species. To add to the variables, it is often unclear where the tertials end and the scapulars begin. Many of the hindmost scapular feathers have the same shape and coloration as the tertials. There is a saving factor in all this confusion; because the groups may be visually inseparable, it is often not necessary, or practical, to separate the two groups in a painting. Realize, however, that there are two distinct feather groups.

As mentioned previously, the folded wing of a resting duck tucks neatly into the sidepocket feathers on the bottom and is covered on the top by the scapulars and tertials. This protects the wing from weather extremes. On a resting bird the only parts of the wing usually visible are the tips on the outermost primaries and a small part of the speculum. On some resting ducks a patch of color can be seen below the upper scapulars toward the front of the flank. You might think that this is part of the wing, but actually it is a continuation of the scapulars. These smaller upper and lower scapulars

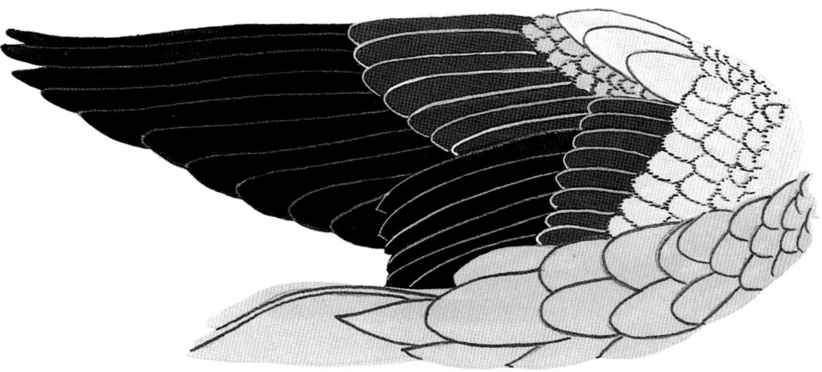

A partially folded wing. The feathers will overlap more when the wing is completely folded and tucked into the body.

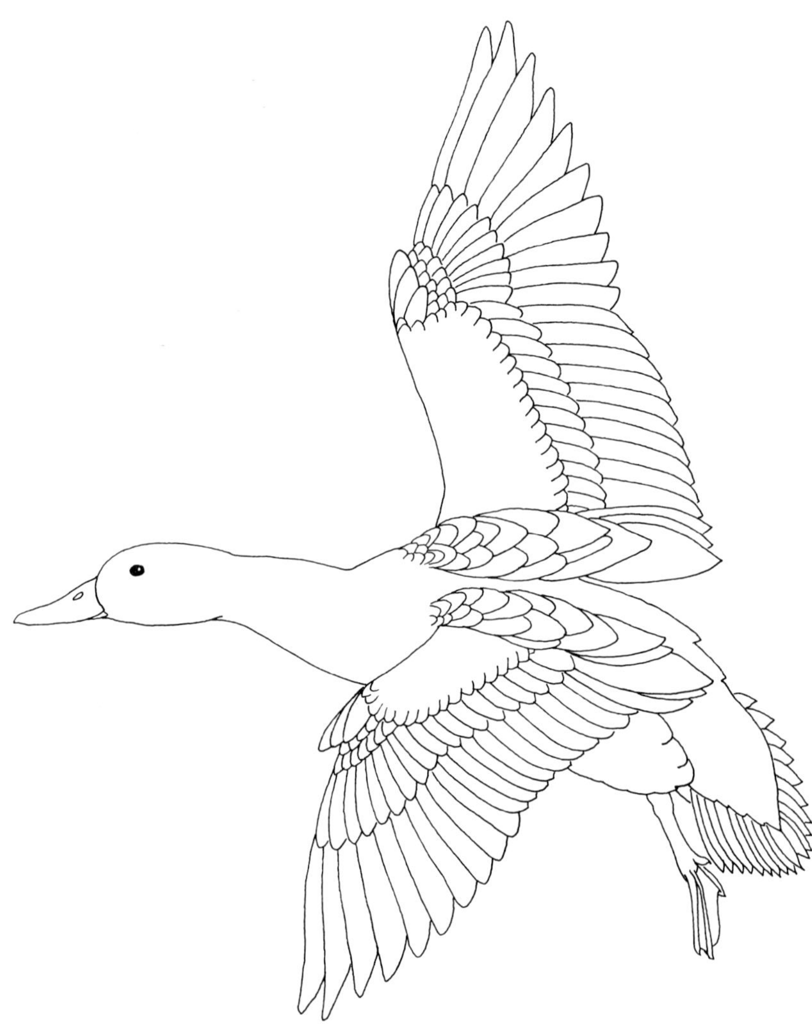

A duck in flight

have indistinct feather margins and either solid colors or patterns that blend into each other, making individual feathers difficult to separate. These feathers are usually just painted as a group. Though the main part of the wing is hidden on a resting duck, the wing feather groups and their relationship to one another are fully visible when the bird is in flight.

Tails

Diversity is the word when it comes to describing the tails of dabbling ducks. One look at the long, modified tail feathers of the pintail or the short, curly tail feathers of the male mallard confirms this. Habitat plays a part too; the tail of the wood duck, a tree-nester, is longer than that of other dabblers to provide the wood duck with greater maneuverability and braking. The number of tail feathers also varies between species; the feathers are all visible, however, only when the tail is fanned out. When the tail is folded only a small part of the feather edges shows; this may conceal a pattern on the central portion of the tail feathers. When painting a fanned tail you need good reference material so you can check to see if there is a pattern or not.

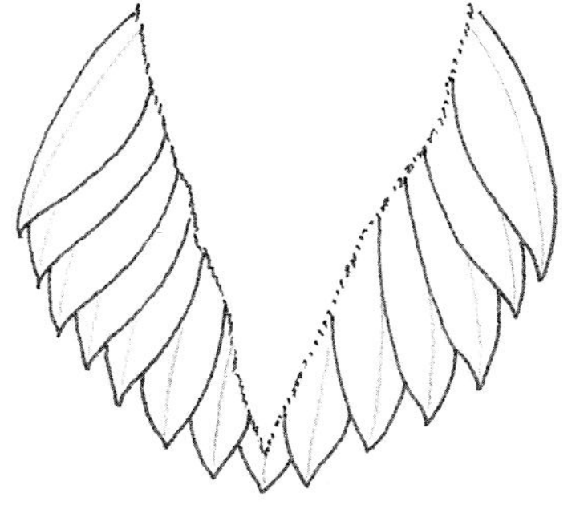

Undertail

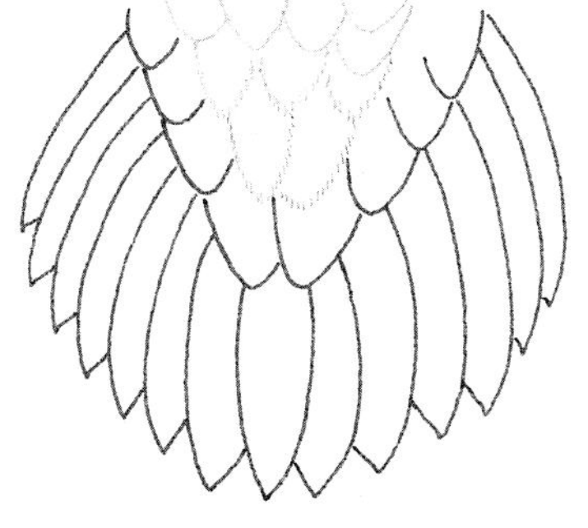

Upper Tail

Tail of a green-winged teal. The upper-tail coverts that cover the oil gland are shown with broken edges. Note that the undertail coverts extend almost to the tip of the tail.

The innermost upper tail coverts are large feathers that cover the oil gland used in preening. The feather shaft on the tail feathers changes placement as the feathers progress from the outside of the tail toward the center. On the outer feathers it is closer to the outer edge, but moves toward the center of the feathers as they go inward. (On the innermost feathers the shaft is almost exactly in the center.) The exception to this rule is the upper tail coverts immediately adjacent to the tail.

The under tail coverts tend to blend together with no distinct margins. These feathers are actually quite large and, in most cases, extend almost to the tips of the center-tail feathers.

Bills

The bill is one of a duck's most distinctive features. Although it is common to all ducks, its shape, size, color, and angle to the head varies between species. Look at the bills of a northern shoveler and an American wigeon to see the differences between the two; they vary in size, length and width, and at the angle with which they are carried to the head.

There are several features that are common to most duck bills. Bills have

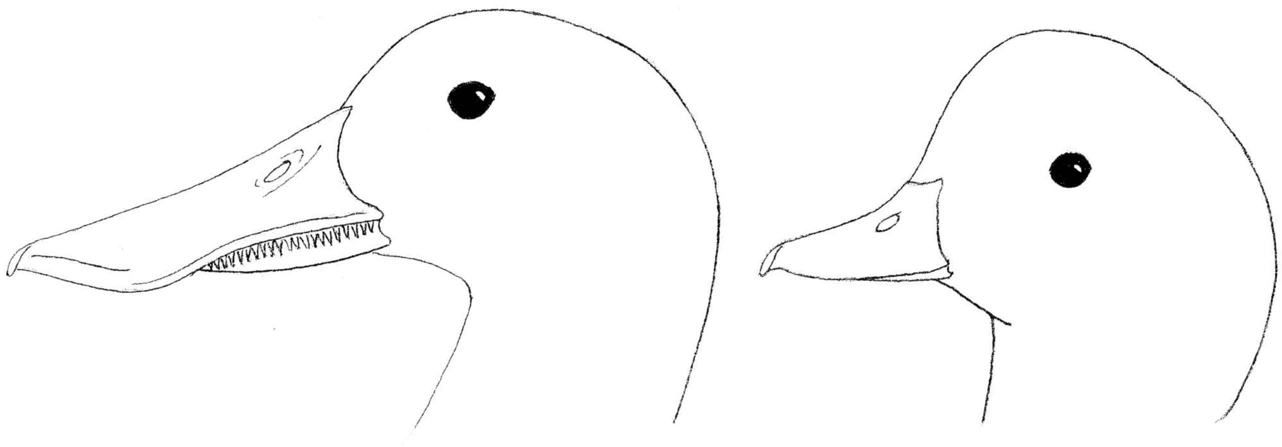

Northern shoveler bill *Wigeon bill*

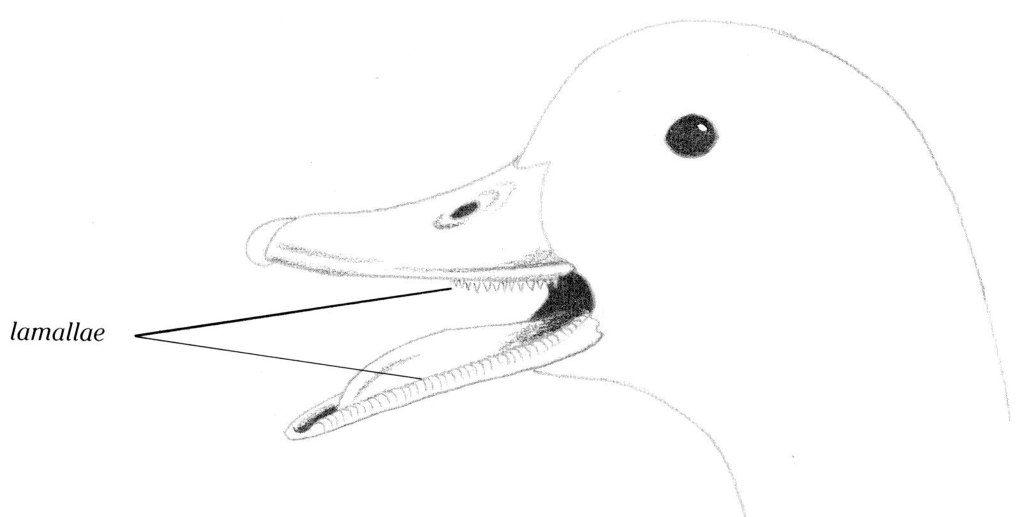

an upper and lower mandible and, typical of all birds, only the lower mandible moves; the upper is fused to the skull. The two bill parts are attached by skin, and this becomes obvious when the bill is opened wide. When closed, the lower mandible tucks under the upper except at the edge closest to the head. Lamallae are also on both mandibles. These are tiny projections that act as strainers, letting water out of the bill while retaining the food. The lamallae are particularly large in the northern shoveler.

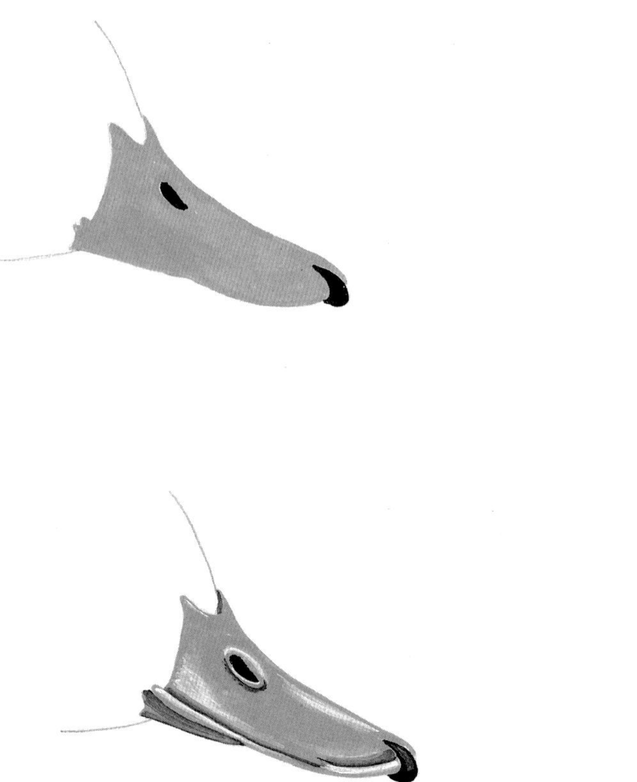

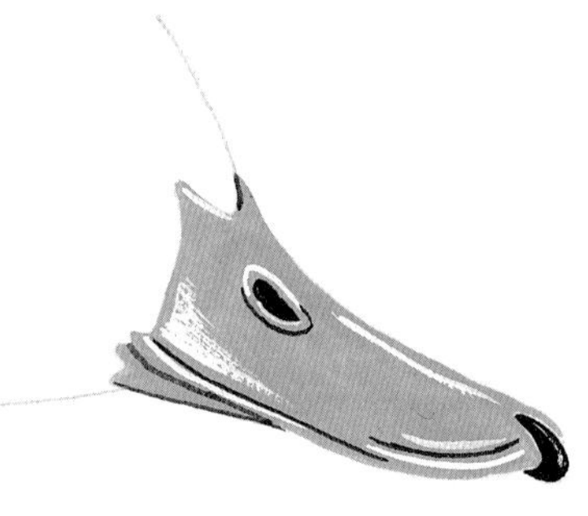

Painting the bill. *The nostril, nail, and main bill are painted with opaque color. Rough opaque highlights and shadows are added. The highlights and shadows are softened by blending the edges, then refined, adding more color to each if needed.*

On the end of the bill is the nail. It is especially apparent on the upper mandible. Again, the shape and size of the nail varies between species. The nostrils of dabbling ducks are located toward the rear of the bill. They are closer to the head in puddle ducks than those on divers, and they usually angle toward the center of the bill, rather than being parallel to each other as in diving ducks. There is also a slight ridge above and below the nostrils.

Bill colors can range from a drab yellow-green to almost black, and to the red, black, white, and yellow bill of the wood duck. The color is contained in a thin membrane that covers the hard, bony bill, and the color quickly fades in death. Some bills have patterns and although the pattern for a given species is fairly consistent, slight differences do occur. Seasonal plumage changes also affect the color of the bill; it may become blotchy or lose some of its color intensity.

Feet

Webbed feet are another distinctive feature of ducks. Folding forward on the upstroke and fanning out on the backstroke, the feet are beautifully designed for propelling ducks through the water. The webbed feet, short legs, and chunky body do not lend themselves to a graceful walking motion, however (although dabbling ducks fare much better on land than do diving ducks). The legs of dabblers are located toward the center of the body (as opposed to divers, whose legs are further to the rear). Notice, too, how the leg and foot are angled toward the center of the body to maintain balance.

The foot has four toes: three forward toes and one small hind toe. The forward toes are slightly curved and each has a different number of joints.

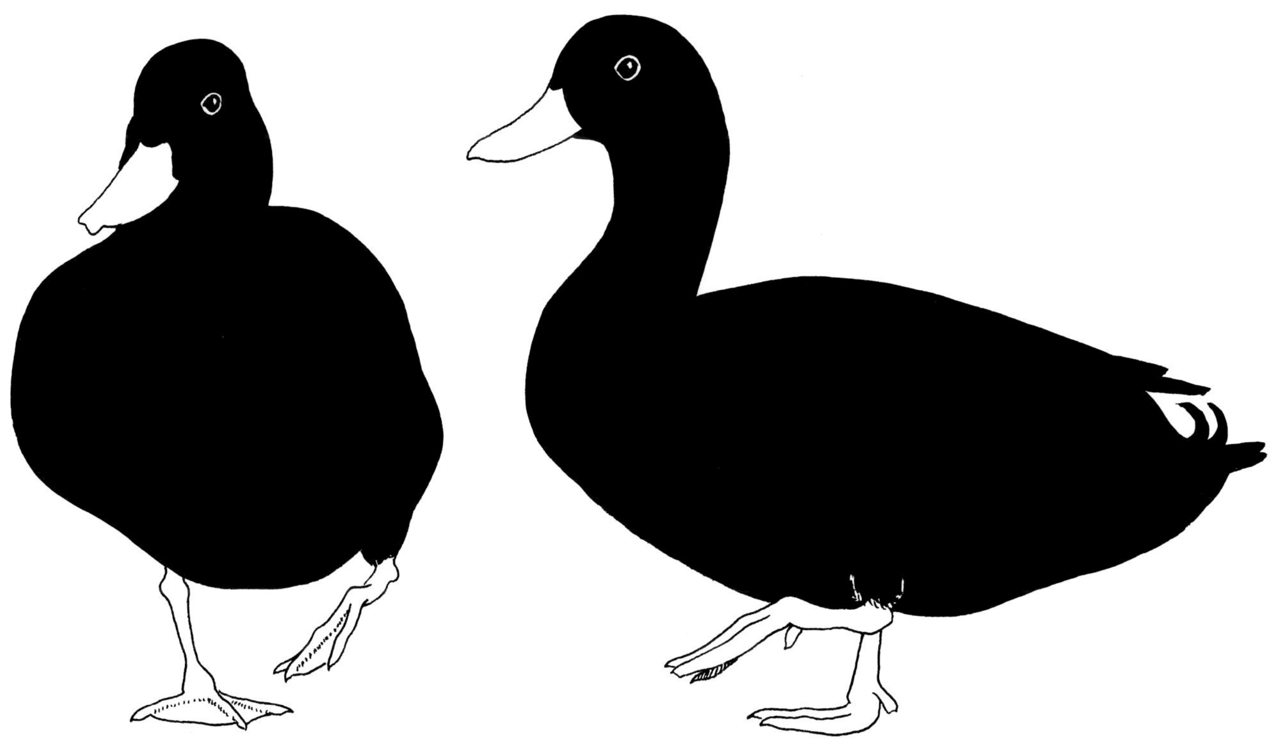

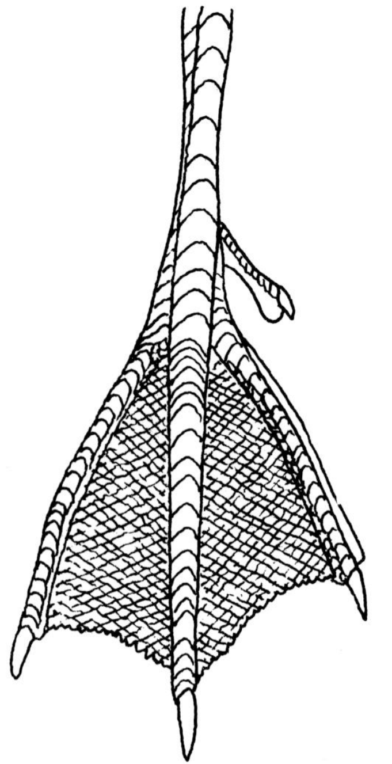

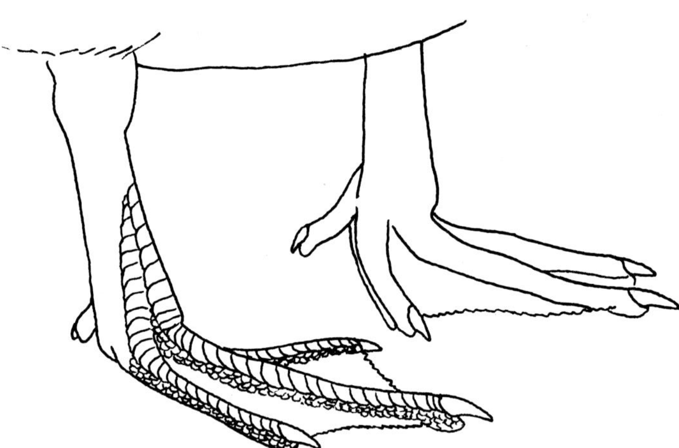

Right foot of a dabbling duck

The outside toe has three joints, the center toe has two, and the inside toe only one. The inside toe also has a small flap of skin on its outside edge. The small hind toe angles toward the inside of the foot and has no flap on it, as does the hind toe of divers. The hind toes of a dabbling duck face toward the inside of the foot and the feet angle inward. The web of the foot is flexible and, when on land or logs, will conform to the surface on which the duck is standing. The surface of the web has a reticulated pattern. The colors of legs and feet range from solid bright colors to drab shades, and some dark spotting can also occur.

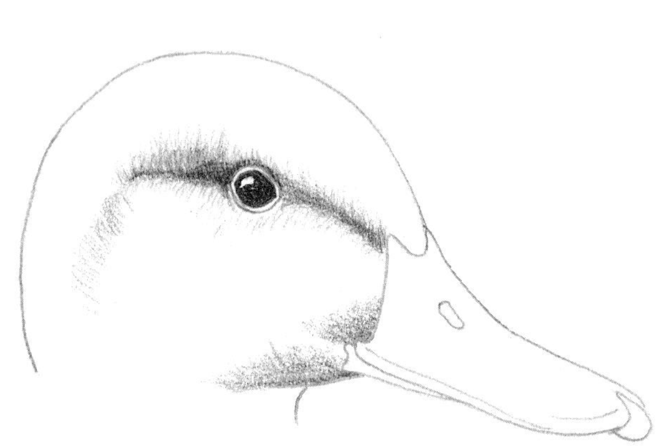

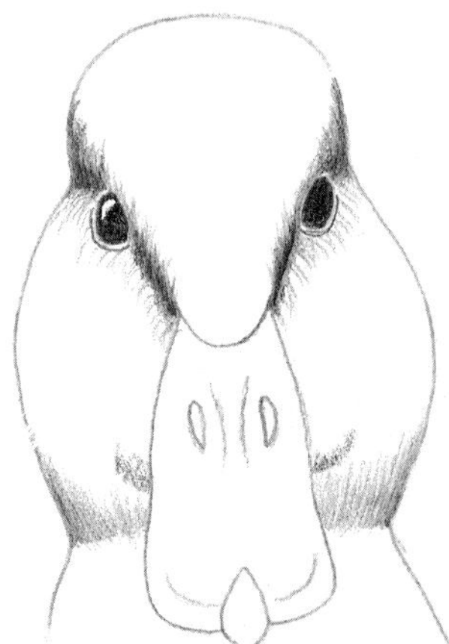

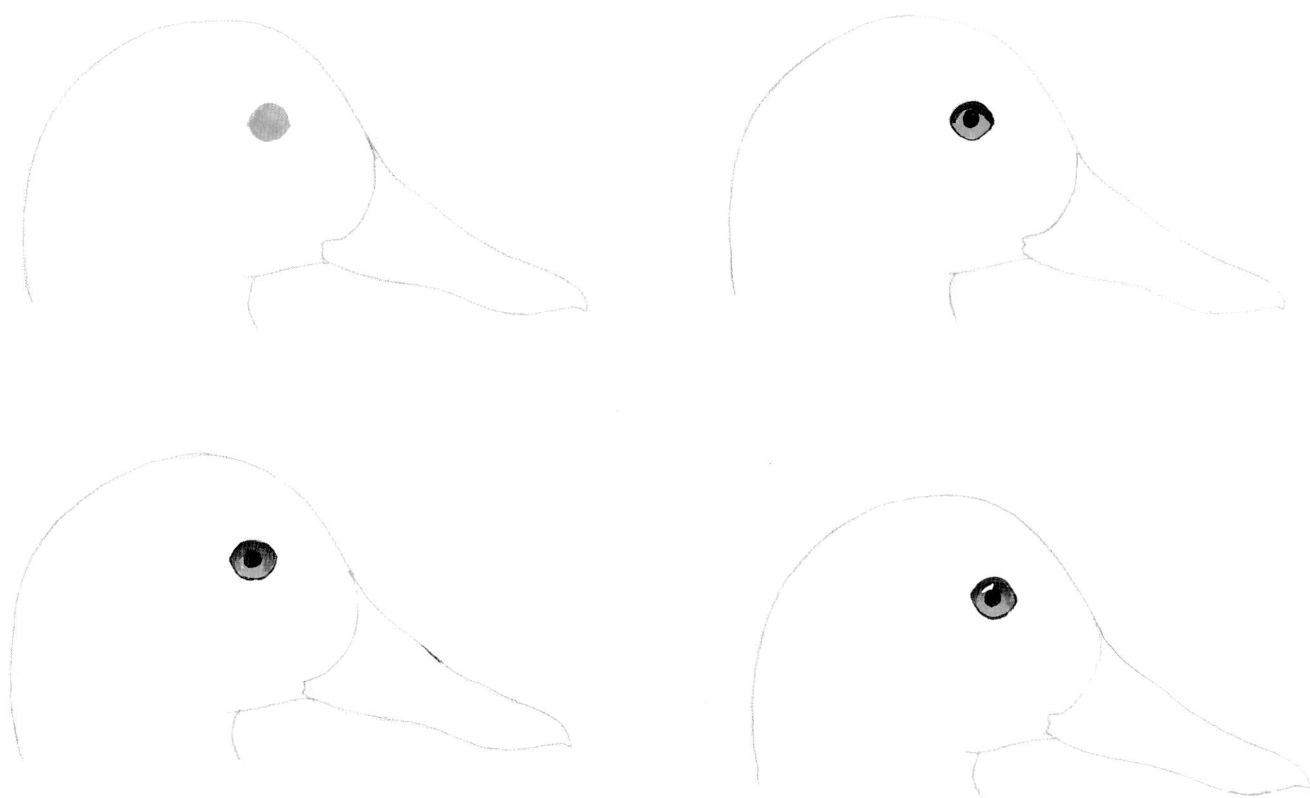

Eyes

Although the eyes of ducks are placed on the side of the head, they are set in a deep indentation that is not found in other birds. This indentation runs from the bill past the eye and toward the back of the head where it disappears; undoubtedly it allows for better vision around the bill. When looking straight ahead, ducks have binocular (two-eye) vision; when looking in other directions, they have monocular (single-eye) vision and, because the eyes do not move in the head, ducks must tip their heads to see in different directions. The eyeball is saucer-shaped when viewed from the front and round when seen from the side (although the skin surrounding the eye gives it an elliptical look). In a painting, the curvature of the eye into the head is shown by a shadow; this creates a believable-looking eye. The iris color of dabblers is usually a shade of brown; the exception is the bright red iris of the wood duck.

Painting the eye. *The iris color is painted. Opaque black is used to paint in the pupil and the shadow at the top of the iris. The shadow is blended down into the iris to give it depth. An opaque white highlight adds "life" to the eye.*

7
Painting Examples

Random Notes Prior to Painting

When following the examples, you will notice that at times certain adjustments are made to the painting in color, value, shape, and so on. This is the way a painting actually progresses; changes are always being made. These examples were not prepainted and then redone for this book. These are first-time examples, done so you could see the real process of bird painting, corrections and all. Very little may be learned from watching the painting of a flawless picture.

Plan ahead when beginning a painting; have at hand only those brushes, colors, and materials that you will need. Excess tubes, brushes, and whatever only add clutter when you need it least. Though the colors on your palette look organized when first squeezed out, don't be dismayed when it all seems a mess after a short time. Very few artists maintain a controlled palette. Have a scrap of watercolor board handy to test brushes for load and stroke, and a rag or paper towel to blot brushes. Give yourself clean water, brushes, all the other materials you may need, and time to paint.

All the examples were painted on cold press illustration board and the paints are gouache (designers colors). Winsor & Newton and Pelikan colors are used interchangeably, except in the case of raw umber, where the brand used is noted. (Winsor & Newton raw umber is yellower than Pelikan raw umber.)

These examples are painted in gouache, but, with a few adaptations of technique, the same methods and colors may be used with acrylics. The variations in technique are noted in the text of the examples.

Drawings

Following the color painting examples are black-and-white line drawings of the individual ducks. By eliminating shading and individual feathers, and only showing significant body patterns and major feather groups, their relationships to one another become more apparent as seen from various angles. The poses show dabbling ducks in different states of excitement, and head and body shapes and the relationship of the eye and bill are seen from some unusual angles. The drawings were done from photographs and specimens to ensure accuracy. These drawings will provide additional references to the form and attitudes of dabbling ducks and enable you to paint a realistic duck no matter what the pose.

Water

Water is the natural habitat of ducks, so it is important to understand some of its properties. Pure water is colorless—a condition that rarely appears in nature. Water usually has a color that may come from a variety of sources: plant life, dissolved materials, chemicals, or turbulence. Water also has another source of color: its surroundings. The surface acts as a mirror and reflects the sky, objects on the bank, or objects resting on the water. An absolutely calm surface would reflect a perfect image; water movement, however, will distort the image. Water and its reflected images must be studied carefully to produce a realistic rendering. In the painting examples the water and reflections are presented in a very simple, straightforward manner because the emphasis of this book is on painting the duck.

Northern Pintail

Anas acuta

The two adjectives used most often to describe the male northern pintail are handsome and elegant. The pintail is sleek and graceful; it has a long, pointed tail and a slender neck with crisp white markings. Very expressive, the neck is curved and swanlike when relaxed and long and thin when excited. The distinctive profile of body and head does not belong exclusively to the male. The female is beautiful, too. Equally as streamlined, she has a more muted coloration of medium-brown feathers that are edged with a lighter shade of brown.

Pintails are second in abundance only to mallards. They have longer, more pointed wings than do most dabblers, and they are swift, strong, and agile fliers. Great numbers of pintails migrate long distances.

The larger scapulars and tertials of the male pintail are similar in shape and color; thus it is difficult to separate the different groups. The two long center-tail feathers are unique, as are the white stripes that extend from the breast onto the neck and head. The dark bill has a bluish stripe on each side; the shape of the stripe may vary slightly between ducks. A pintail painting is rather straightforward; gray, black, and white are the most frequently used colors. The exception is the head, which is a dark, rich brown.

The palette used is white, ivory black, ultramarine blue pale, Payne's gray, Pelikan raw umber, raw sienna, and Vandyke brown. The brushes used are #1 and #3 Kolinsky sable rounds, a #2 filbert and a ½-inch flat sable wash. Unless noted otherwise, the brush used is the #3 round.

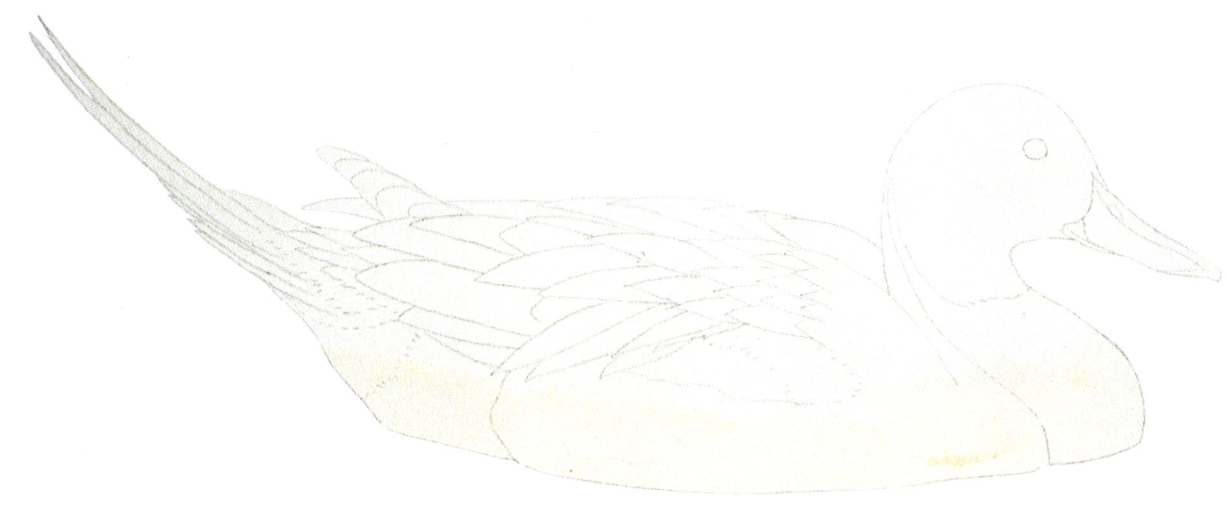

The pintail drawing is transferred to the painting surface and the lower portion of the duck is coated with liquid masking fluid.

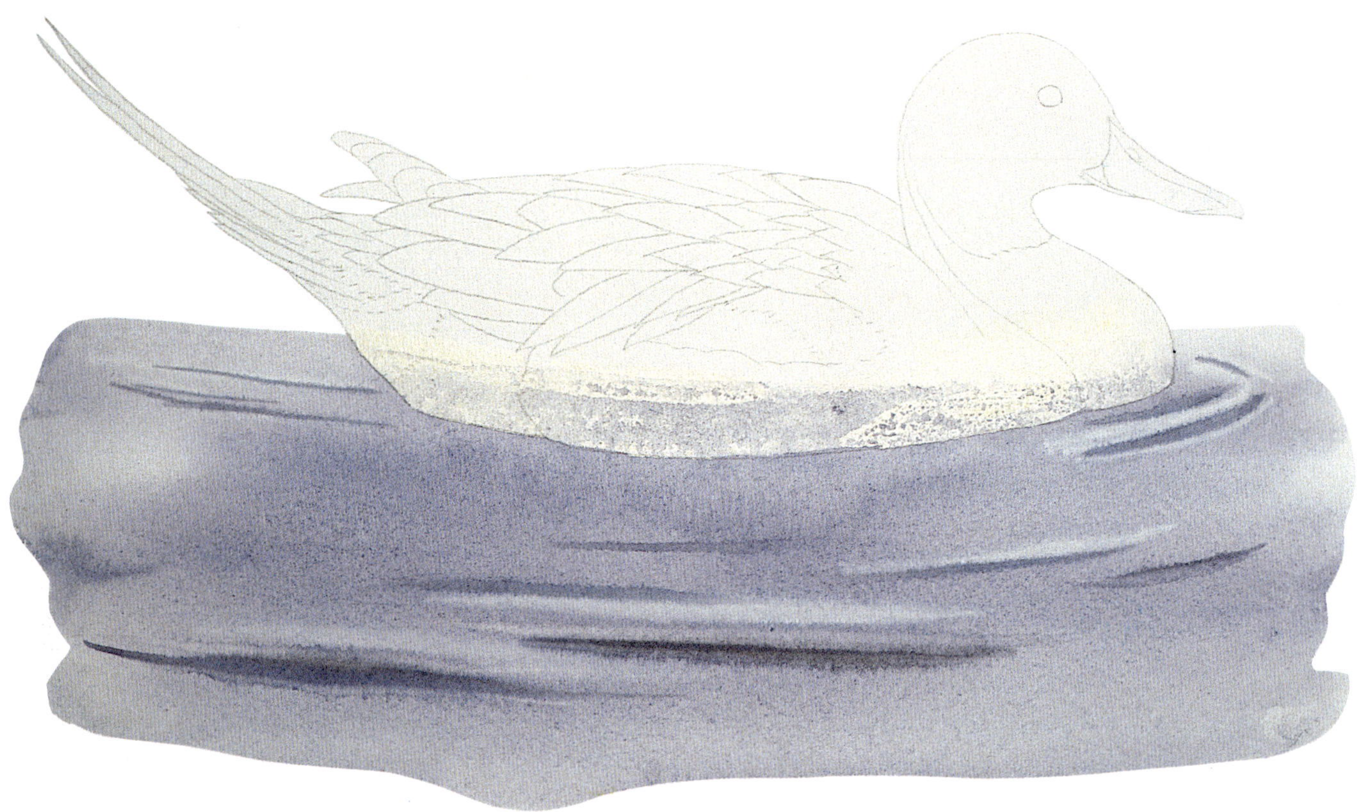

Using the half-inch flat, a wet-in-wet wash of Payne's gray mixed with ultramarine blue pale is painted below the duck to indicate water. While this wash is still wet, opaque white and a mixture of ultramarine blue pale and black are alternately stroked in at random to show water highlights and shadows.

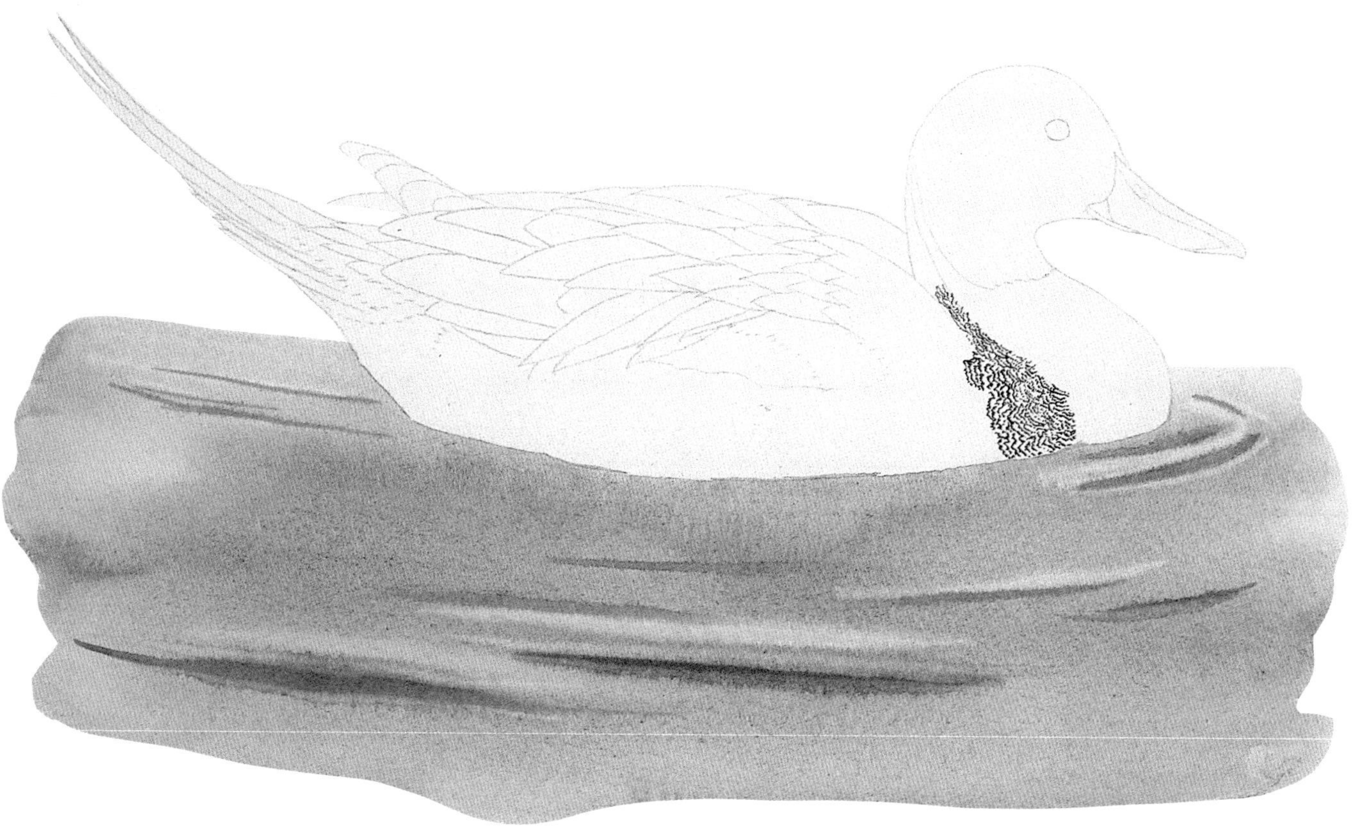

When the water wash is dry, the masking is removed. The rather tedious job of painting vermiculation is begun by using black in the #1 round.

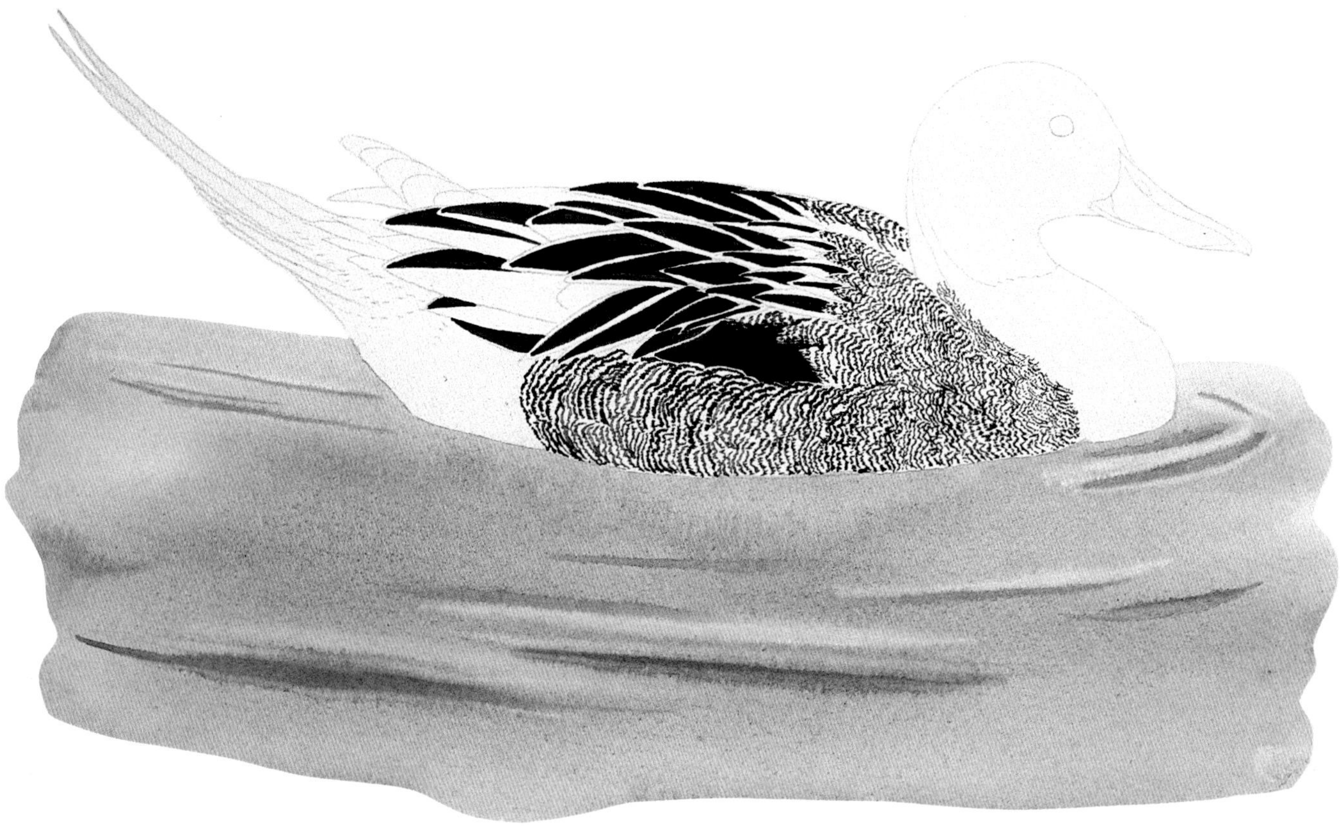

Painting the vermiculation on the breast, flank, and some scapulars is completed. Notice how the width of the vermiculation increases as it progresses toward the rear of the sidepocket. Do not worry if some of the vermiculation is darker or lighter; this is the way it appears in nature because the feathers overlap. Opaque black is then used to paint in the dark patterns on the scapulars and tertials. The black patch on the side is not part of the wing but is comprised of overlapping black scapular feathers. Where this patch meets the sidepocket, black is split-brushed back into the sidepocket to show an irregular feathered edge.

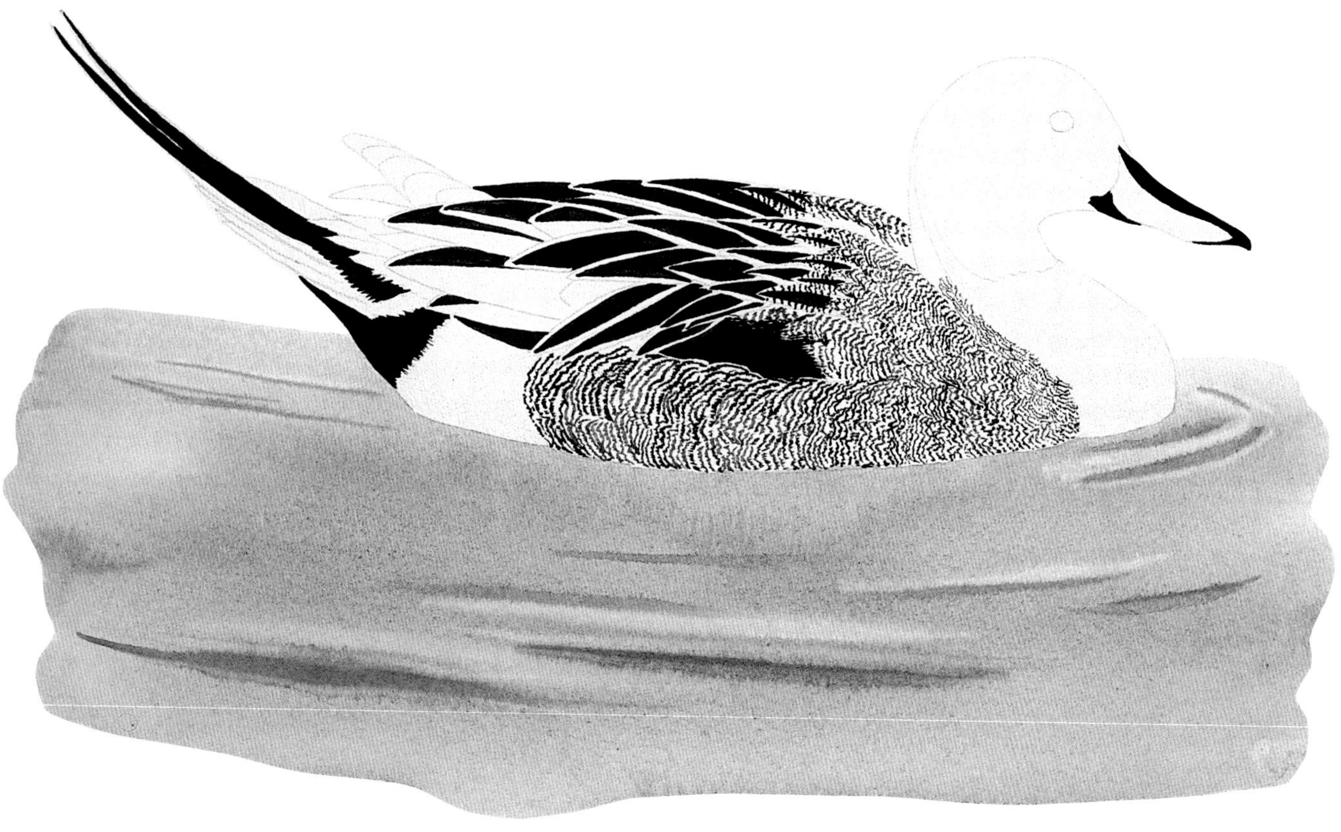

Opaque black is painted on the remainder of the back area, under tail and upper tail coverts, the two long center-tail feathers, and the bill. The #1 round is filled with black and used to add vermiculation to some of the forward scapulars with black centers. A base coat of opaque white is painted on the breast, neck stripe, rear of the side-pocket, and on the front-most upper tail coverts.

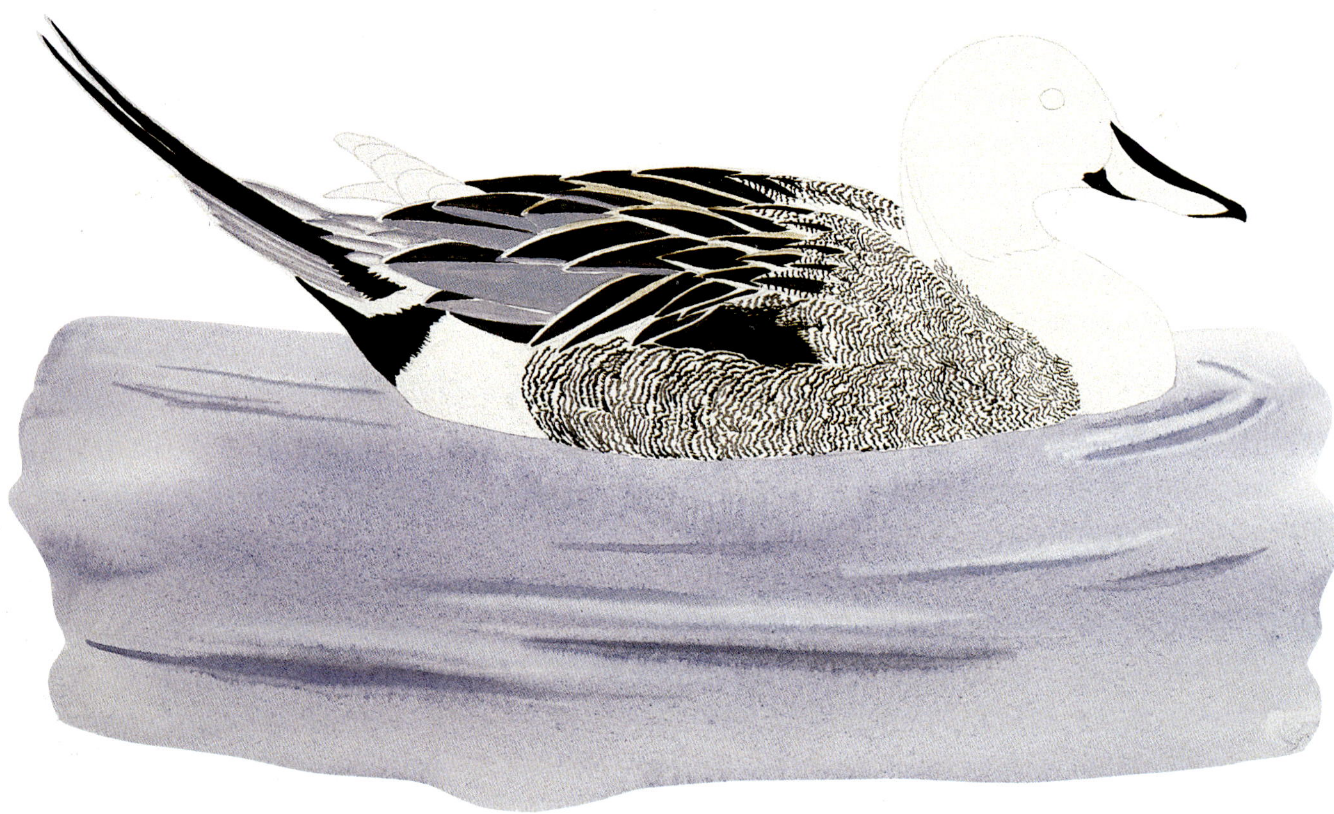

A mixture of Payne's gray and white is painted at the top of each white upper tail covert and individually graded down onto each feather. The same mixture and technique is used on each white tail feather. This mixture is also painted opaquely on the tertials and some of the larger scapulars. A thin coat of diluted raw umber is detailed on the inner white edge of the remaining scapulars.

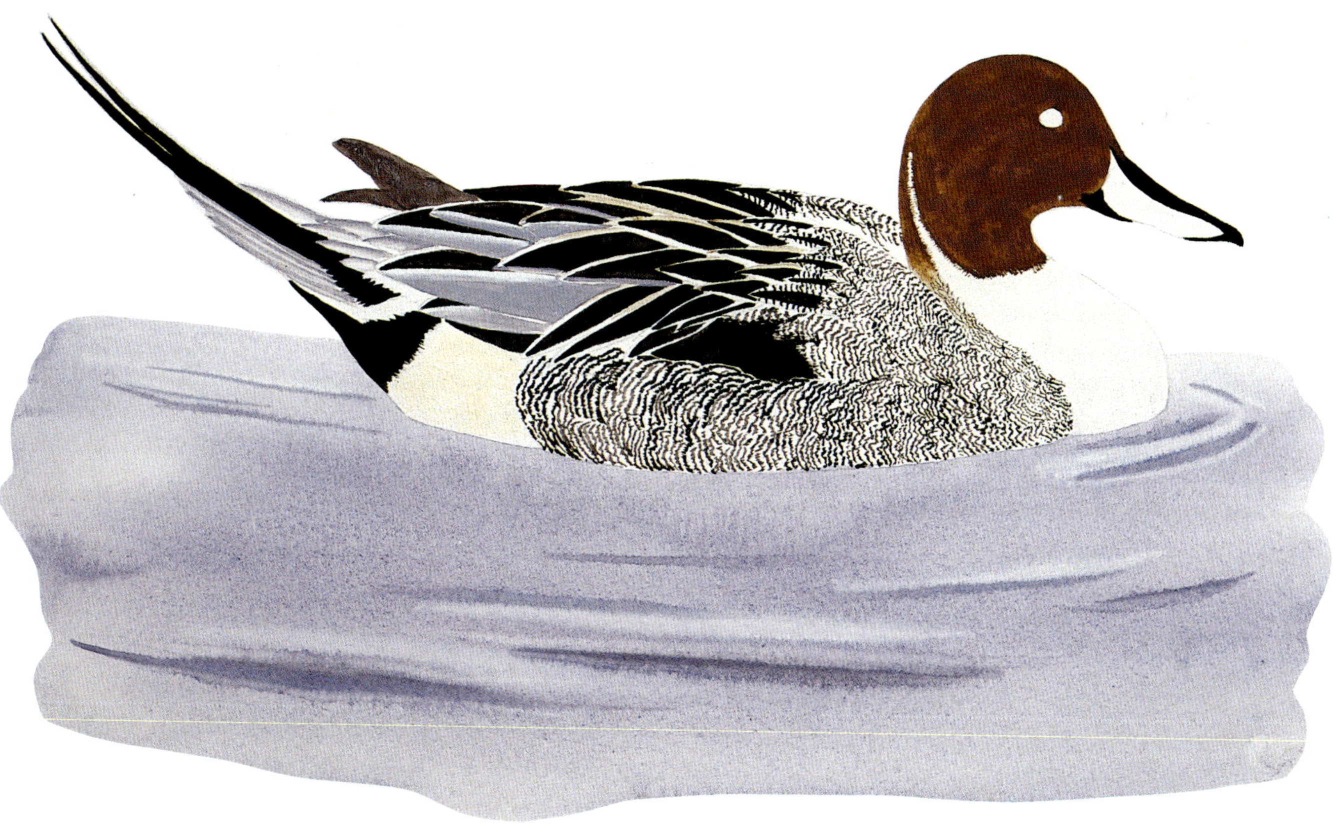

Opaque white is painted along the shaft of the black and gray tertials and scapulars, then graded down over the gray. A thin mixture of raw sienna and white is lightly split-brushed over the white area at the rear of the sidepocket. The head is painted wet-in-wet with a mixture of Vandyke brown and a very small amount of raw umber. Where the brown of the head meets the white of the neck, the edge is broken up by splitbrushing the brown into the white. Where the neck tucks into the body, the brown is graded to a soft blend. The tips of the primaries are painted with an opaque mix of raw umber and Payne's gray.

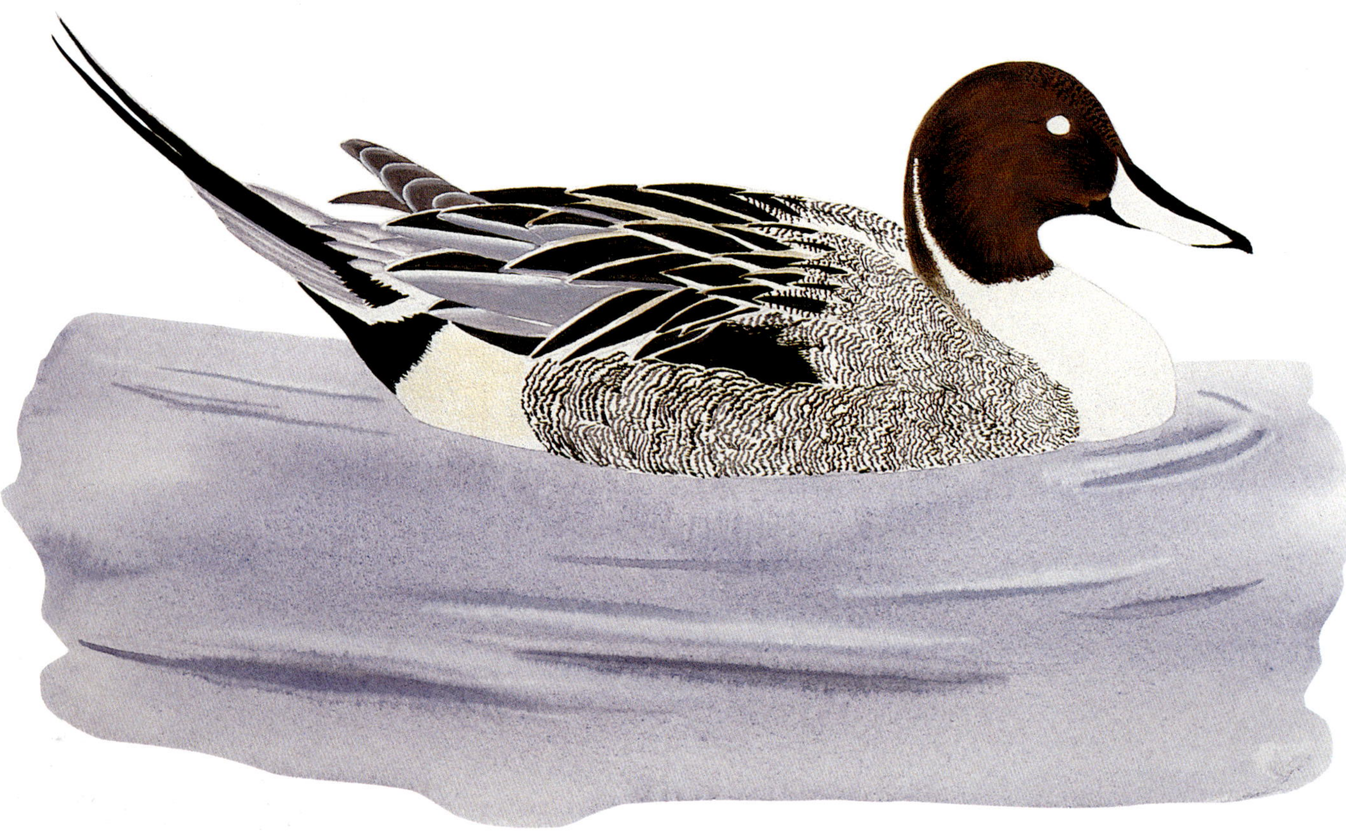

The head is refined by lightly tipping in the forehead with opaque black in the #2 filbert. The dark areas of the head are shaded and defined with thin black in the splitbrush, carefully following the direction of the head feathers. The tips of the primaries are painted with white that is graded down into each feather.

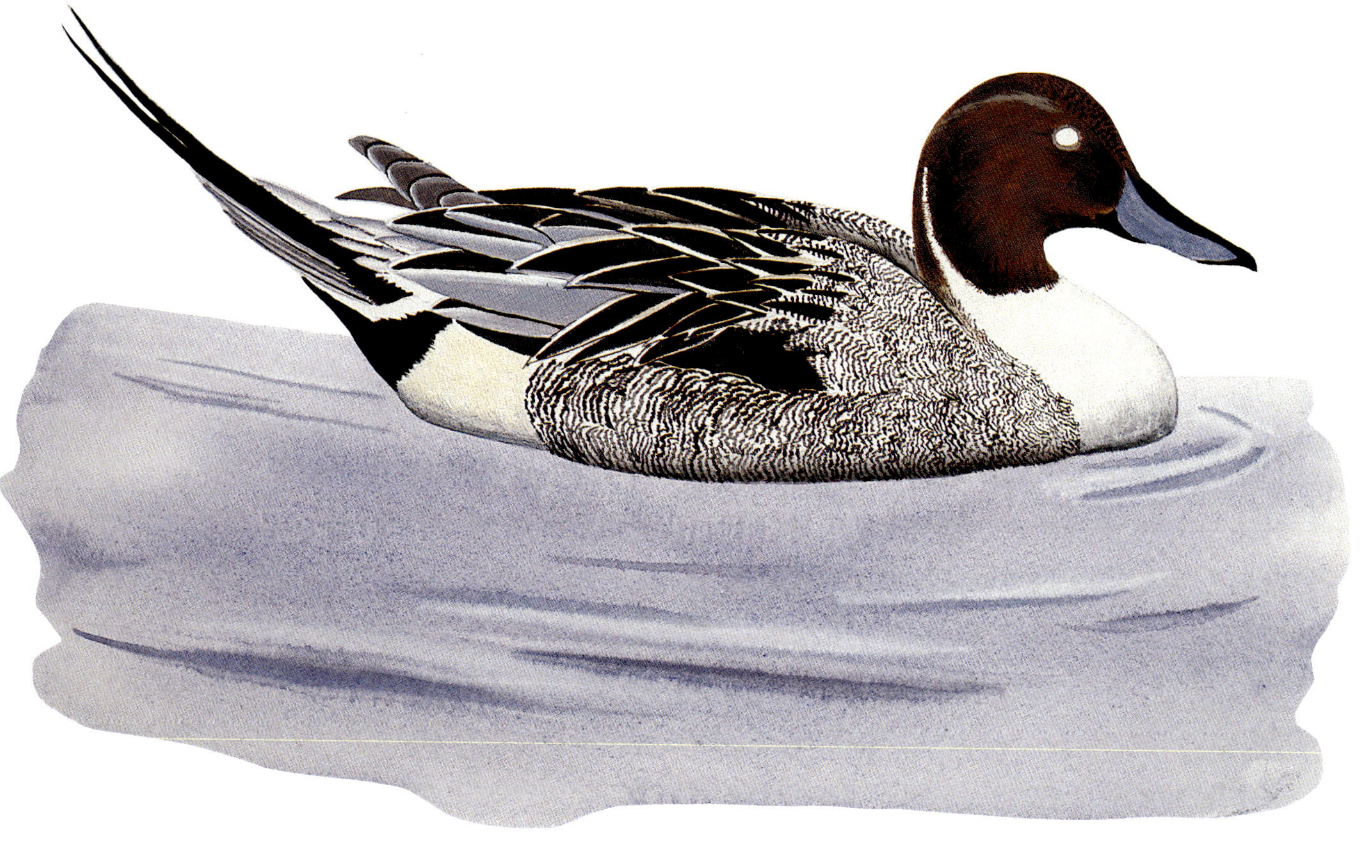

The light areas of the head—around the eye and at the back of the crown—are detailed with an opaque mixture of white, raw umber, and Vandyke brown. The blue stripe of the bill, which may vary in shape, is painted with a mixture of ultramarine blue pale and white. Opaque black in the #1 round is used to show small shadows under the tail feathers, upper tail coverts, primaries, tertials, and scapulars. To give roundness and form to the body and to separate the two sets of scapulars, thinned black is graded and glazed over all of the lower body and the far set of scapulars. To accomplish this, the picture is turned upside down and thinned black is painted along the area to be darkest, then graded and glazed with a clean, damp brush until a rounded effect is achieved.

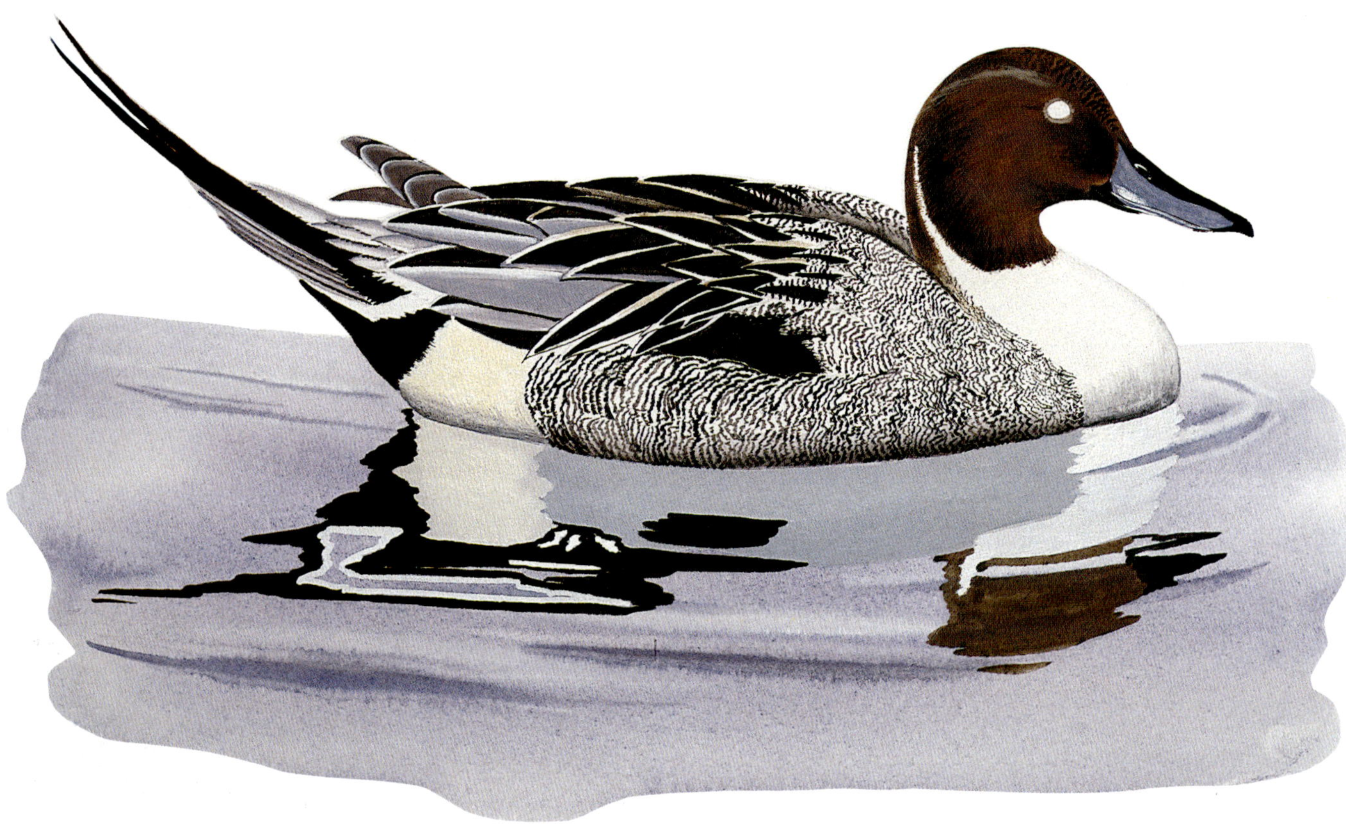

The water and the duck looked too separated, so it was determined to add the reflection. (The reflection could be added at almost any point during the painting steps.) The reflection painted here is very basic. At this point rough black and white highlights are painted on the bill.

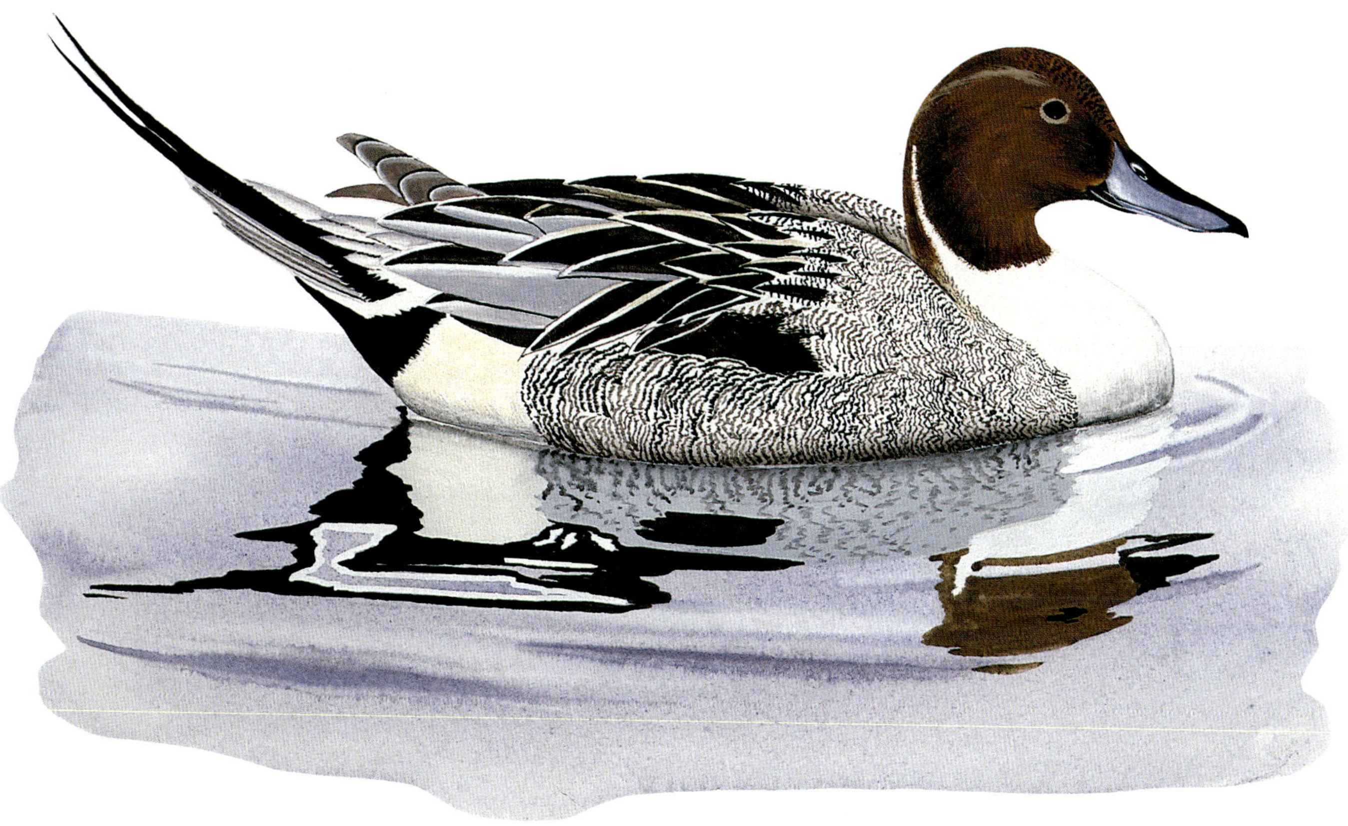

Additional simple shading and patterns are painted on the reflection to achieve a realistic effect. The highlights and shadows on the bill are softened with a clean, damp brush. The eye of the pintail is very dark so it is painted in with opaque black; no attempt is made to show the pupil. (Acrylics note: The highlights and shadows on the bill must be blended while the paint is still wet.)

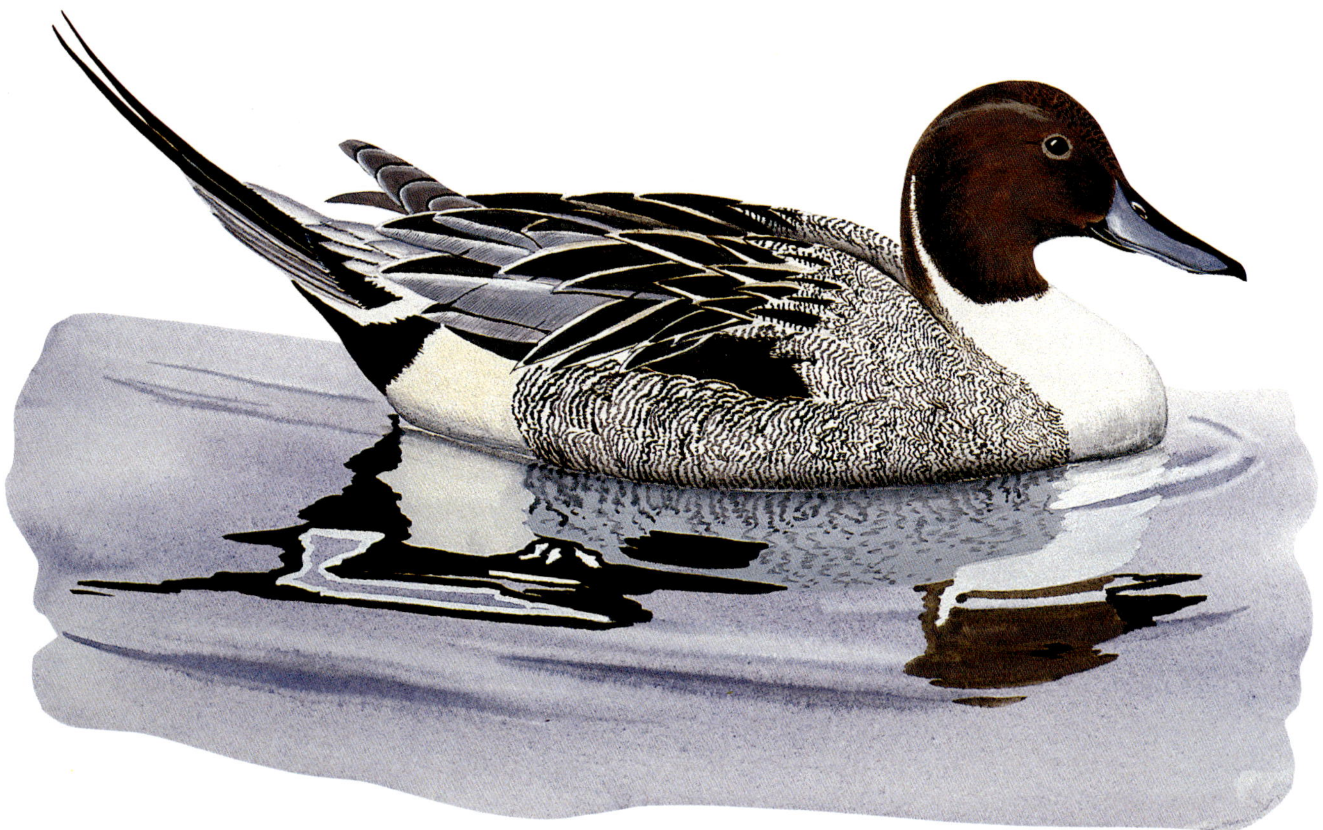

Thinned black is splitbrushed on the gray of the tertials to show light featheration. Opaque black in the #1 round is used to detail in random feather splits. Ultramarine blue pale mixed with white is used in the #1 round to detail the edges of the black upper tail coverts and to paint an edge on one of the long tail feathers. An opaque white highlight is placed in the eye to finish the pintail.

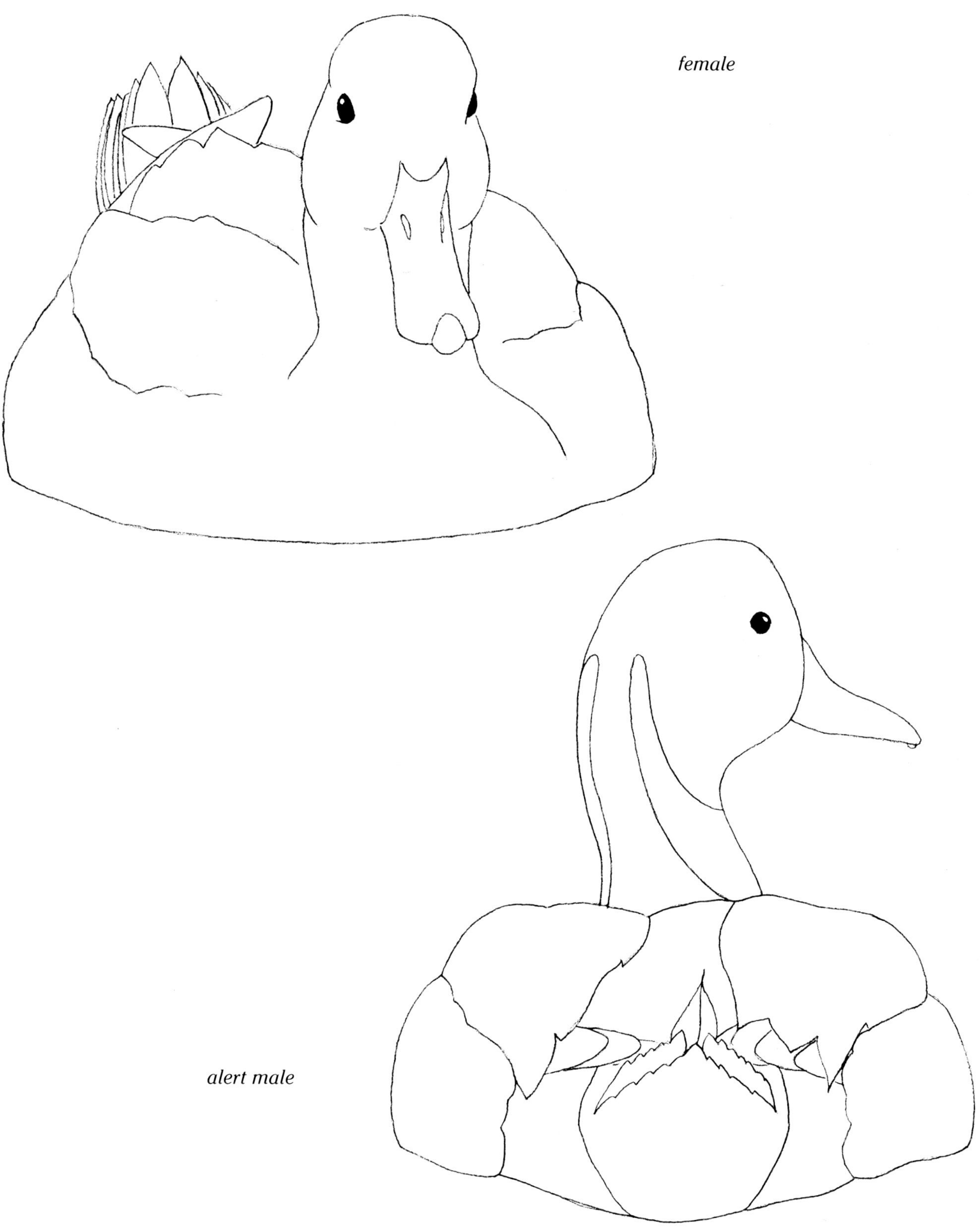

Pintail

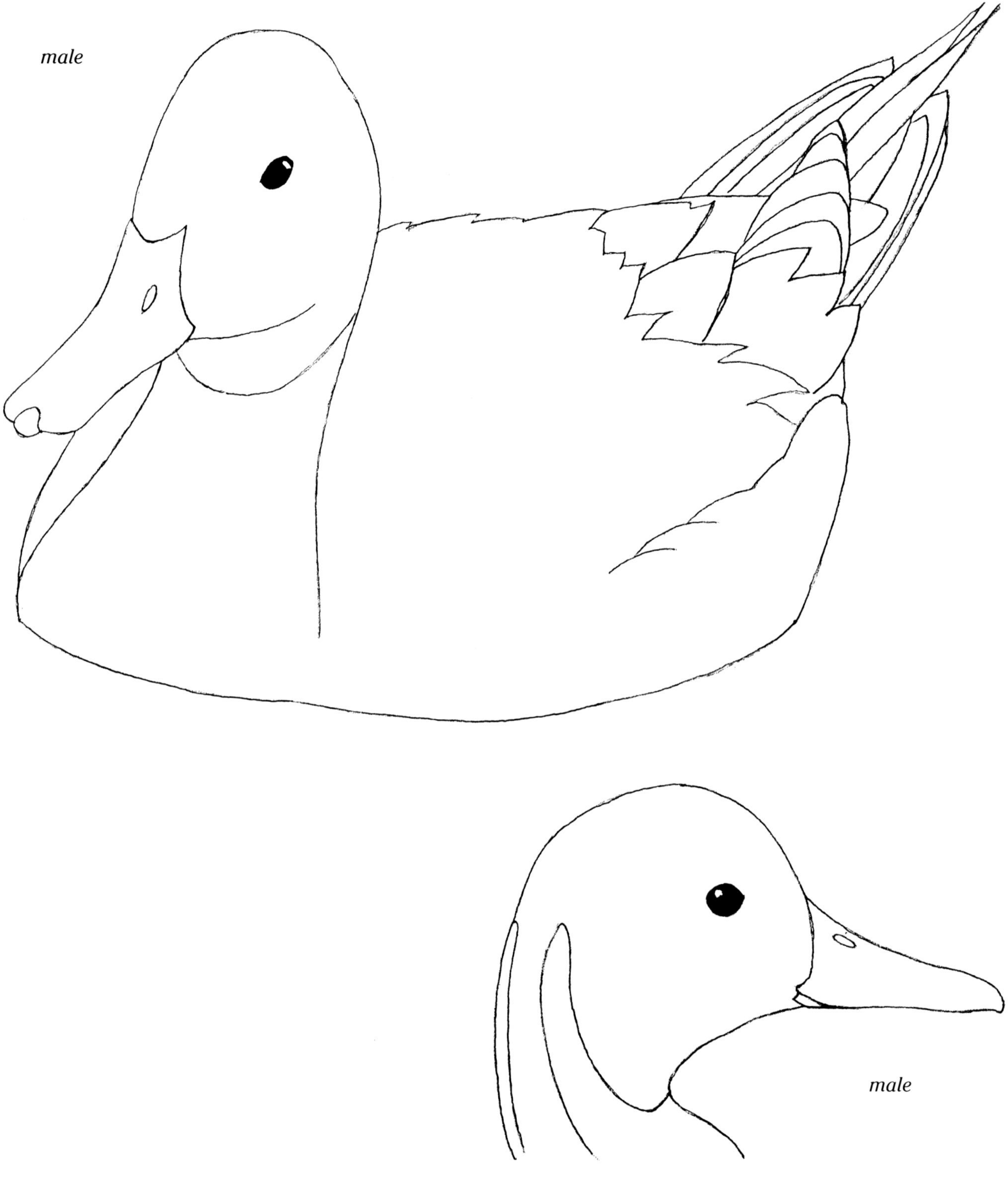

Pintail

Blue-winged Teal

Anas discors

The small blue-winged teal seems to have an aversion to cold weather; it is the first duck to leave the north in the fall and the last to migrate from the south in the spring. When feeding, these ducks dabble on the surface or stick their heads under the water while cruising along; they rarely tip up as do other dabbling ducks.

The blue-winged teal gets its name from its blue wing coverts, which are present on both males and females. When the females are at rest and the blue is hidden, their coloration is similar to that of the female green-winged teal, with which they are easily confused. In breeding plumage the male is quite distinctive, with a white crescent on its blue-grey head and boldly marked scapulars. During molt, which begins in July and lasts into fall, the males closely resemble the females. Thus, in painting this species close attention must be paid to coordinating the background with the seasonal featheration of the bird.

The standing male blue-winged teal painted here has its wing partially flexed to show the blue coverts. The speculum iridesces green and at the rear of the head there is a tiny amount of pink-purple iridescence. Notice that the individual feathers of the breast and sides have more than one spot on each feather. As the feathers progress toward the sidepocket and grow larger, they also have many more spots. The blue-winged teal male is colorful and rather straightforward to paint. It should present no particular painting problems.

The palette used is white, Pelikan raw umber, ultramarine blue pale, burnt umber, raw sienna, brilliant green, sap green yellowish, cadmium yellow pale, yellow ochre, ivory black, violet, and cadmium red pale. The brushes used are #3 Kolinsky sable round, #1 Kolinsky sable round, and the ½-inch flat sable wash. Unless specifically noted, the #3 round is the brush used.

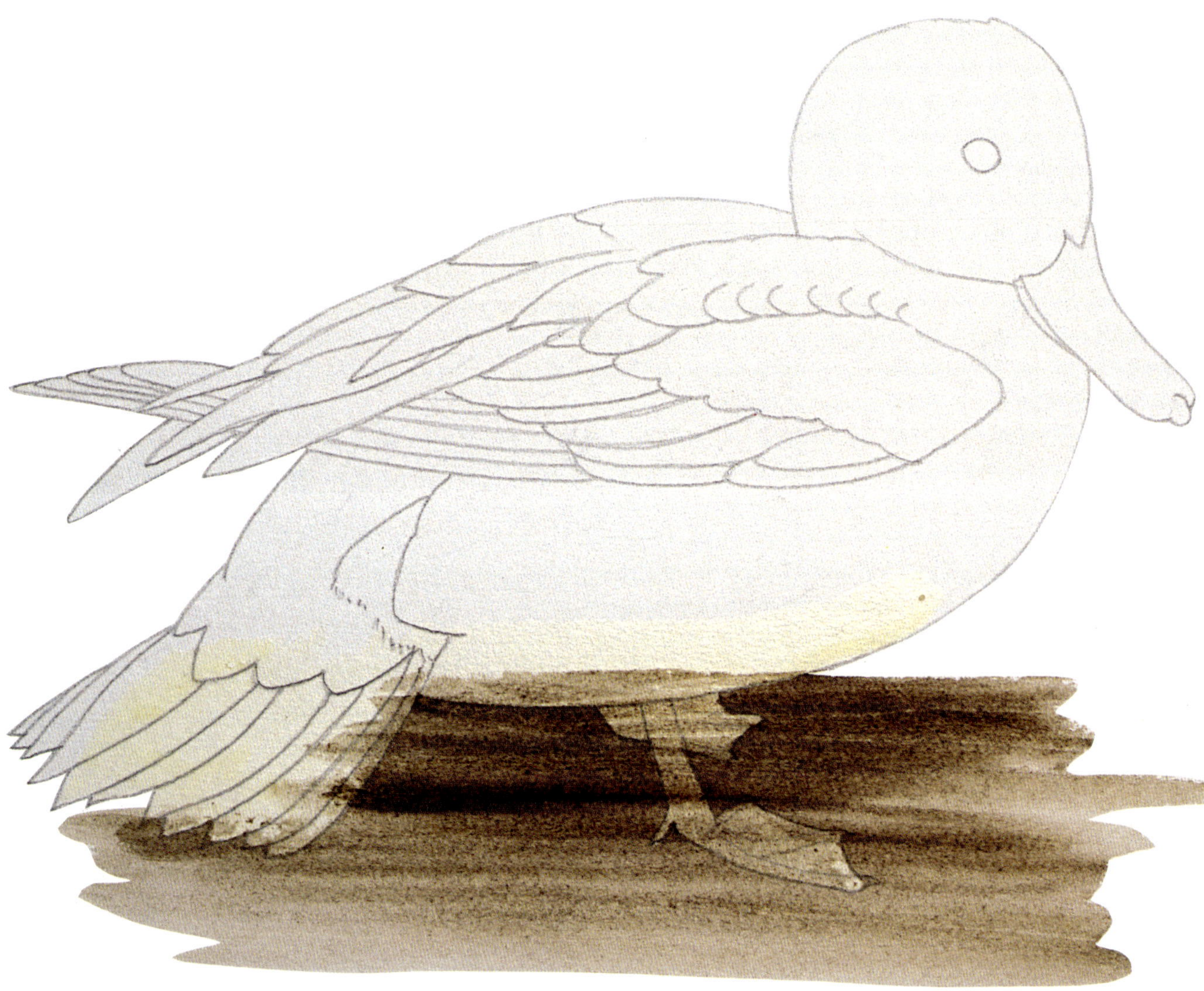

The drawing is transferred to the painting surface. Liquid masking is painted on the feet, legs, lower portion of the body, and tail. When the liquid masking is dry, an uneven wet-in-wet wash of thinned raw umber is painted with the half-inch sable brush to show ground.

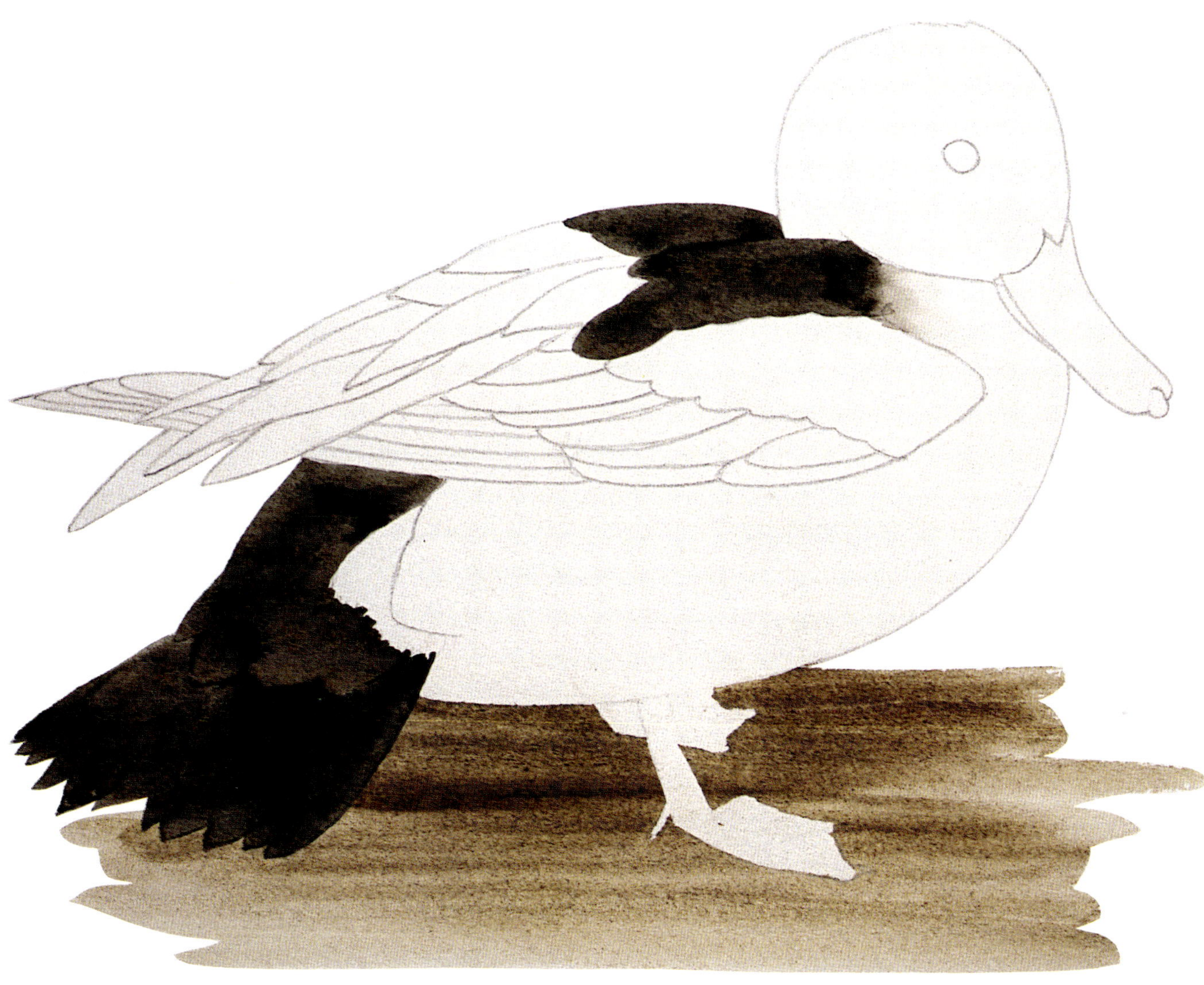

When the ground wash is dry the masking is removed. A thin mixture of raw umber and black is painted on the tail and upper tail coverts. The same mixture is used to paint the scapulars. Where the scapulars meet the breast, the color is graded out with a clean damp brush.

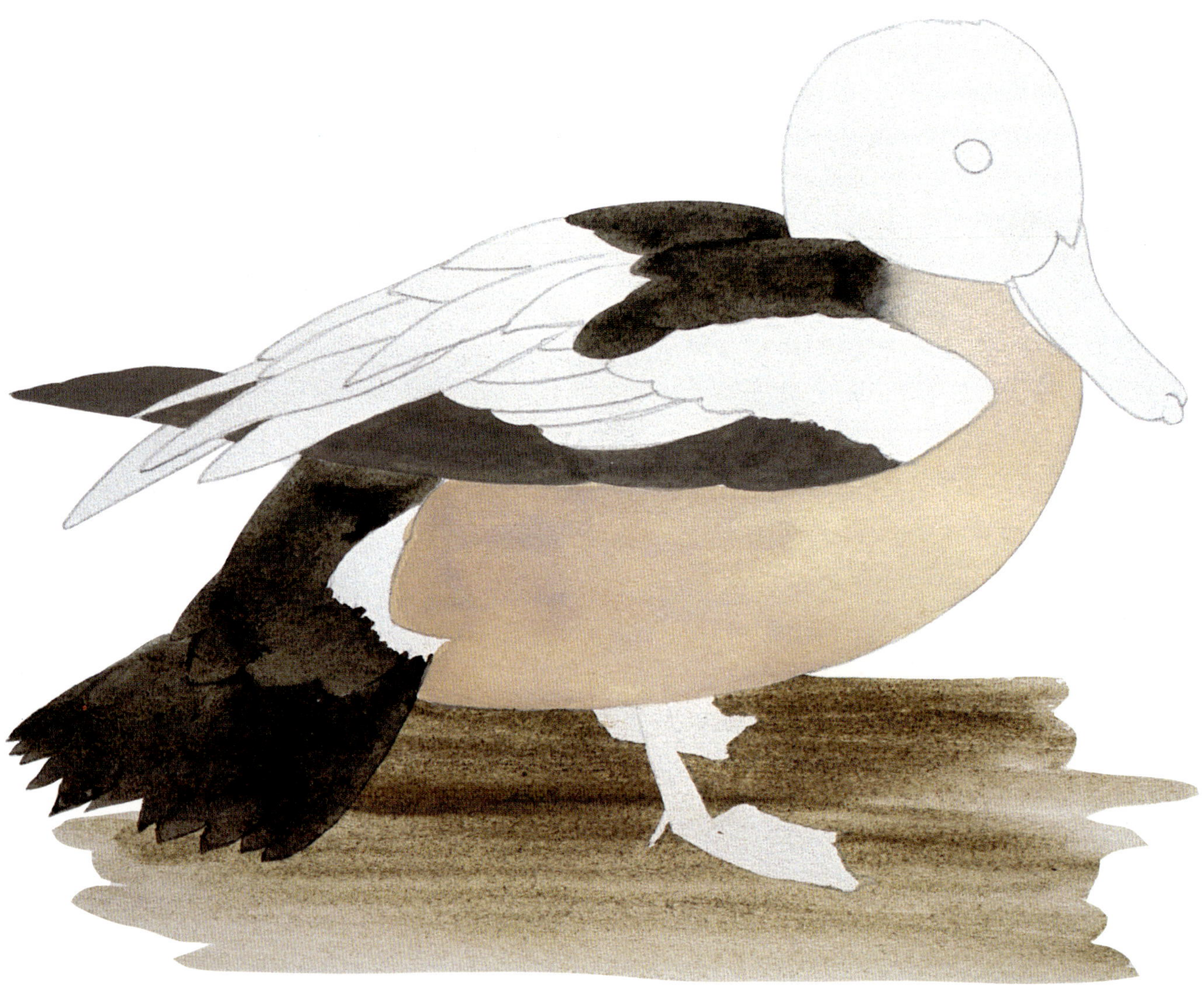

This step is rather tricky because there is a slight color change in the large wash of the breast and underparts. A mixture of white, raw sienna, and burnt umber is washed wet-in-wet over the breast. As this wash progresses back toward the belly and flanks, it is darkened slightly by adding more raw sienna and burnt umber. The color transitions need not be perfectly even since the dark patterns to be painted later will cover any irregularities. A mixture of white, black, and raw umber is painted over the primaries, alula, and some of the secondaries that are grayish. If the wing feather lines become obscured by the paint, reposition the tracing and transfer them again.

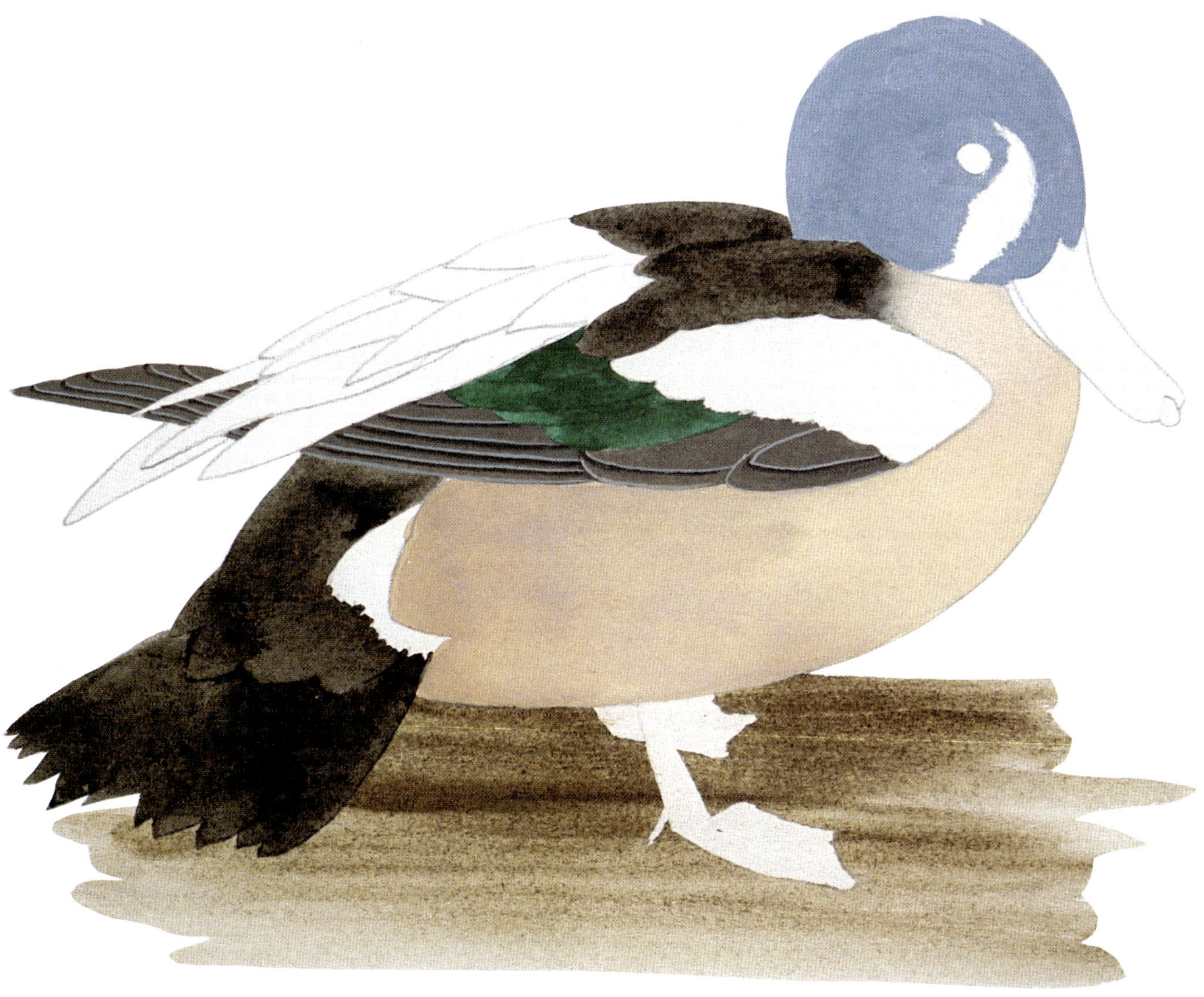

Thinned black in the #1 round is used to detail a light shadow under each dark wing feather, then thin white in the #1 round paints in a light feather edge above each shadow line. Brilliant green is painted on the iridescent inner secondaries (speculum). The base color of the head is a mixture of white, ultramarine blue pale, and black.

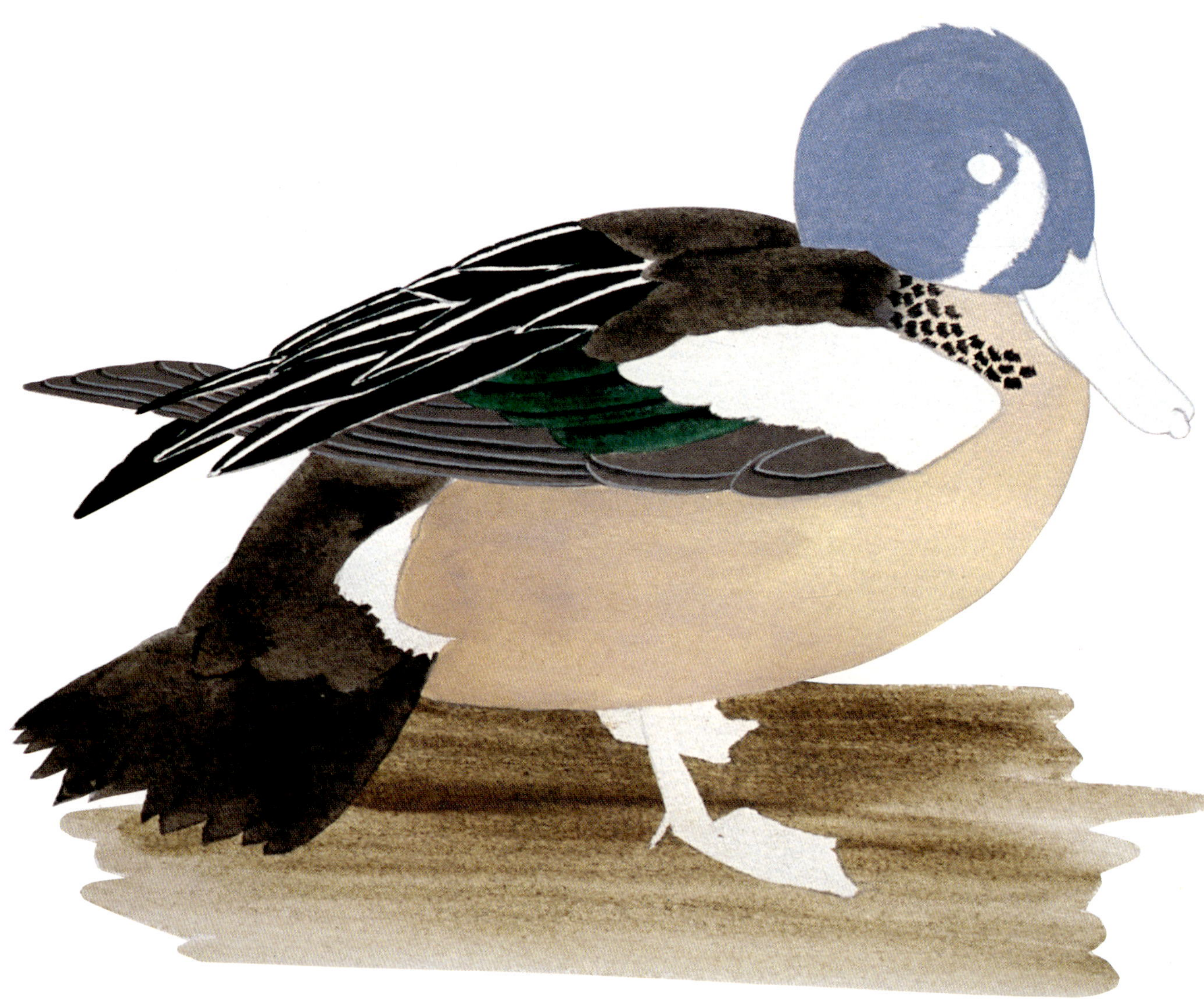

Opaque black is painted on the tertials and larger scapulars, then used in the #1 round to begin the spotted feather pattern on the upper breast. A black shadow line is painted under each green secondary and, while still wet, glazed and graded with a clean, damp brush.

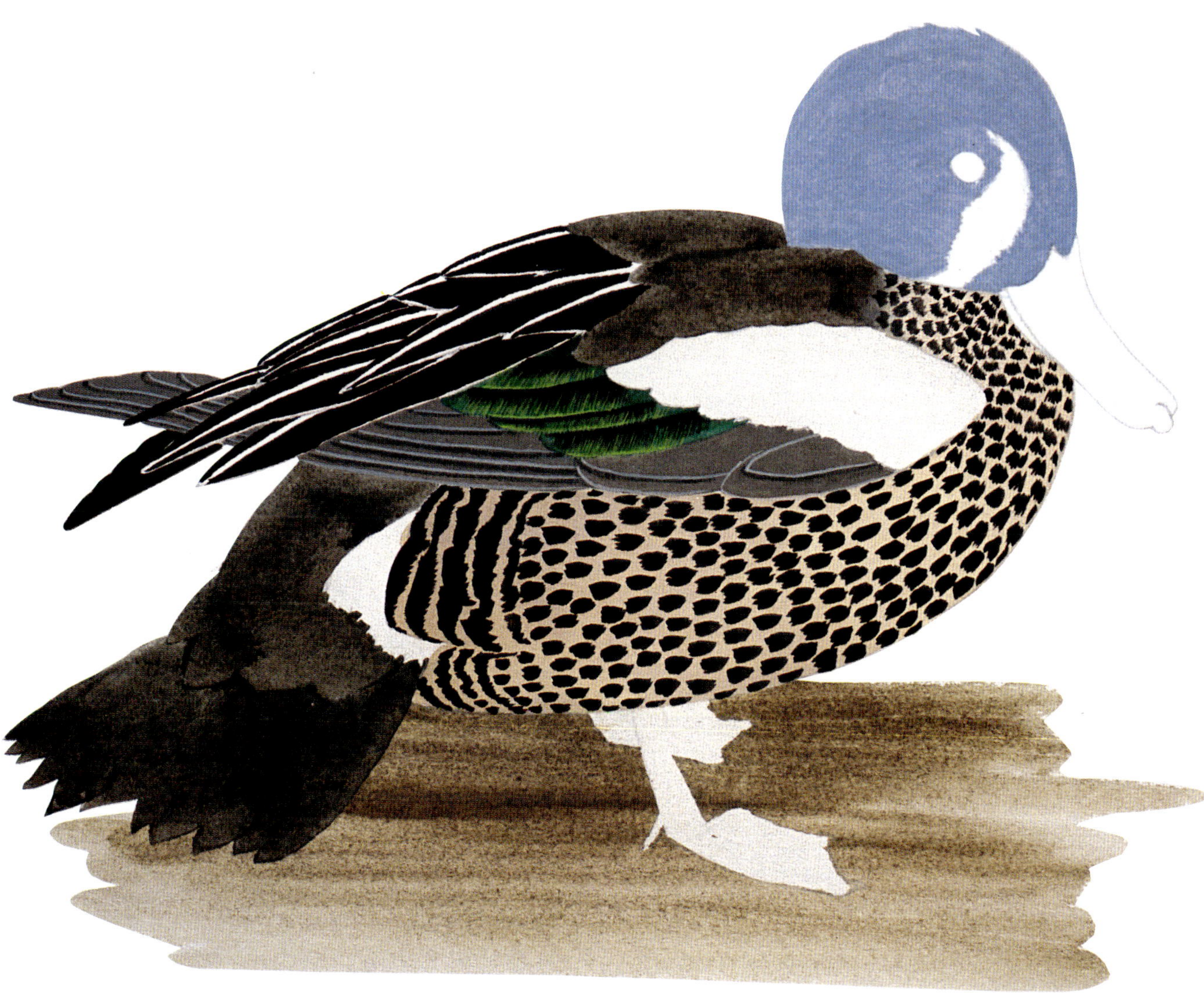

The black patterns on the breast, belly, and flank are completed. Notice how the size and shape of the patterns change and how they follow the contour of the body. Opaque sap green yellow is splitbrushed upwards from the edge of each green secondary to give them an iridescent sheen.

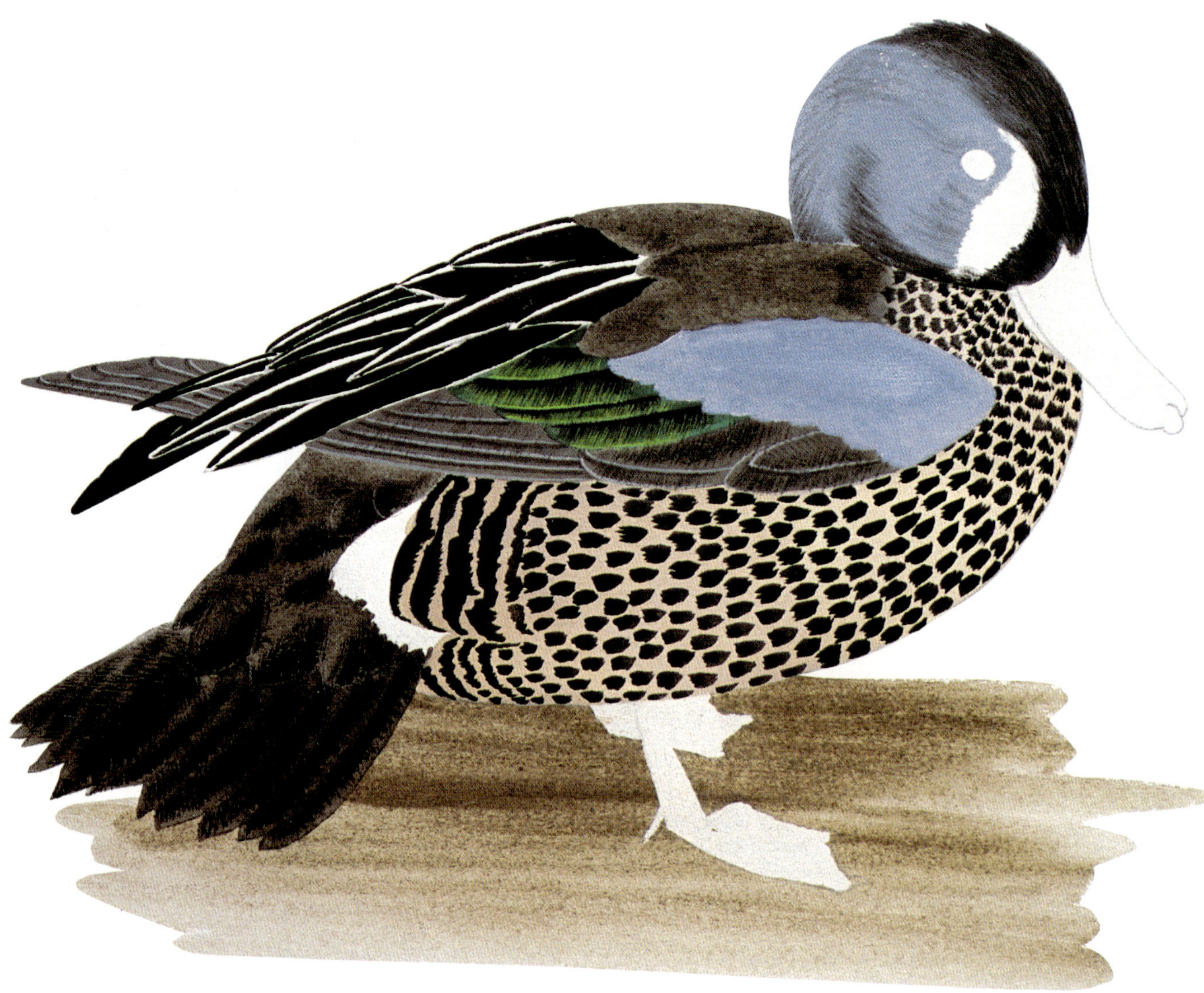

The wing coverts are painted in with an opaque mixture of white and ultramarine blue pale. Opaque black is used in the splitbrush to paint the inner portion of each tail feather and the lower feather edges of the upper tail coverts. The black in the splitbrush is also used to show featheration on the secondaries and alula. Thinned black in the splitbrush is used to paint in the dark forehead and crown and to shade the bottom of the head and cheek.

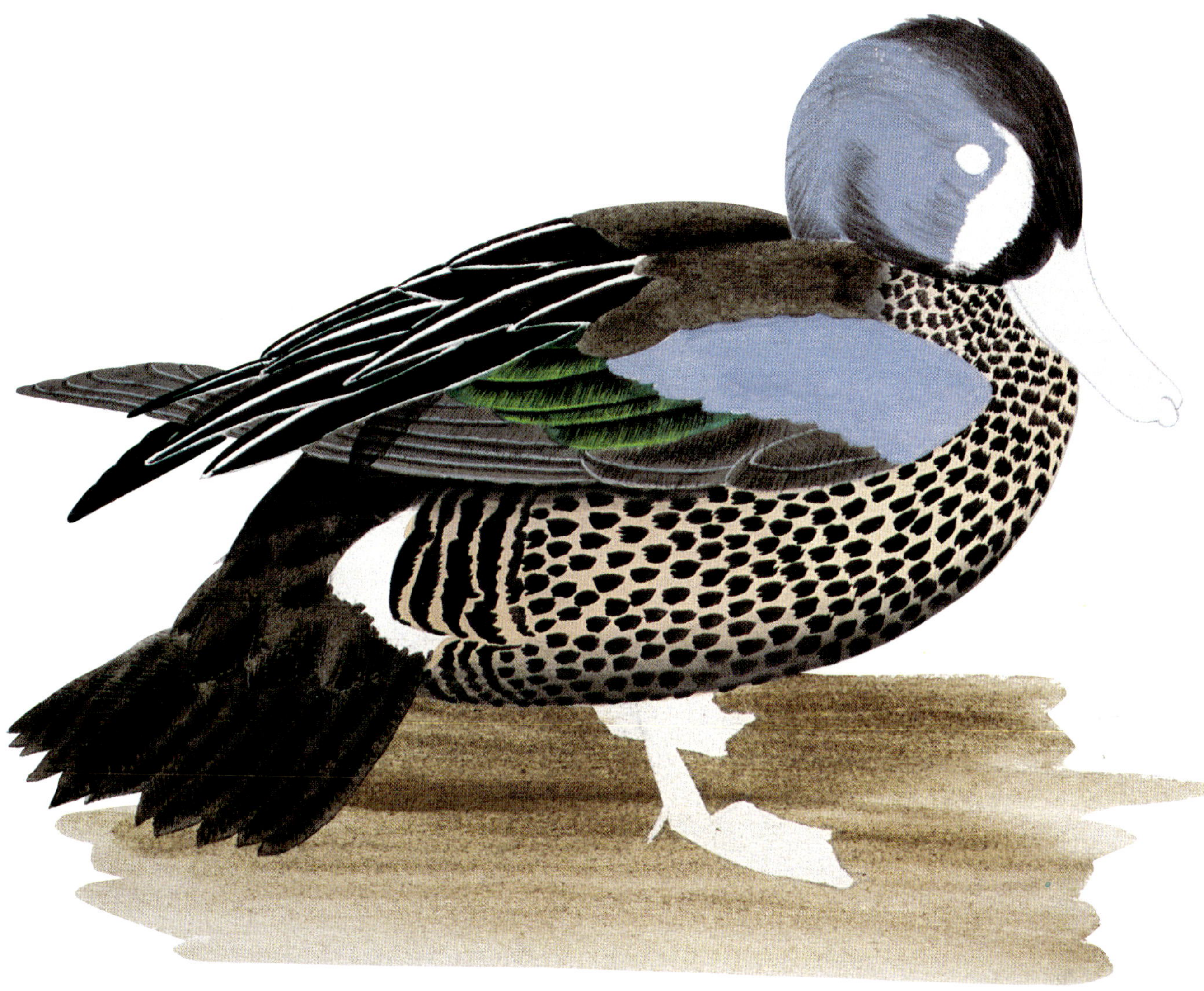

A series of glazed and graded washes defines body form and adds shading to the blue-winged teal. The painting is turned upside down and, beginning at the bottom of the belly, a broad line of thinned black is painted on the area to be darkest. This black is then glazed and graded over the belly with a clean, damp brush until a gentle shaded effect is achieved. This same technique is used to shade the far set of scapulars to add separation. The painting is now righted, and a line of thinned black is painted under the near wing over the top of the flank and upper tail coverts. This line is graded and glazed downward to show separation between the wing and the body. Light black shadows are painted on the primaries underneath the tertials to show the separation between them.

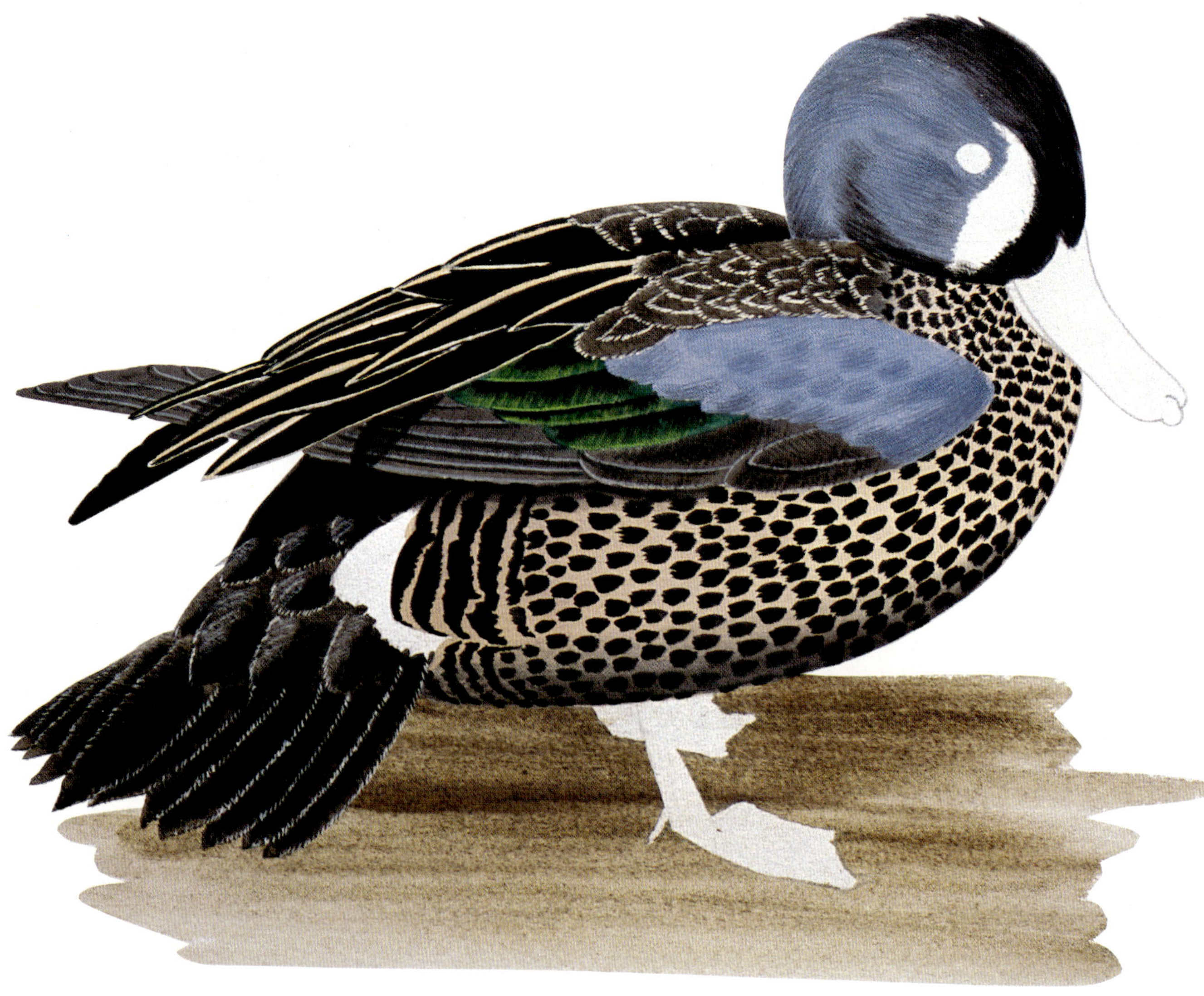

A mixture of black, white, and ultramarine blue pale is used in the splitbrush to add more feather detail on the head and on the blue wing coverts. A mixture of white and raw sienna in the #1 round details the feather edges and patterns of the small scapulars; this color also details the edges of the upper tail coverts and tail feathers. A darker shade of the white and raw sienna mixture is used to paint in the centers and edges of the tertials and large scapulars.

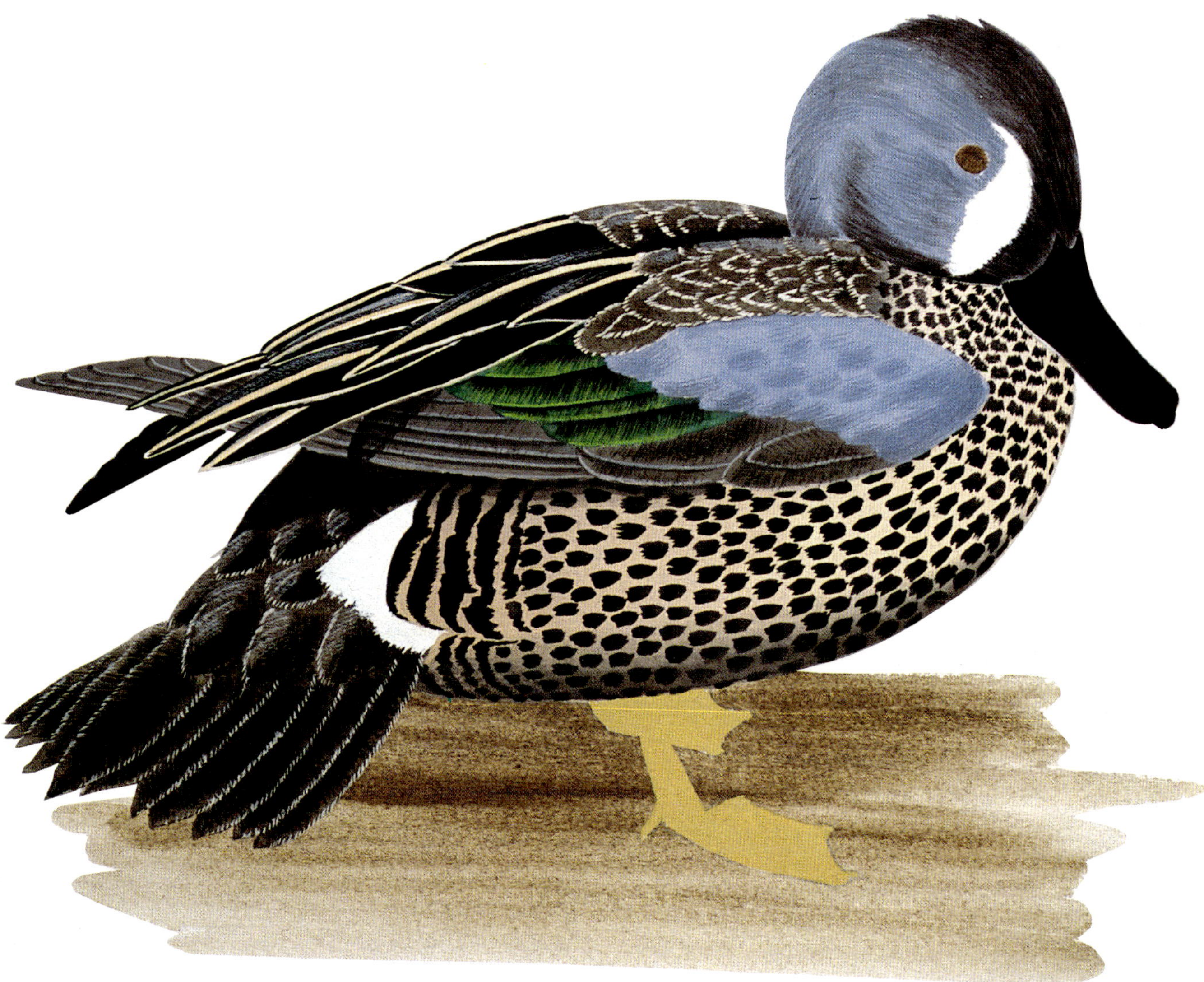

Opaque black is used to paint in the bill. Opaque white paints in the white facial crescent and the white area behind the sidepocket. Yellow ochre mixed with cadmium yellow pale colors the feet and legs. The upper sides of the scapulars and tertials are lightly drybrushed with a white and black mixture for highlights. The iris of the eye is painted in with thin raw umber.

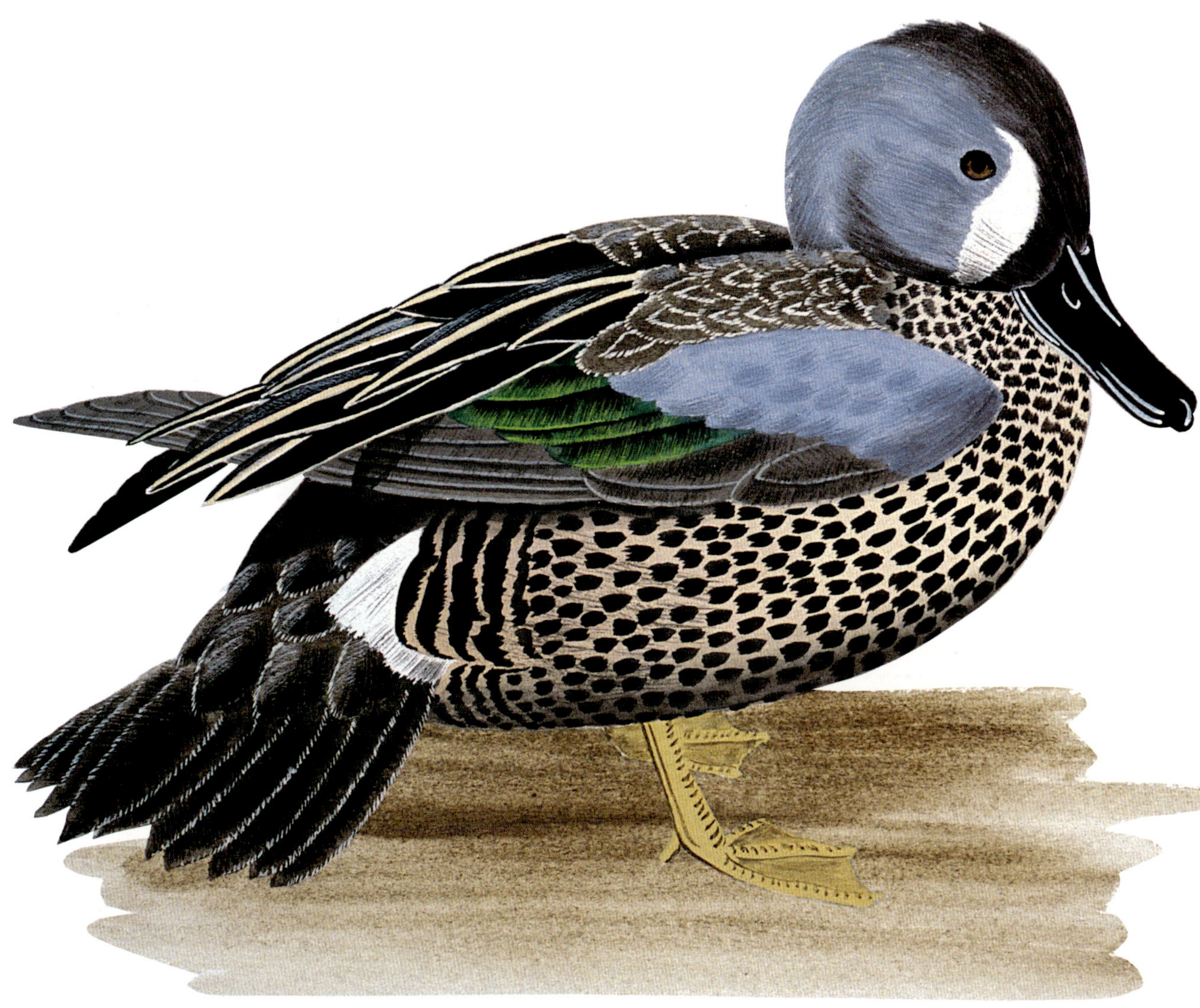

Rough opaque white highlights are painted on the bill. Opaque black in the splitbrush is used to shade the white facial crescent, rump, and blue wing coverts and to add featheration to the flank. Thin raw umber in the #1 round adds shadow detail on the feet and legs. Opaque black paints in the pupil and shadow at the top of the eye.

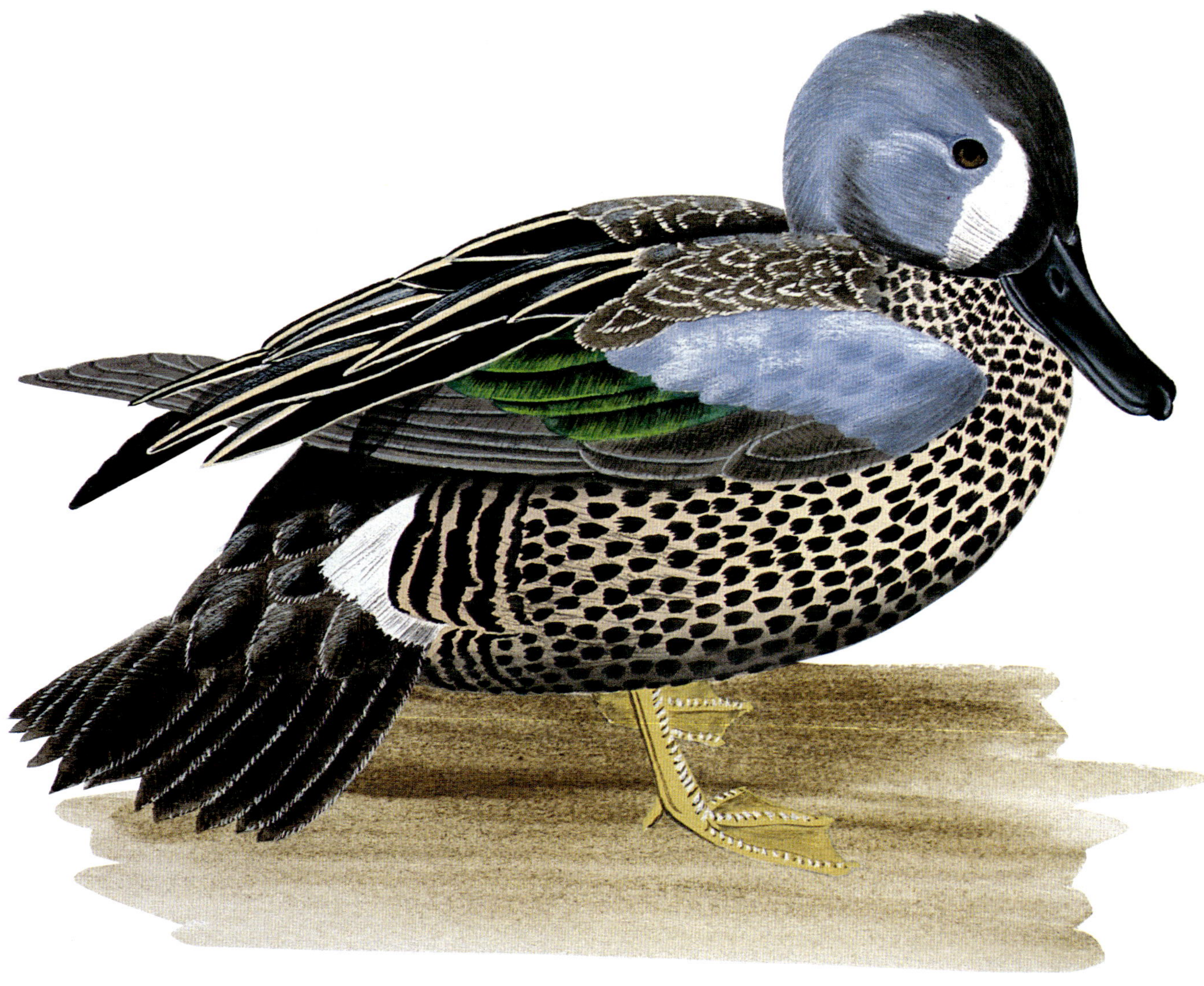

The rough white highlights on the bill are blended and refined with a clean, damp brush and the black shadow in the eye is blended down into the brown iris. Thinned white is dabbed on the scales of the feet and legs to show light highlights. Highlights on the blue wing coverts are indicated by drybrushing with opaque white. (Acrylics note: The white bill highlights and black eye shadow must be blended while wet.)

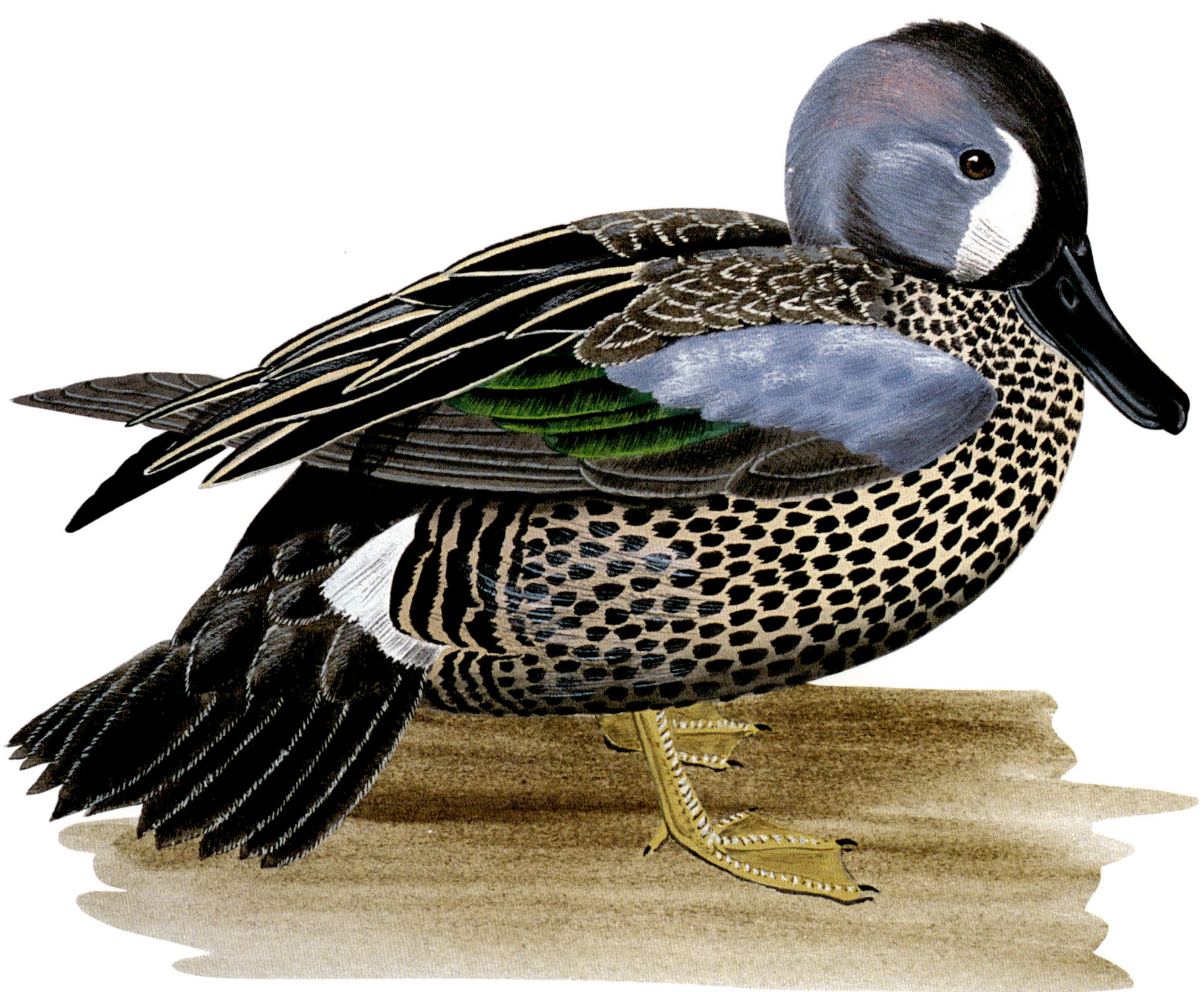

Opaque white in the splitbrush highlights the flank feathers. Opaque black is used to paint in the nails on the feet and to paint a shadow under the feet. To show separation between the small gray scapulars and the wing, tiny opaque black shadows are painted under the scapulars. An opaque mixture of white, violet, and cadmium red pale is used in the splitbrush to show the pinkish iridescence at the back of the head. Finally, an opaque white highlight is placed in the eye.

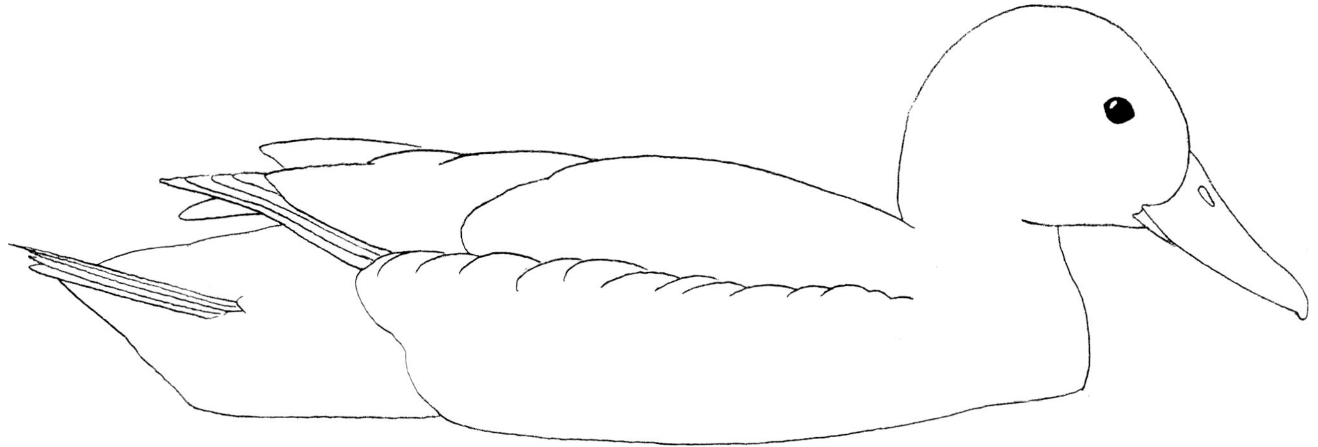

female

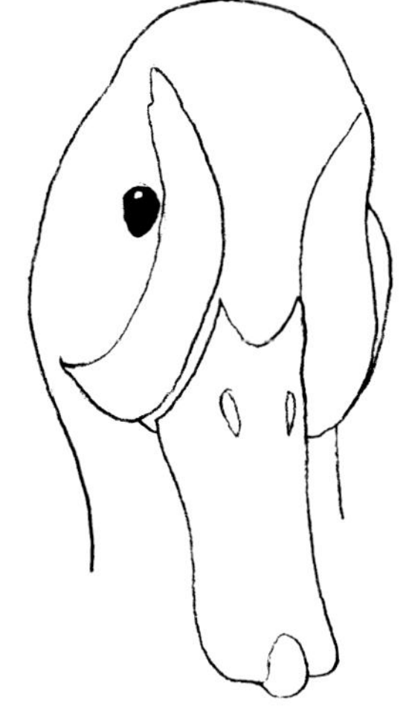

male

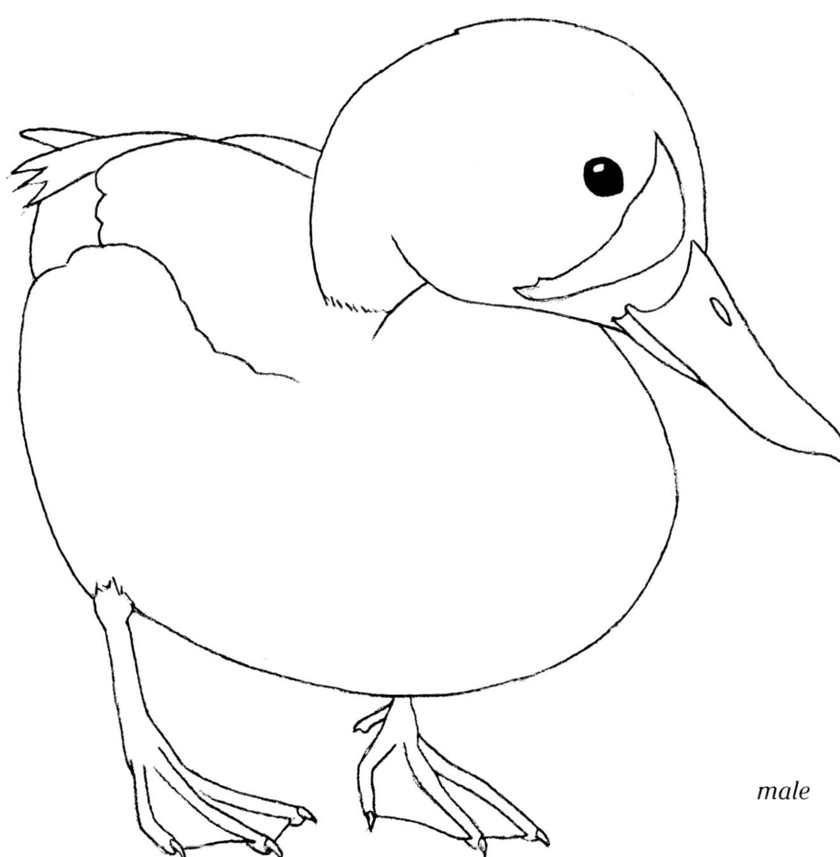

male

Blue-winged Teal

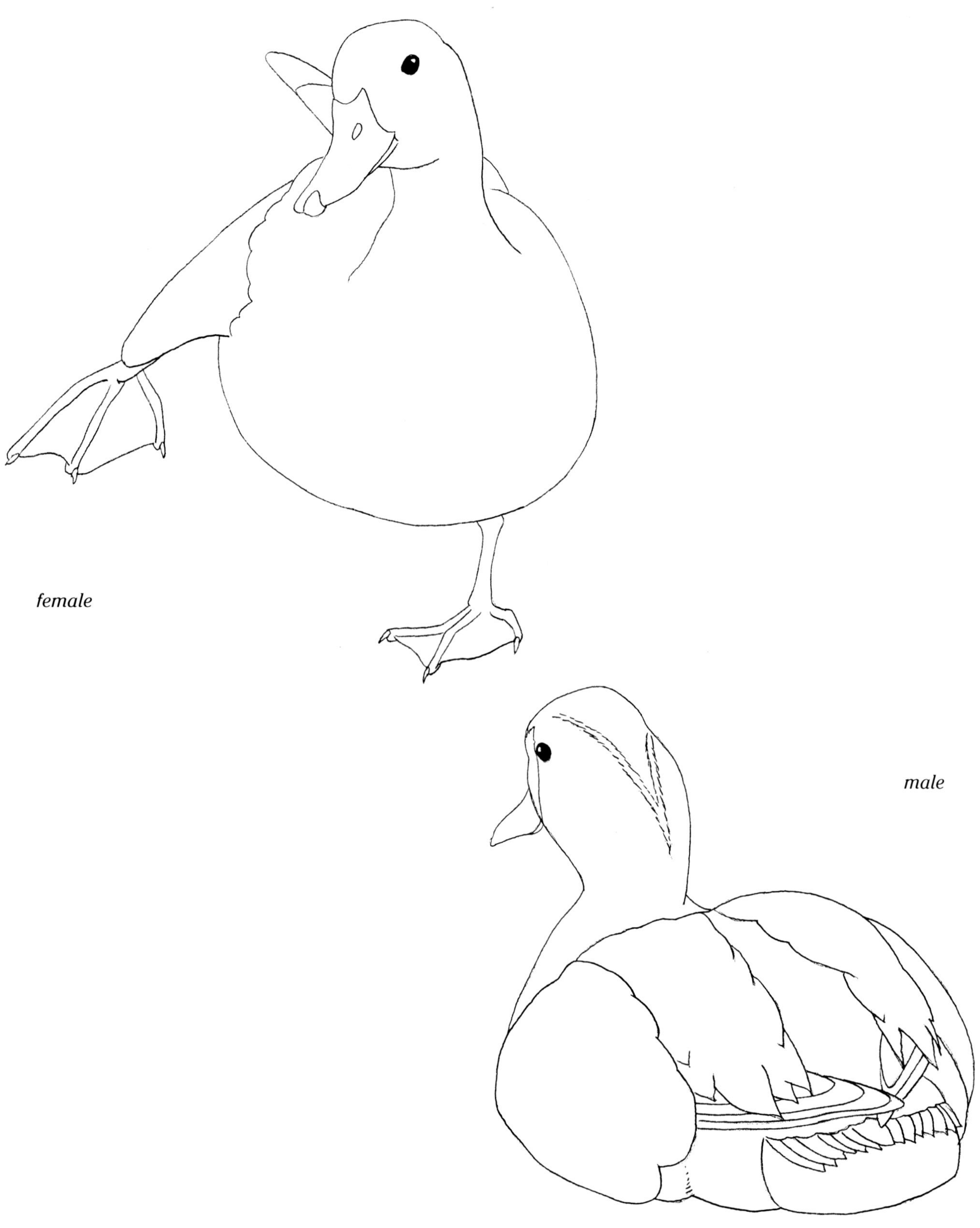

Blue-winged Teal

American Green-winged Teal

Anas crecca Carolinensis

The American green-winged teal is the smallest of all waterfowl. Size notwithstanding, the male green-winged teal is second in bright coloration only to the male wood duck. Its reddish brown head has a dark—sometimes glossy green—broad eye stripe that begins in front of the eye and stretches to the back of the head. Female green-winged teals lack the colors of the male. They are brown overall, with light cream or orangish margins on the brown feathers. The speculum of the female's wing is iridescent green. The degree of darkness may vary between each duck.

The green-winged teal is one of the most agile ducks on land and runs fairly easily. It is also one of the few dabbling ducks that will dive readily to escape danger. In flight, they have very rapid wing beats and are fast fliers. One of the earliest ducks to migrate north in the spring, their long flights are rather leisurely with frequent stops. Their diminutive size, quick wing beats, and two-tone under tail coverts make them one of the easiest duck species to identify in flight.

Painting the male green-winged teal requires a good deal of patience because of the extensive vermiculation, which begins at the back of the breast and extends onto the scapulars, down the sides, and onto the side-pockets. The rich brown color of the head is rather tricky to achieve so test mixtures should be made to find the proper shade. The degree and richness of the iridescent green on the broad dark eye stripe depends on the angle and quality of light striking the head. On the breast, the dark spots are of varying intensity because some light feather tips overlap the spots, slightly obscuring them. The tertials and longer scapulars may vary in color from gray to light brown depending on the bird and quality of light.

The palette used is white, yellow ochre, burnt sienna, ivory black, Pelikan raw umber, Vandyke brown, permanent green dark, permanent green light, raw sienna, Payne's gray, and ultramarine blue pale. The brushes used are #1 and #3 Kolinsky sable rounds and ½-inch sable flat. Unless otherwise noted, the brush used is the #3 round.

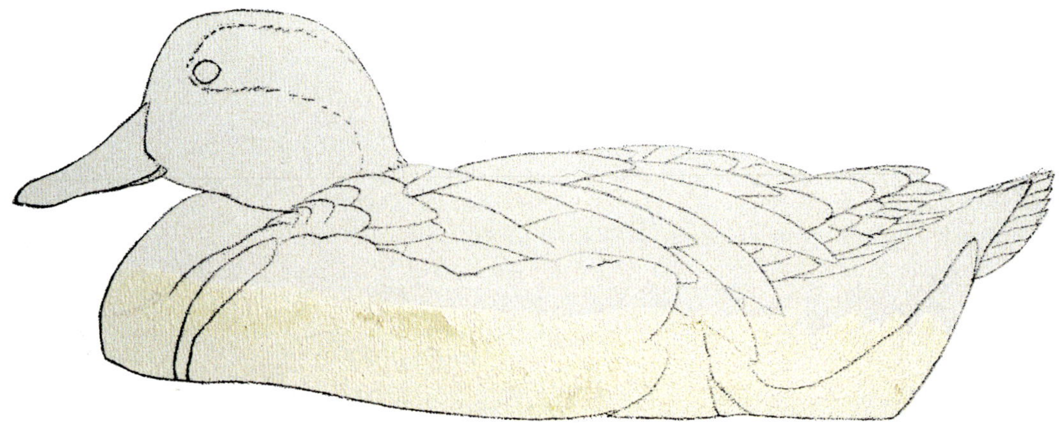

The Green-winged teal drawing is transferred to the painting surface and the lower portion of the duck is coated with liquid masking fluid.

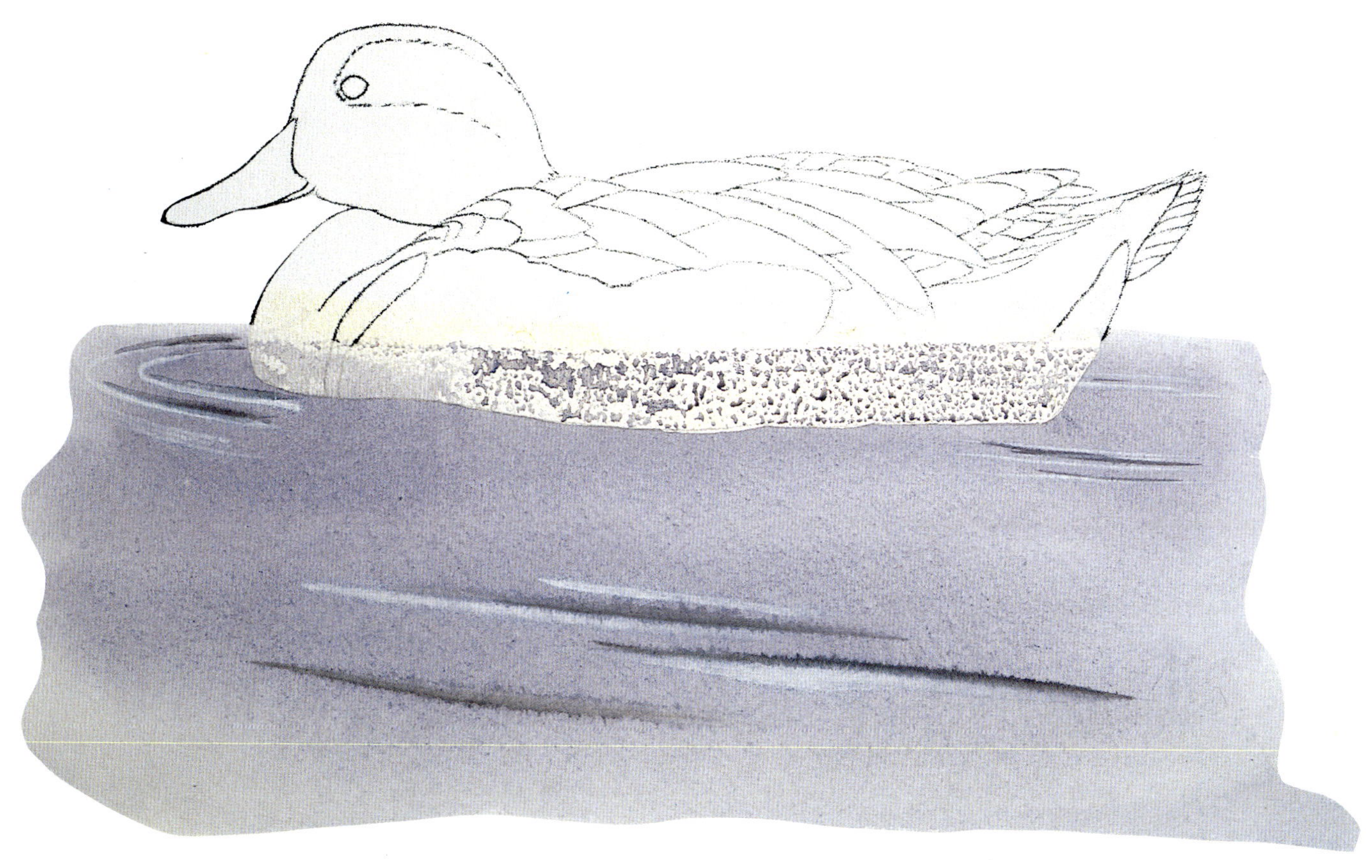

Using the half-inch flat, a mixture of ultramarine blue pale and Payne's gray is washed wet-in-wet from the bottom of the duck downward to indicate water. While this wash is still wet, opaque white highlights and a mixture of ultramarine blue pale and black for shadows are added.

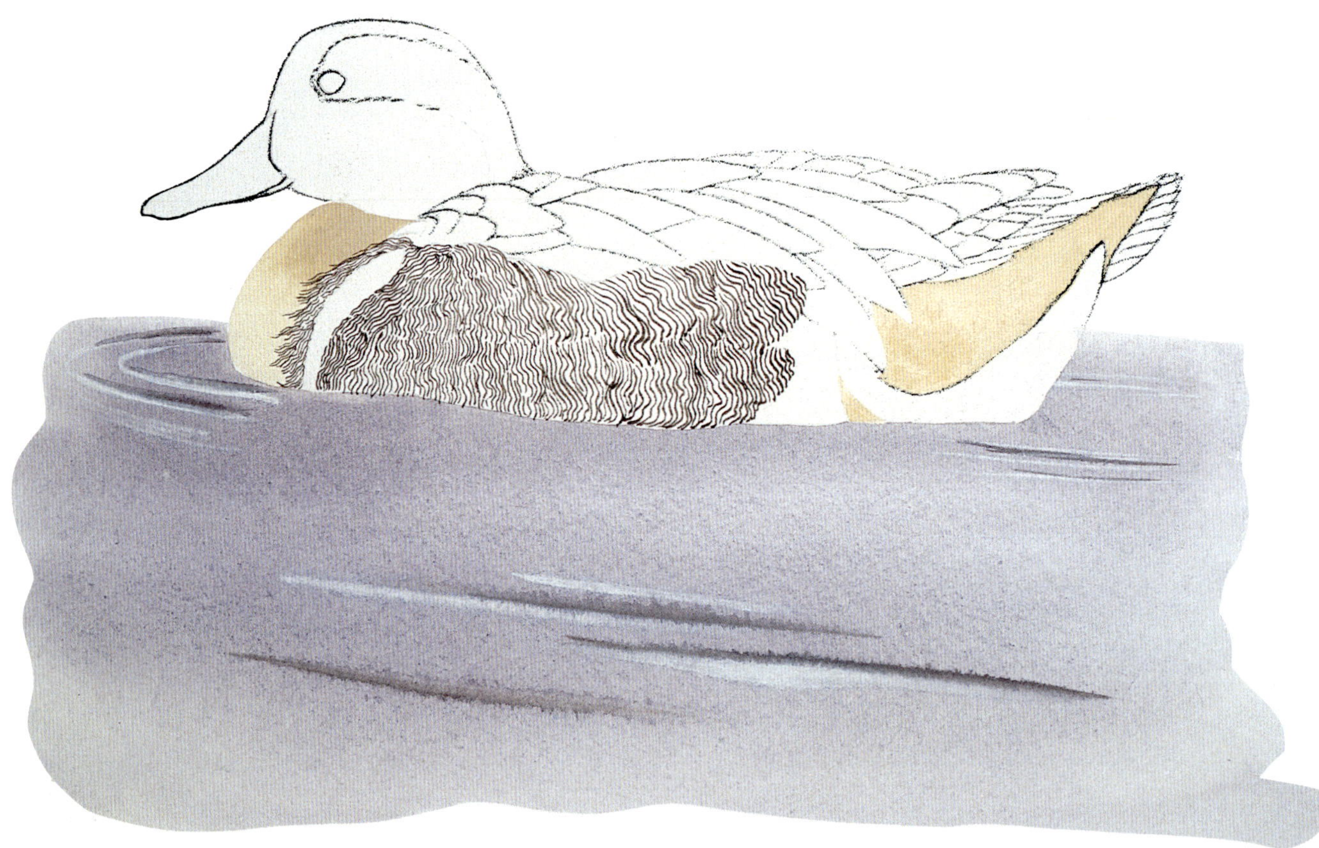

The breast is painted with a graded wash comprised of white, yellow ochre, and a touch of burnt sienna. The concentrated mixture is painted at the top of the breast, then pulled down the breast with a clean, damp brush. The yellowish under tail coverts are painted with a thin mixture of white and raw sienna. Black in the #1 round is used to detail vermiculation on the lower breast and sidepocket.

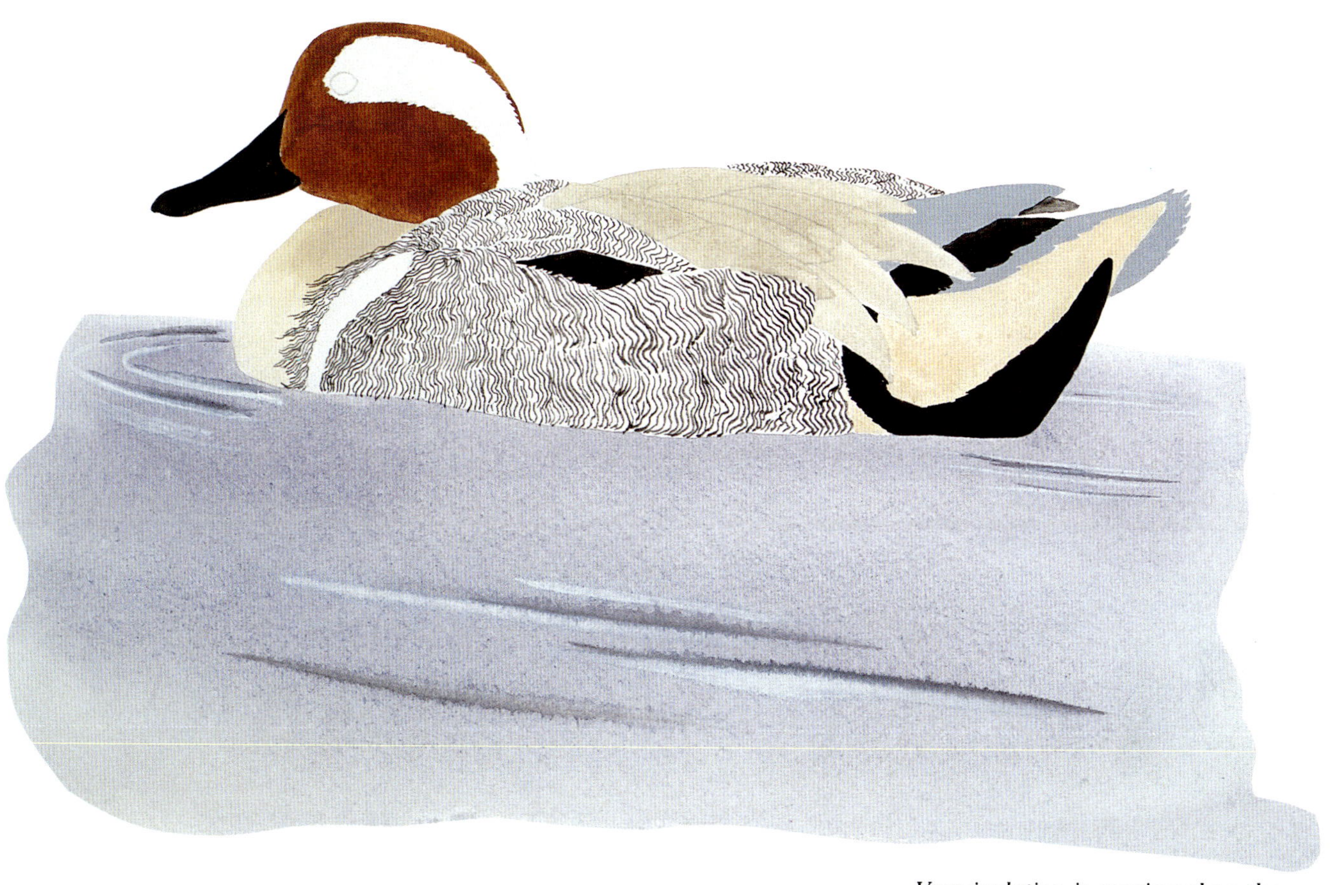

Vermiculation is continued on the forward scapulars, the area at the back of the sidepocket, and on the exposed back feathers. Raw umber and white are mixed and thinly washed on the scapulars and tertials. Black and white are mixed to form a neutral gray and used opaquely to paint the tail and primaries. A thin wet-in-wet wash of Vandyke brown and burnt sienna is used for the base color on the head. Opaque black is painted on the bill, upper tail and lower under tail coverts, and on the dark side spot, which is part of the scapulars. Black is then thinned and painted on the far primaries.

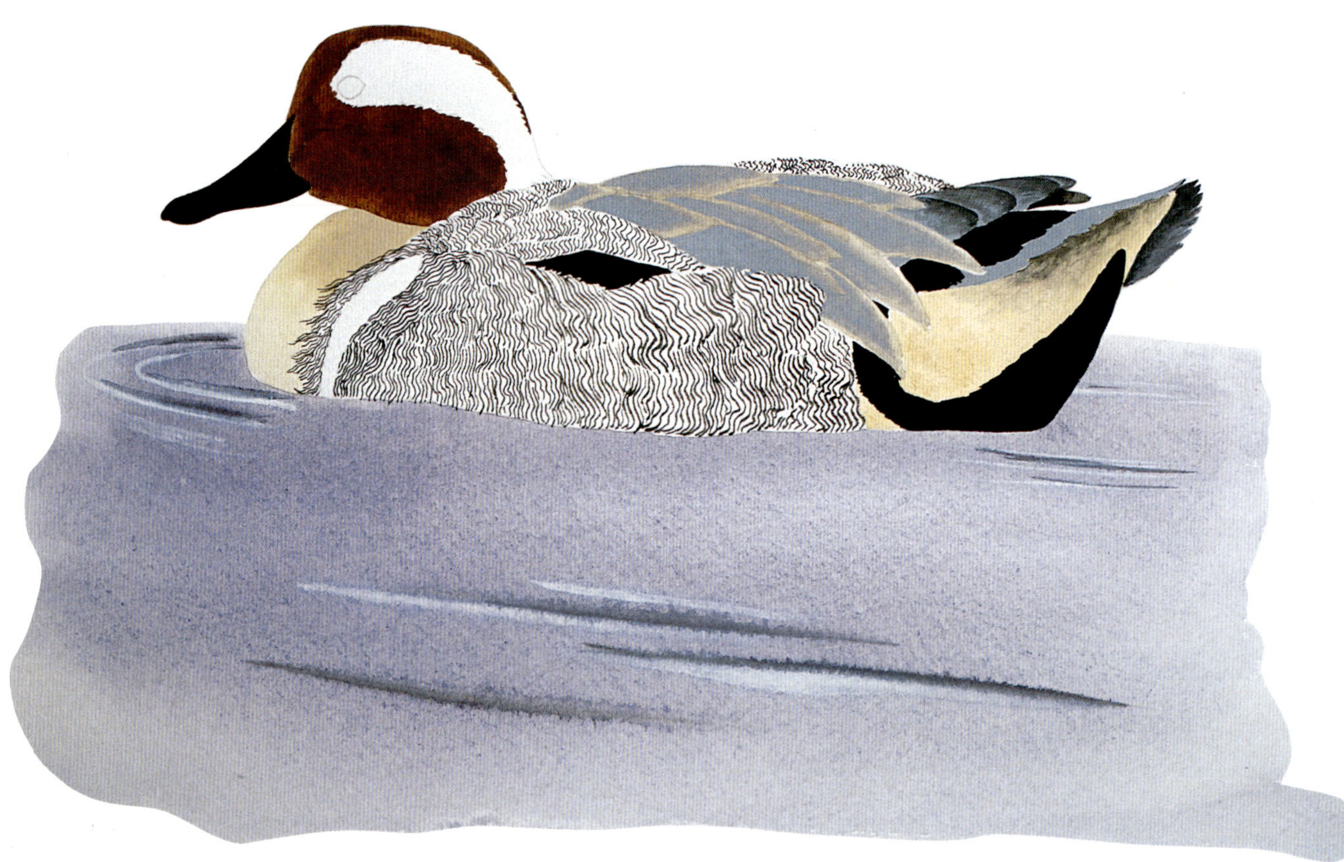

Several graded dark washes are painted to show shading and form. Thinned black is graded on the far under tail feathers, on the yellowish under tail coverts, and on the tips of the gray primaries. Payne's gray is painted in the centers of the brown scapulars and tertials. The gray is thinned and graded toward the edges of each feather so a gray-brown blend is achieved. This is accomplished by blending the gray on each feather while the gray is still wet.

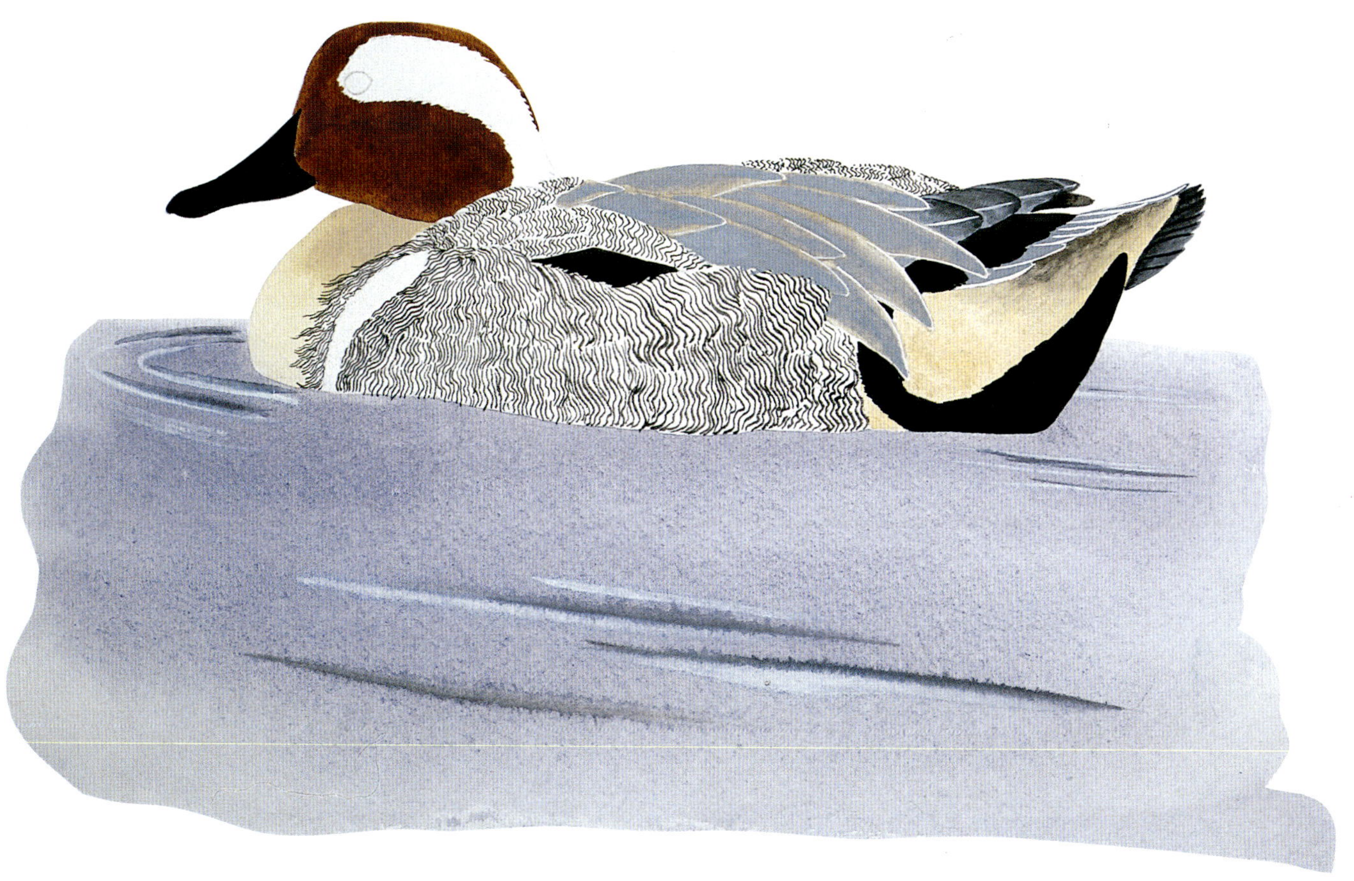

The outer edges of the upper (near) tail feathers are detailed with an opaque white line, while the inner edges of the lower (far) tail feathers are given a dark shadow line detailed with opaque black. It is determined that not enough contrast exists between the tertials and scapulars, so opaque white in the #1 round is used to detail the feather edges and more gray is added to darken those feathers' inner tips. Opaque white is also used to detail a shaft on each primary.

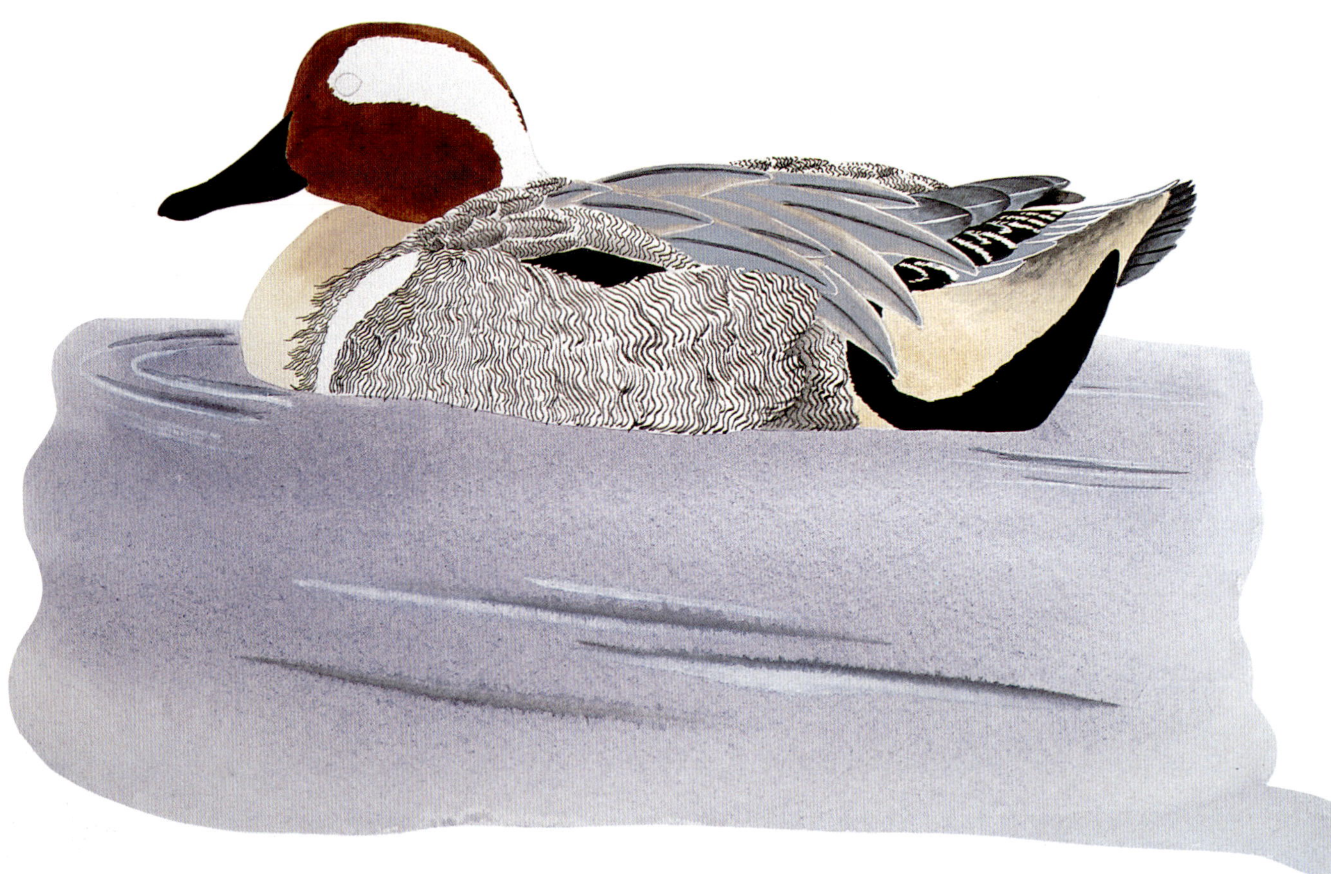

To separate the sidepocket from the area behind it, thinned black is graded onto the duck's back, then it is pulled into the sidepocket feathers with the splitbrush to create irregular feather edges on the sidepocket. To show individual feathers on the vermiculated front scapular and back feathers, very thin black is lightly brushed on the bottom of each feather. Black shafts are painted on the tertials and scapulars with opaque black; as each line is painted it is softened with a clean, damp brush. Opaque white details the edges of the black upper tail coverts.

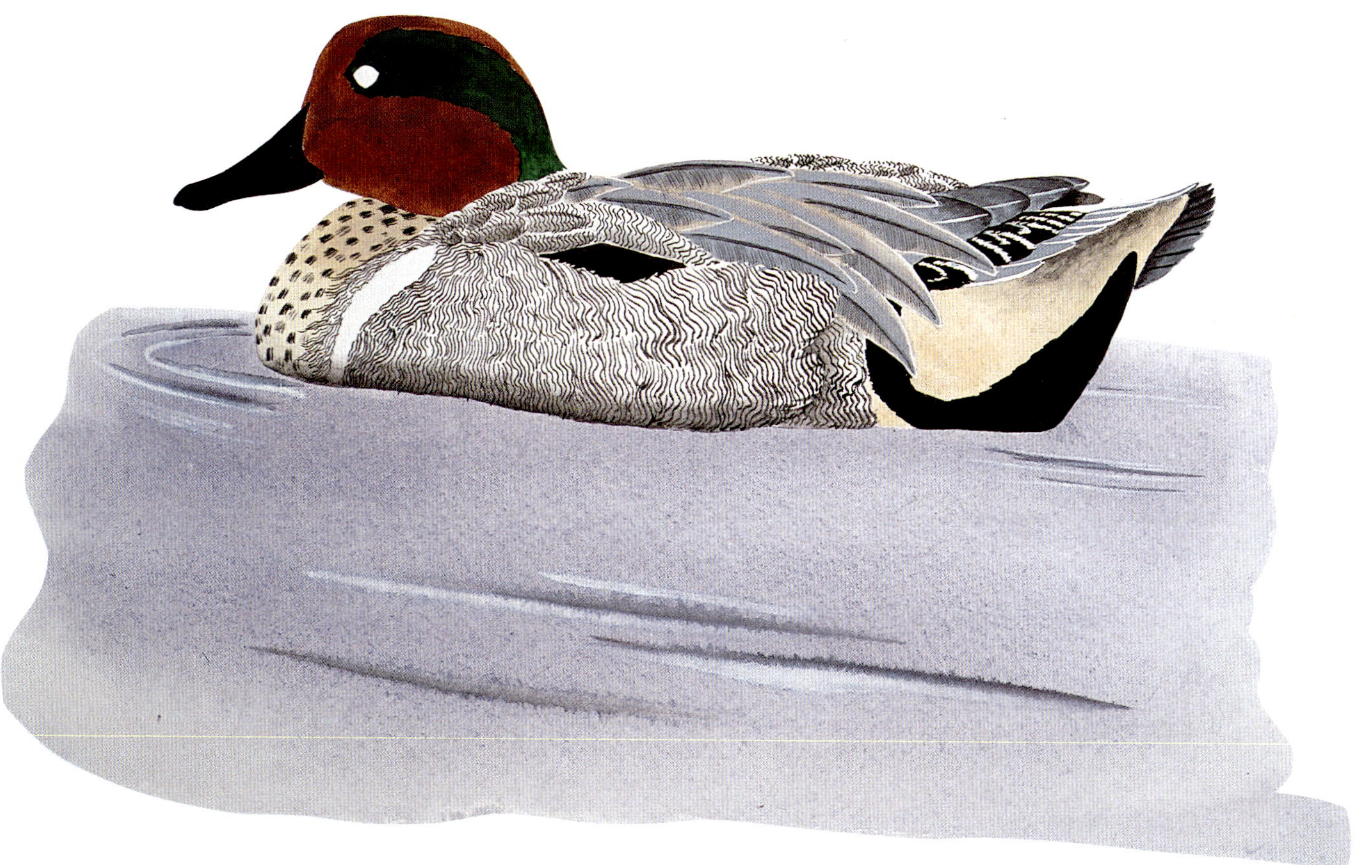

Thinned black is lightly splitbrushed on the bottom of each gray scapular and tertial to show featheration. A thinned black graded wash is painted on the lower part of the body by turning the painting upside down. The thinned black is painted along the darkest area, then graded and glazed with a clean, damp brush to achieve a rounded effect. Permanent green dark is painted thinly on the green head band. With the tip of the brush split slightly, black is used to paint the dark breast spots. Be careful to have the spots follow the contour of the breast, and remember that not all of the spots have the same color intensity because some are under overlapping feathers.

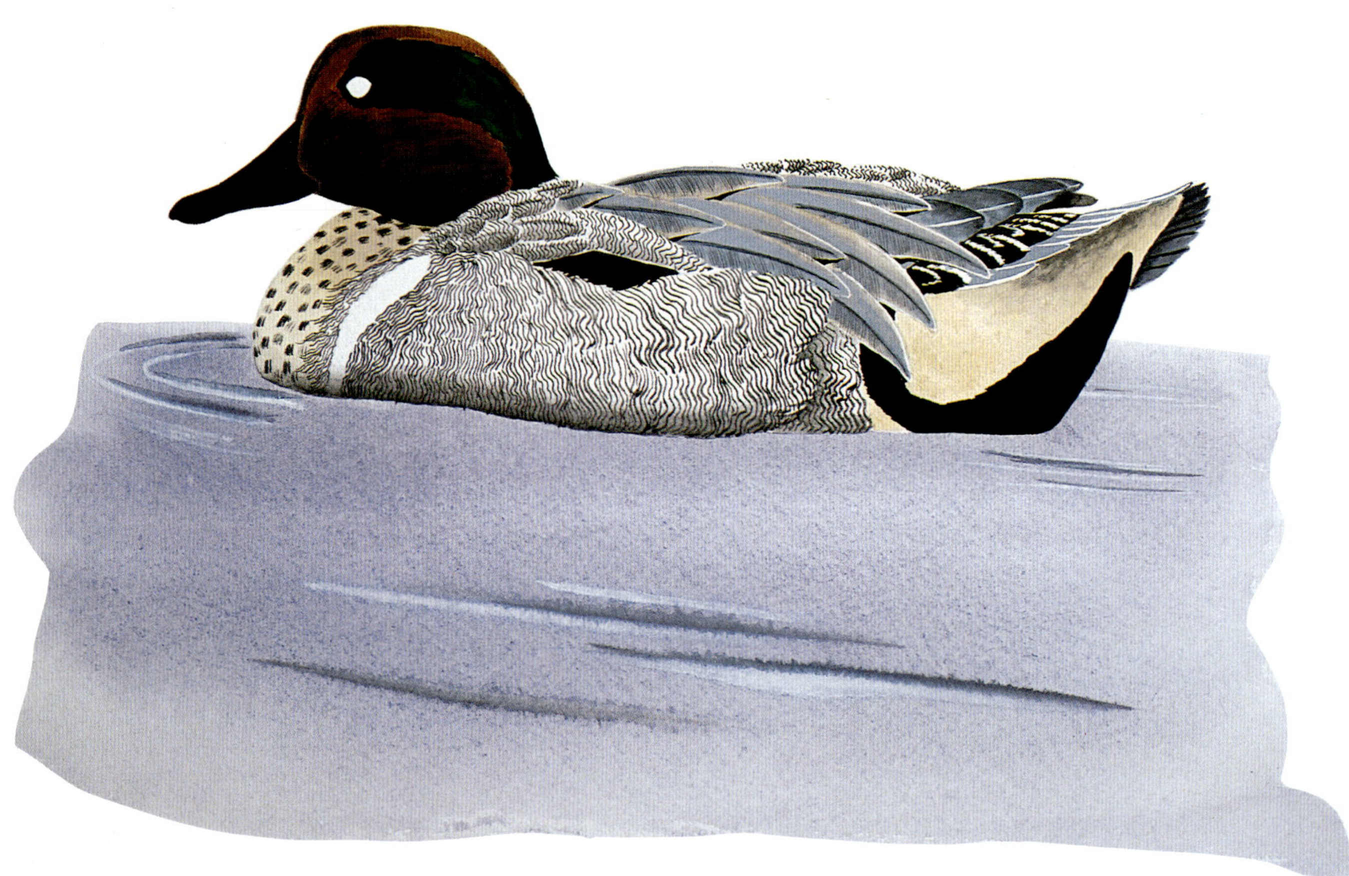

The splitbrush, loaded with black, is used extensively on the head to show shading on both the brown and green. Opaque black in the #1 round details dark shadows under overlapping scapulars and tertials.

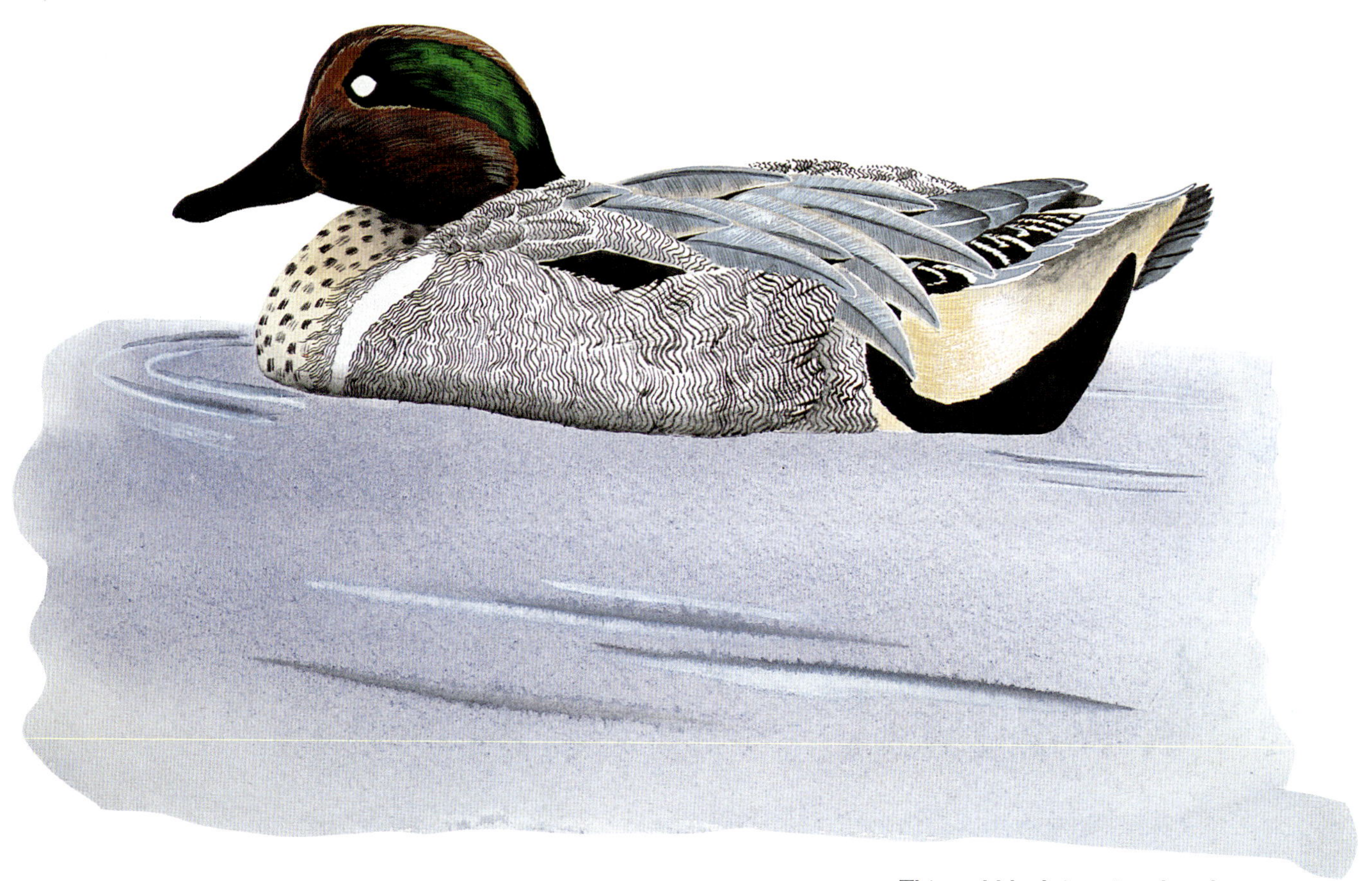

Thinned black is painted at the top of the breast and graded down onto the breast to show the head tucked into the breast and body. Opaque permanent green light is splitbrushed on the dark green head band to indicate iridescence. Light highlights on the brown of the head are splitbrushed in with a mixture of Vandyke brown, white, and raw sienna. Opaque raw sienna and white are alternately splitbrushed on the yellowish under tail coverts to achieve a rounded, feathered effect. Splitbrushed opaque white is painted on the upper part of the scapulars and tertials to show feathered highlights. Feather splits and unevenness in the sidepocket are shown by splitbrushing with thinned black. Deep feather breaks in the sidepocket are added by detailing with opaque black in the #1 round.

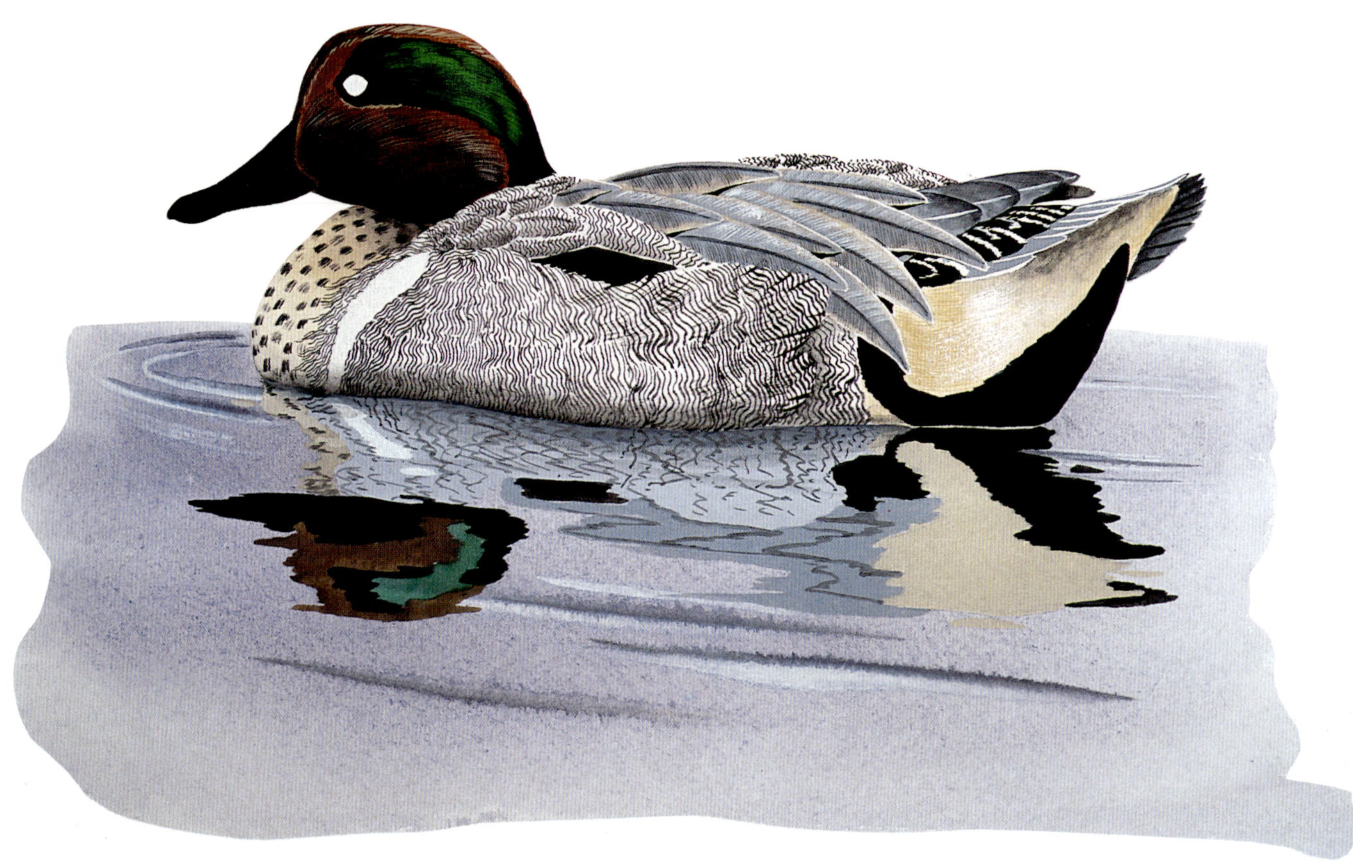

The reflection is now added, although it could have been painted at any step. Always remember the reflection is a less bright and almost always imperfect image of the floating teal.

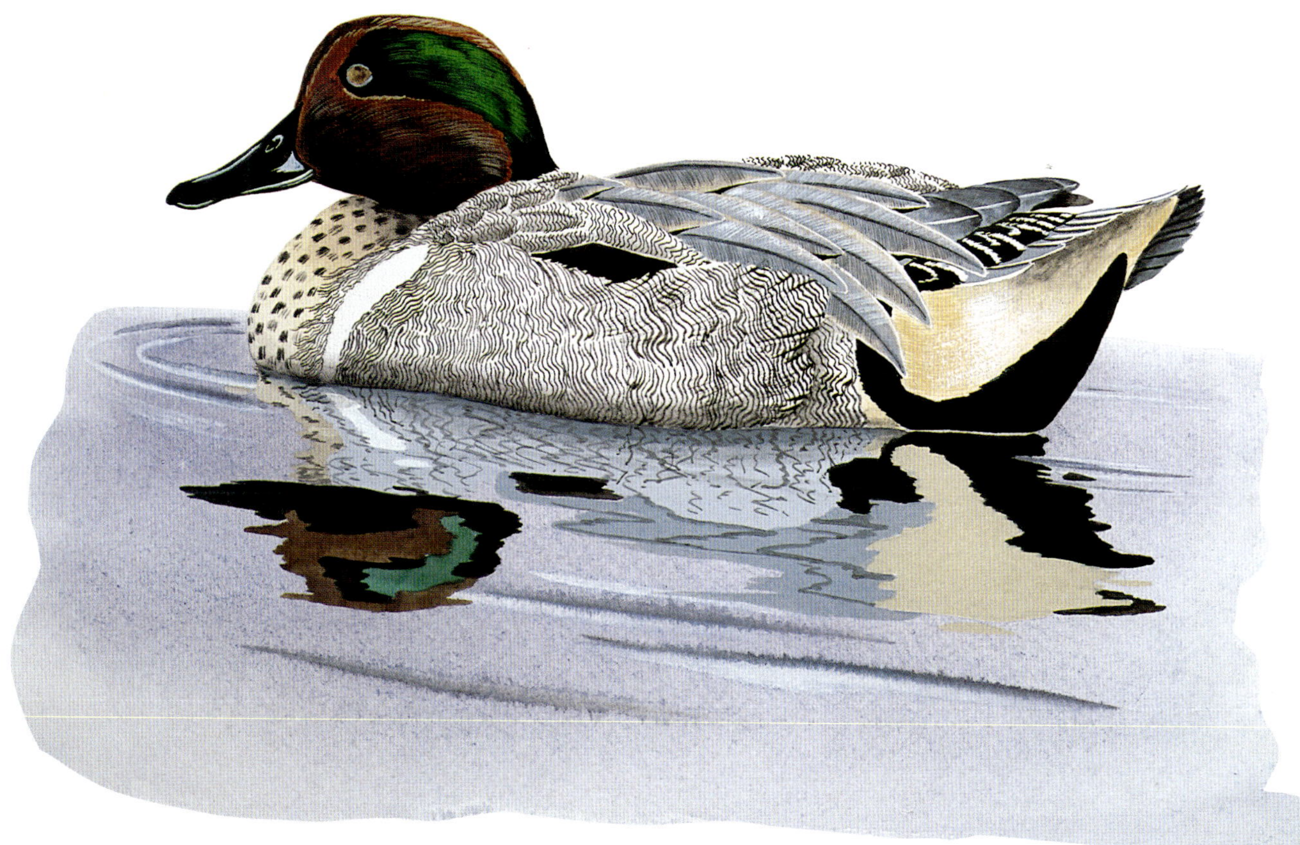

The eye is painted with thin raw umber. Opaque white is applied to the bill to show rough highlights. Thinned black is detailed between the upper tail feathers to indicate separation. Payne's gray and white are mixed to paint a light gray in the eye ring.

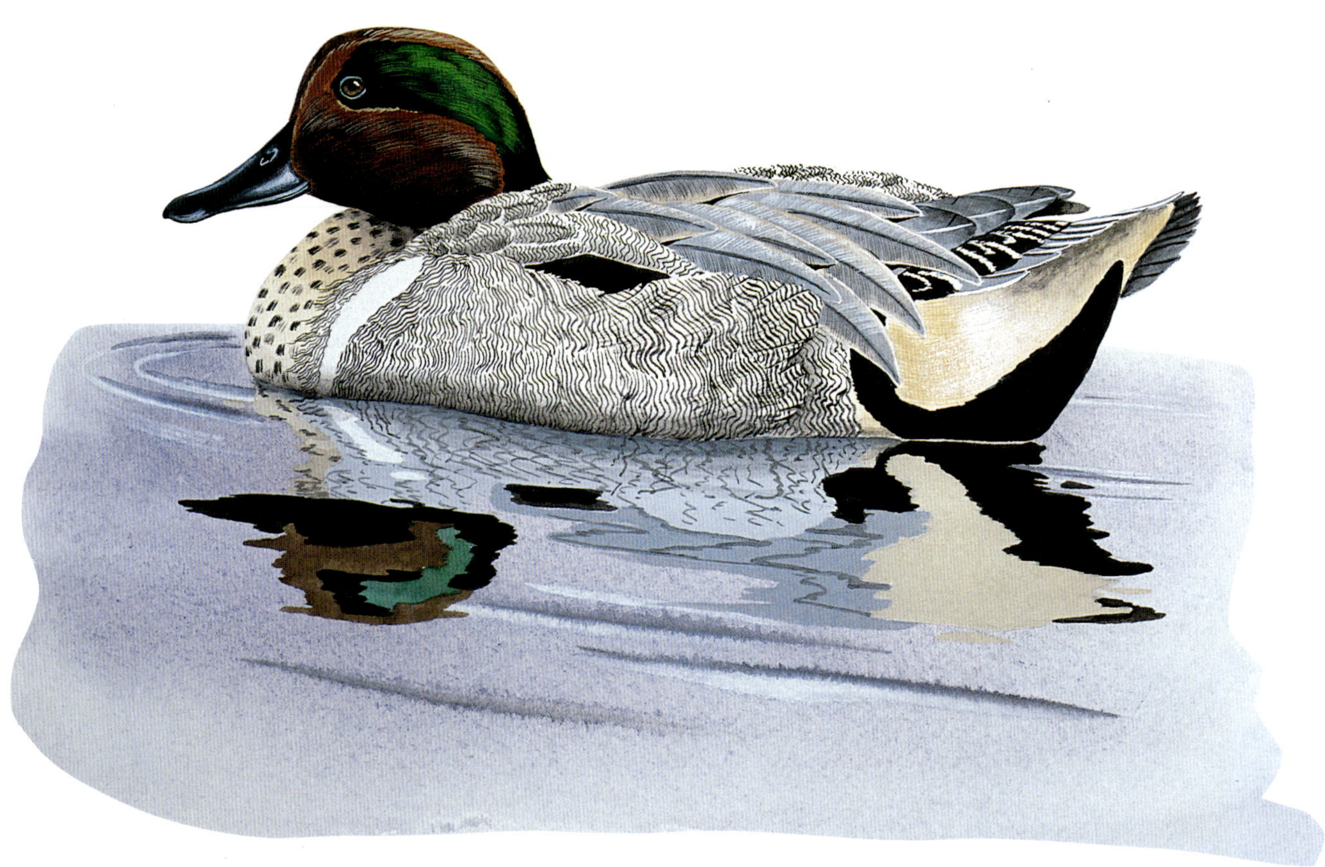

White highlights on the bill are refined and softened with a clean damp brush. Opaque white in the #1 round is used to highlight the dark feather breaks in the sidepocket. Opaque black in the #1 round adds random feather breaks in the primaries. The pupil and shadow in the eye are painted with opaque black, then the shadow is blended down into the brown iris. When the black in the eye is dry, an opaque white highlight is placed in the eye. (Acrylic note: The white highlights on the bill must be blended while the white is still wet.)

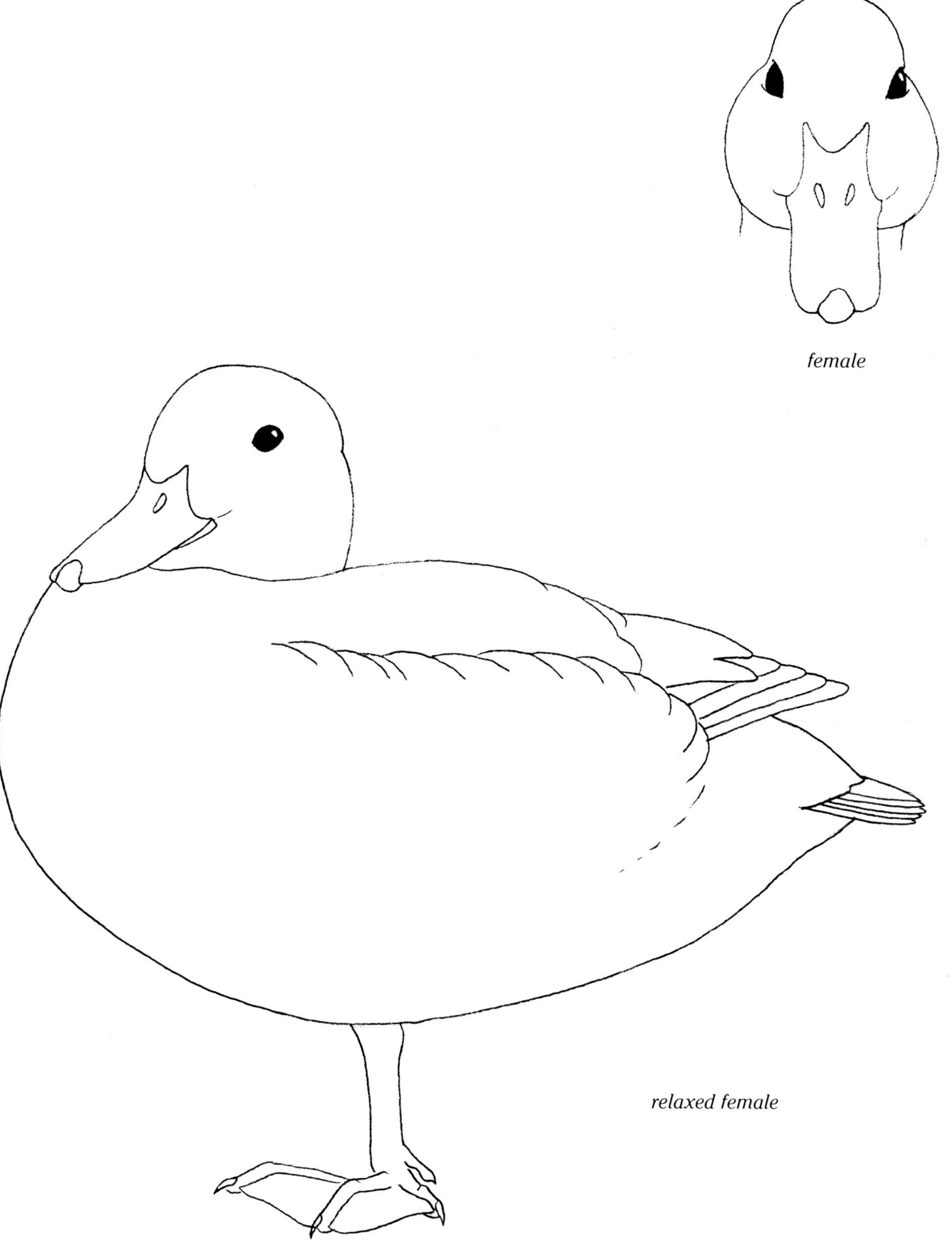

female

relaxed female

Green-winged Teal

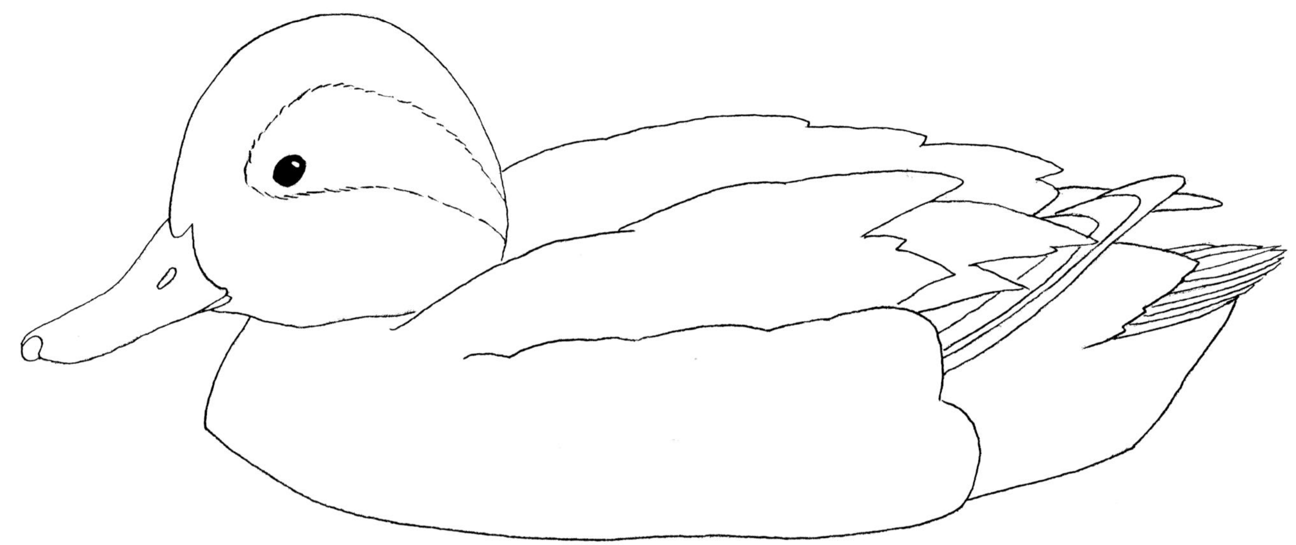

relaxed male

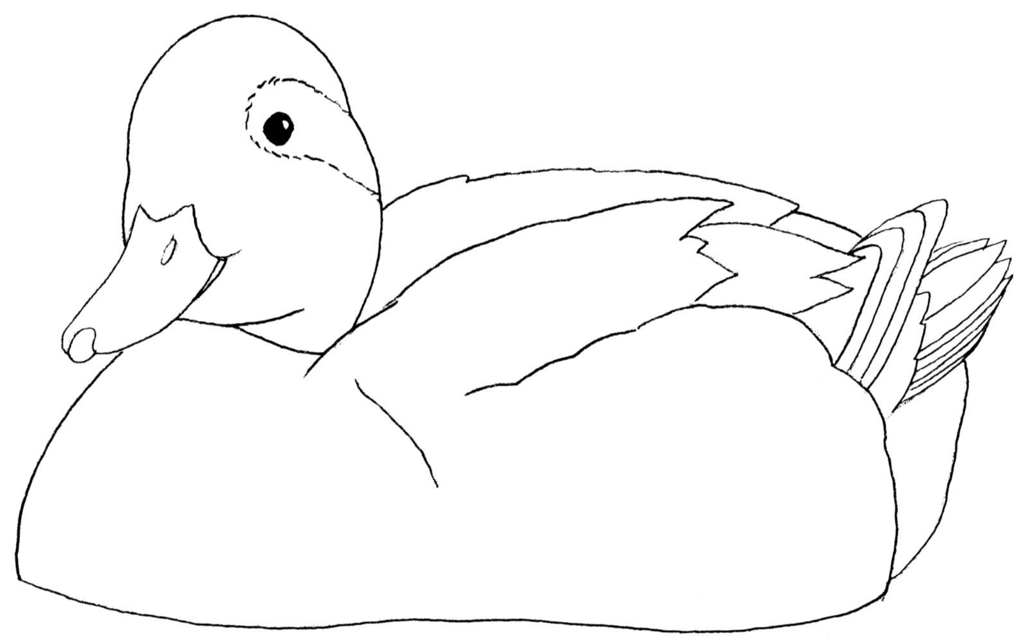

wary male

8
Practice Birds

Wigeon

Anas americana

This is the duck that has two spellings for its name and a common name that was changed to a more common name. Confused? Well, here it is: the common spelling is now wigeon, it used to be widgeon, and before that the duck was called a baldpate—so all of the above are the same duck. While wigeons feed in the same manner as other dabbling ducks, they also have a fondness for plants found only in deep water. Unfortunately, they are poor divers, but by hanging around diving ducks, such as canvasbacks, they pick up scraps and will even take plants away from the divers as they bring them to the surface. Wigeons are also excellent at walking on land, and they graze on grasses and grains with their very small bills, which are well suited to this purpose.

At first glance, wigeons are not as strikingly colored or patterned as are other dabblers. On more careful examination, though, the full range of coloration, vermiculation, and patterns is seen. With its subtle color changes, a wigeon can be more difficult to paint than, say, a wood duck. The breast blends softly into the sidepocket and may be colored from pink to brown, the scapulars are delicately colored, the tertials are boldly patterned, and the dark eye band boasts a green iridescence. All in all, this duck must be carefully painted to achieve a realistic portrait.

Palette: white, ivory black, phthalo blue, Pelikan raw umber, brilliant green, sap green, yellow ochre, red ochre, and Payne's gray.

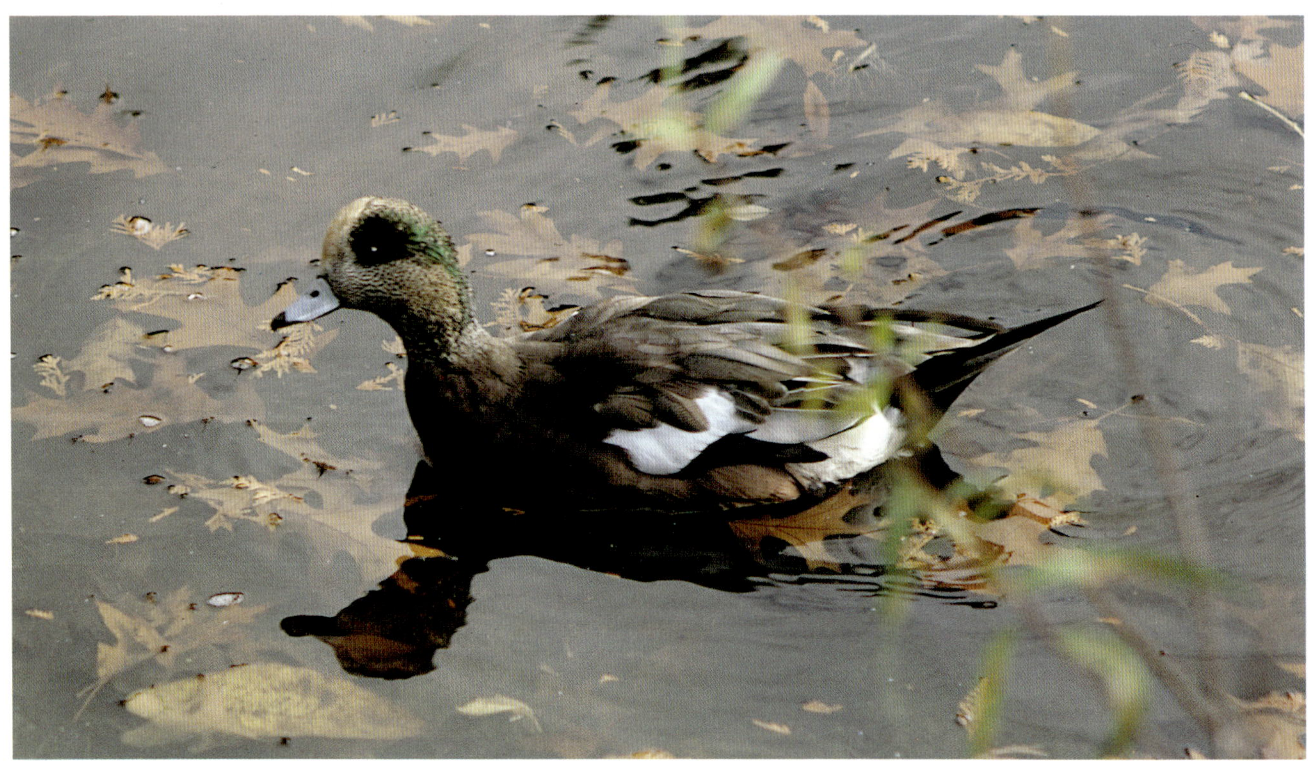

American Wigeon (Dave Mohrhardt photo)

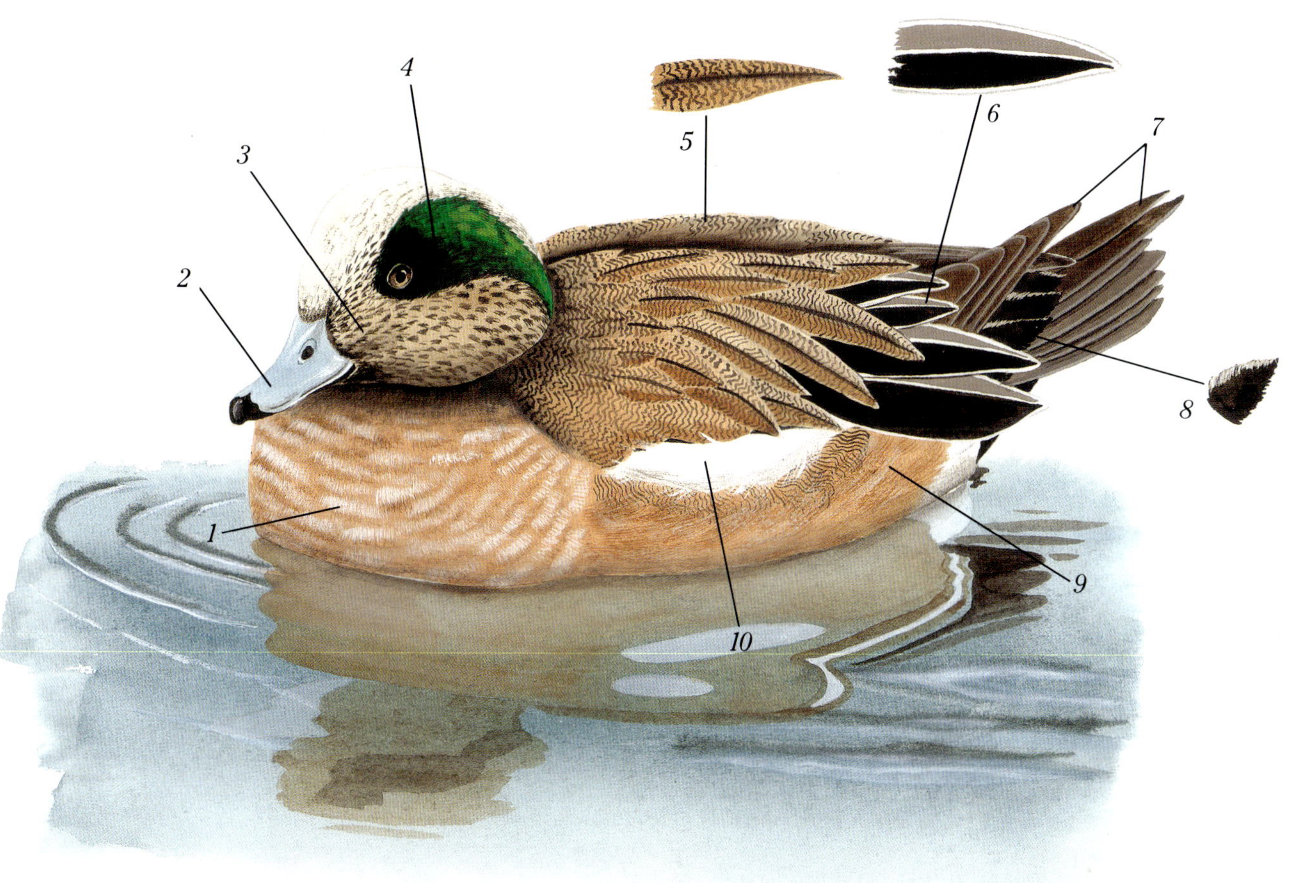

1. The base breast color is a mixture of red ochre, yellow ochre, and white. Feather shadows are splitbrushed with opaque raw umber, and the light feather edges are splitbrushed with opaque white.

2. The bill is a mix of white and phthalo blue.

3. Thinned raw umber is washed wet-in-wet on the lower part of the head and graded to a very thin color on the forehead and crown. Thinned black in the split-brush is used to paint in the dark pattern.

4. Brilliant green is highlighted with sap green yellow and shaded with opaque black for the eye band.

5. The scapulars are a thin wash of Vandyke brown mixed with yellow ochre. Thinned black details in the vermiculation and feather shafts.

6. The tertials are black, Payne's gray, and white. The separation between the colors is very distinct.

7. Tail and primaries are a mixture of black and raw umber.

8. Upper tail coverts are opaque black with a white or yellow-white margin on the inner edge.

9. The sidepocket is a mixture of white, yellow ochre, and Vandyke brown with a small amount of red ochre. Thin black is used to detail vermiculation. The vermiculation extends down the sidepocket but is often obscured.

10. The opaque white is part of the wing coverts.

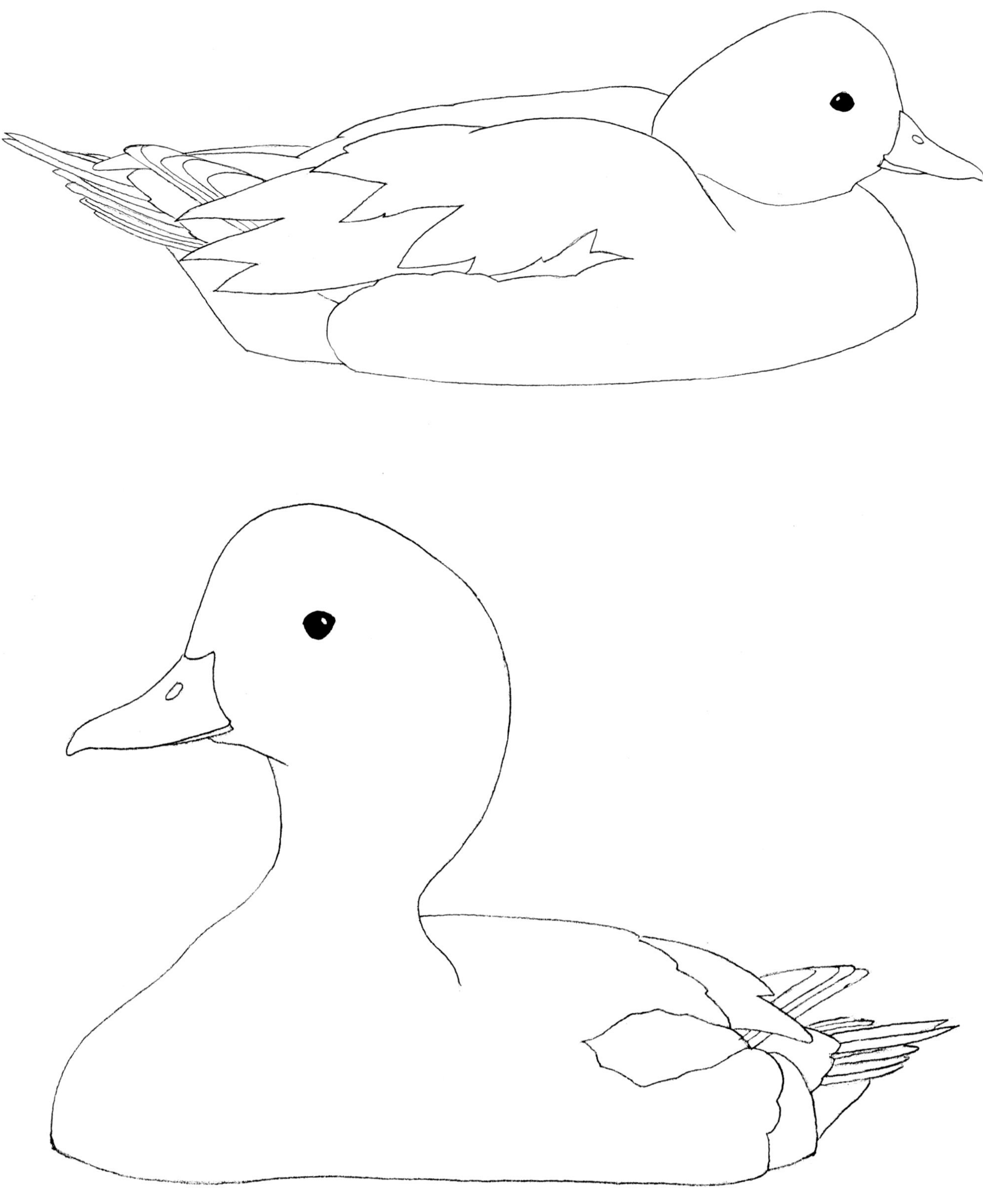

Wigeon

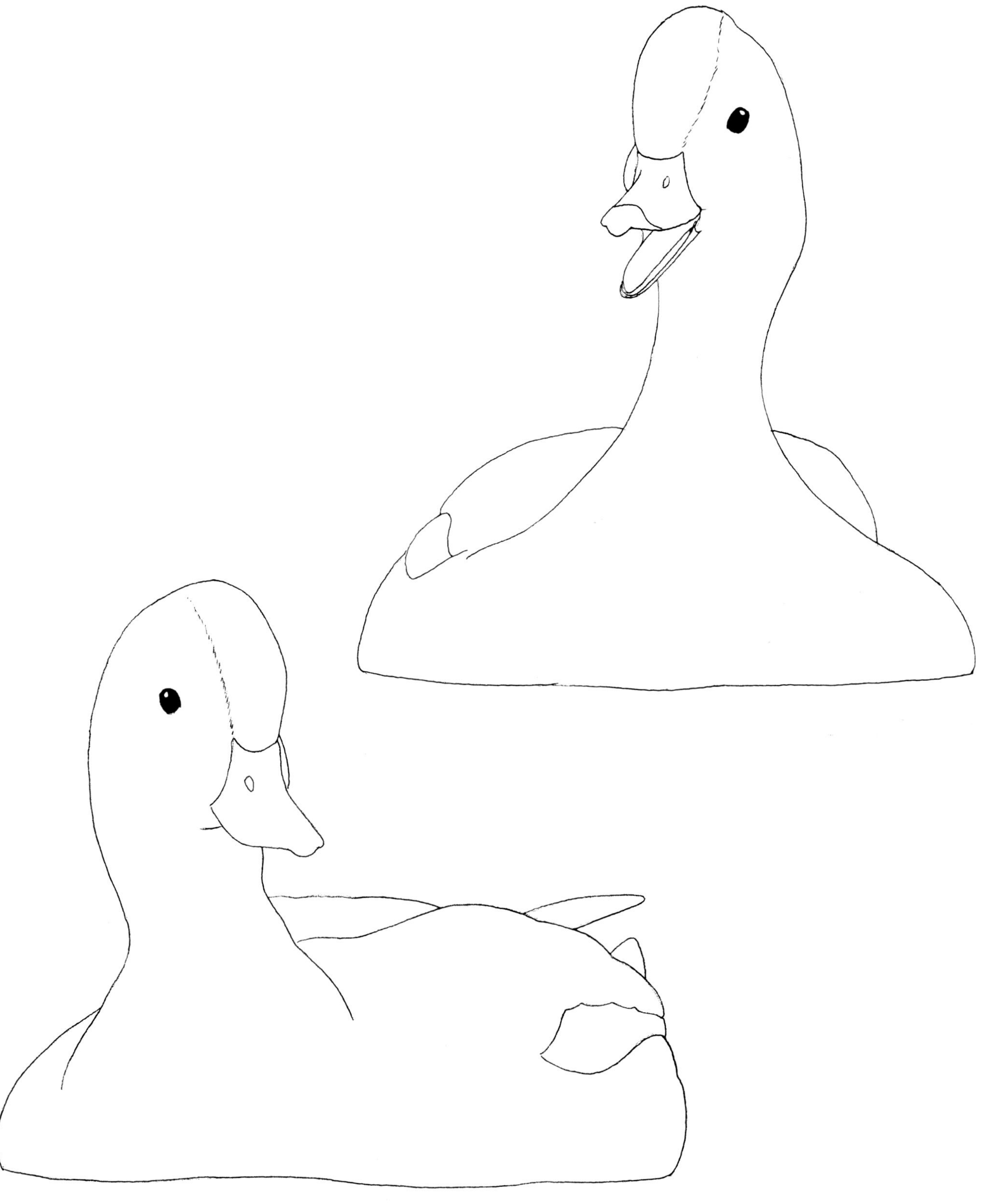

Wigeon

Mallard

Anas platyrhynchos

The mallard is the most common duck. Mallards have easily adapted to the proximity of man and, for that matter, to other species of ducks, crossbreeding to produce some unusual hybrids. They are able to live on almost any size body of water—from small ponds to large lakes. The females resemble black ducks but have a lighter coloration. While the male mallard structurally resembles the male black duck, the male mallard is distinctively colored and cannot be confused with any other dabbler. Its iridescent green head, chestnut-colored breast, light underparts, and curved center-tail feathers are unmistakable.

Painting the male mallard is not difficult, but there is a lot of painstaking vermiculation, which is emphasized in this picture to show how extensive it is. The scapulars have indeterminate margins so much of the vermiculation runs together and is painted as a group. The speculum on both males and females iridesces a blue-violet. The legs range in color from orange to orange-red.

Palette: white, ivory black, cadmium orange, red ochre, burnt umber, cadmium yellow pale, brilliant green, sap green yellowish, and Payne's gray.

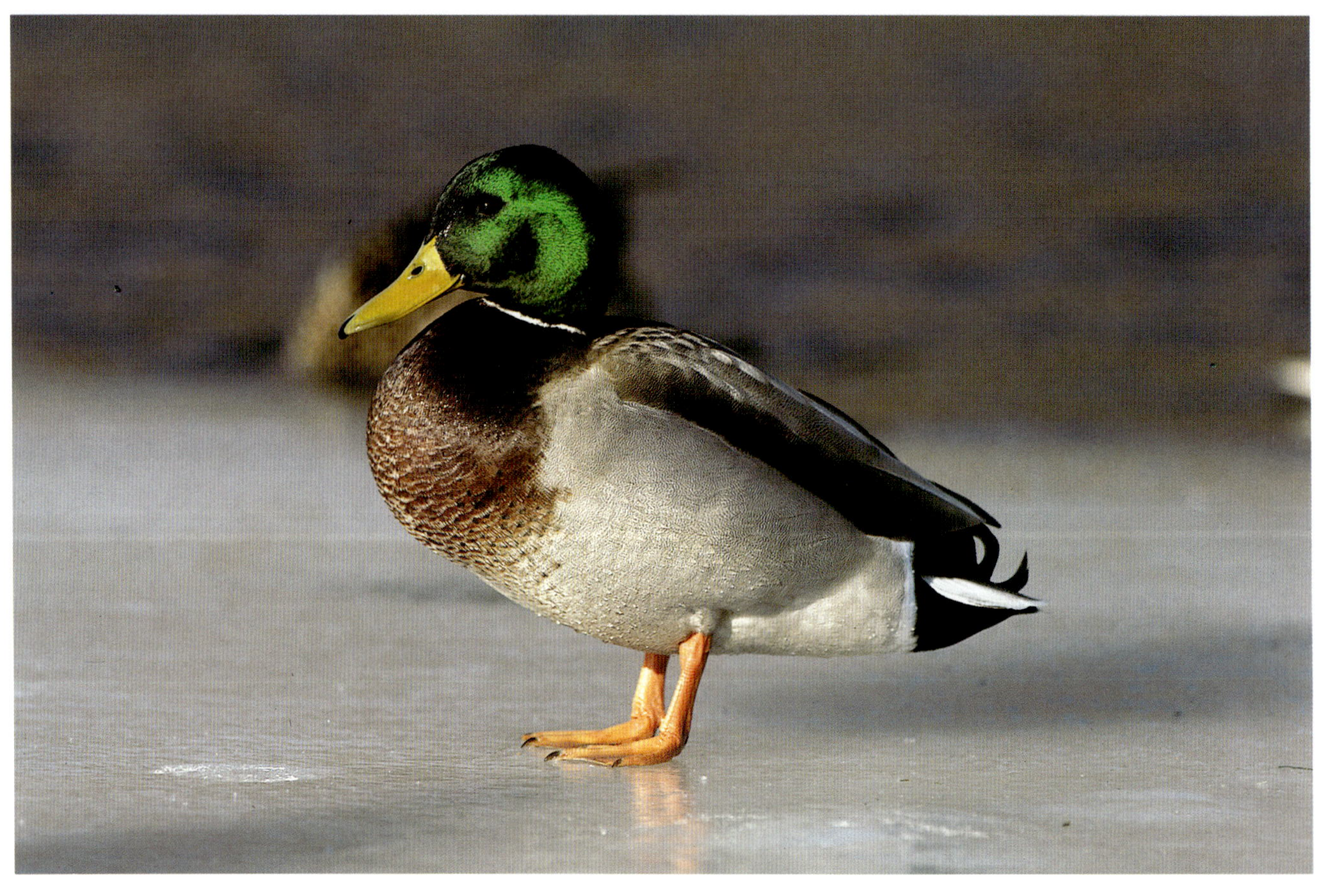

Mallard (Rod Planck photo)

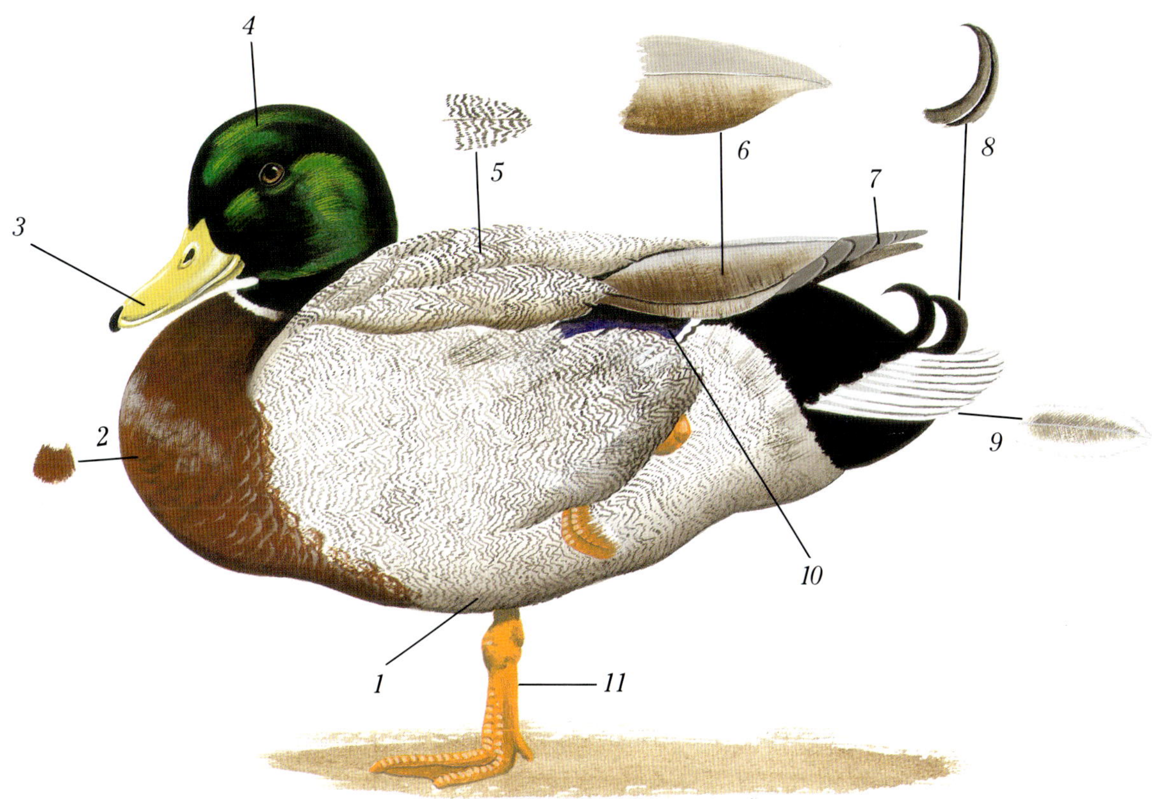

1. Shading on the light-colored body areas is done with graded washes of thinned black. Each area is painted separately.

2. The base breast color is an opaque mix of red ochre and burnt umber. Payne's gray is tipped on to show light feather edges, and it is also used in the splitbrush to show highlights.

3. The bill is cadmium yellow pale mixed with white.

4. Green iridescence on the opaque black of the head is shown with brilliant green highlighted with sap green yellow. The depth of the iridescence is determined by the angle and intensity of light.

5. The vermiculation is thinned black detailed with a #1 round.

6. The tertial is washed with thinned Payne's gray. The brown shading is washed and splitbrushed from the outer edge. The brown used here may be painted with a more gray tone on some birds.

7. The primaries are opaque Payne's gray.

8. Opaque black is used for the upper and lower tail coverts and the central tail feathers. Notice how the curved tail feathers are V-shaped.

9. When the tail is folded, only the white edges of the tail feathers can be seen; they actually have a brown-hued central pattern that becomes more pronounced as the feathers progress toward the center.

10. The exposed speculum is thin ultramarine blue pale shaded with black.

11. The legs and feet are cadmium orange mixed with a small amount of white. The dark shading is a mixture of cadmium orange and ultramarine blue pale.

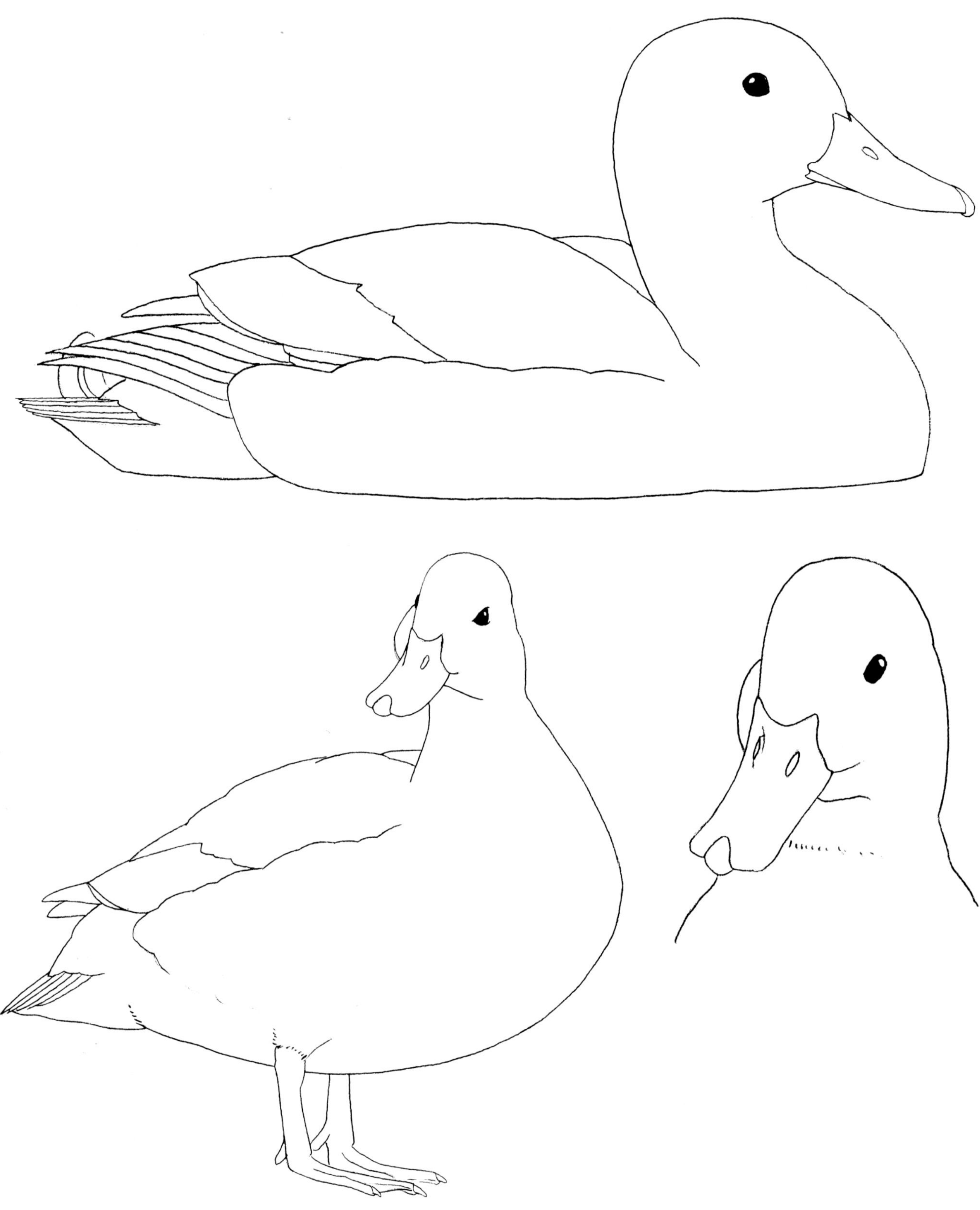

Mallard

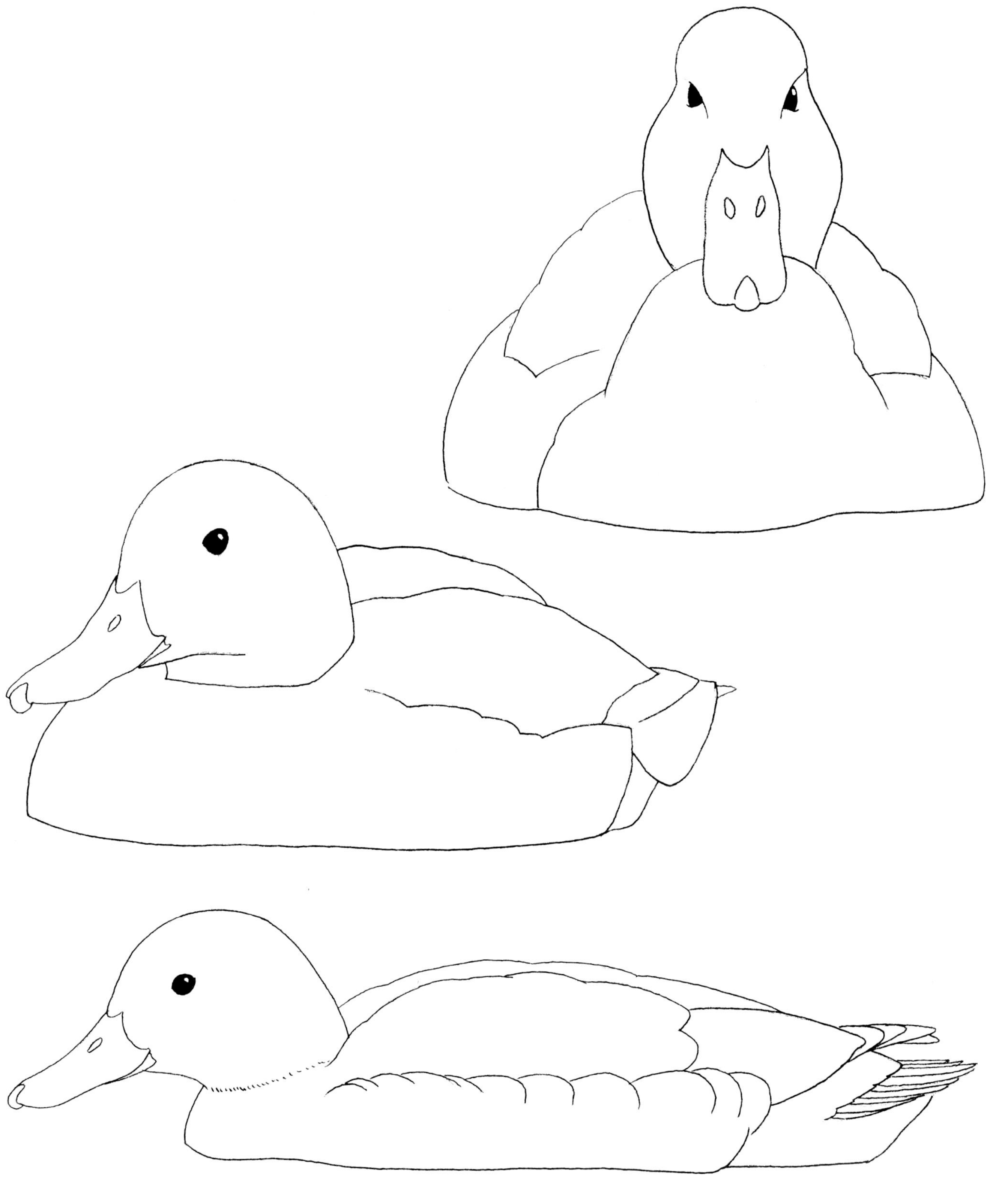

Mallard

Black Duck

Anas rubripes

Black ducks are similar in shape and size to mallards and are often called black mallards. The males of mallards and black ducks, of course, are quite disparate in coloration. The females of the two species, however, are very alike, although the female black duck is somewhat darker and has more color contrast between the head and body than does the female mallard. Male and female black ducks are almost identical except for minor differences in feather shape and bill color. The female has a yellow-green bill, while the male's bill is a brighter yellow. Black ducks are the wariest and most alert of the dabblers and, consequently, are difficult to closely approach. Their dark bodies and light-colored underwings make them easy to identify in flight. Black ducks are strong fliers and travel great distances in a single day.

The black duck is the ideal species to study for feather direction and groups because the contrast between the dark feather center and light feather edge makes the feathers easy to identify and separate—even the scapulars and tertials can be easily identified. Good reference material is a must because any discrepancy in feather direction or size is immediately apparent. The body color is basic but close attention must be paid to mixing the color; it is a brown-black, not a solid black. The variable in black ducks is the color of the leg and foot, which can range from brown to red.

The palette used to paint the black duck is very limited. Although there are only a few painting steps, there is much individual feather painting.

Palette: ivory black, raw umber, white, yellow ochre, and cadmium yellow pale.

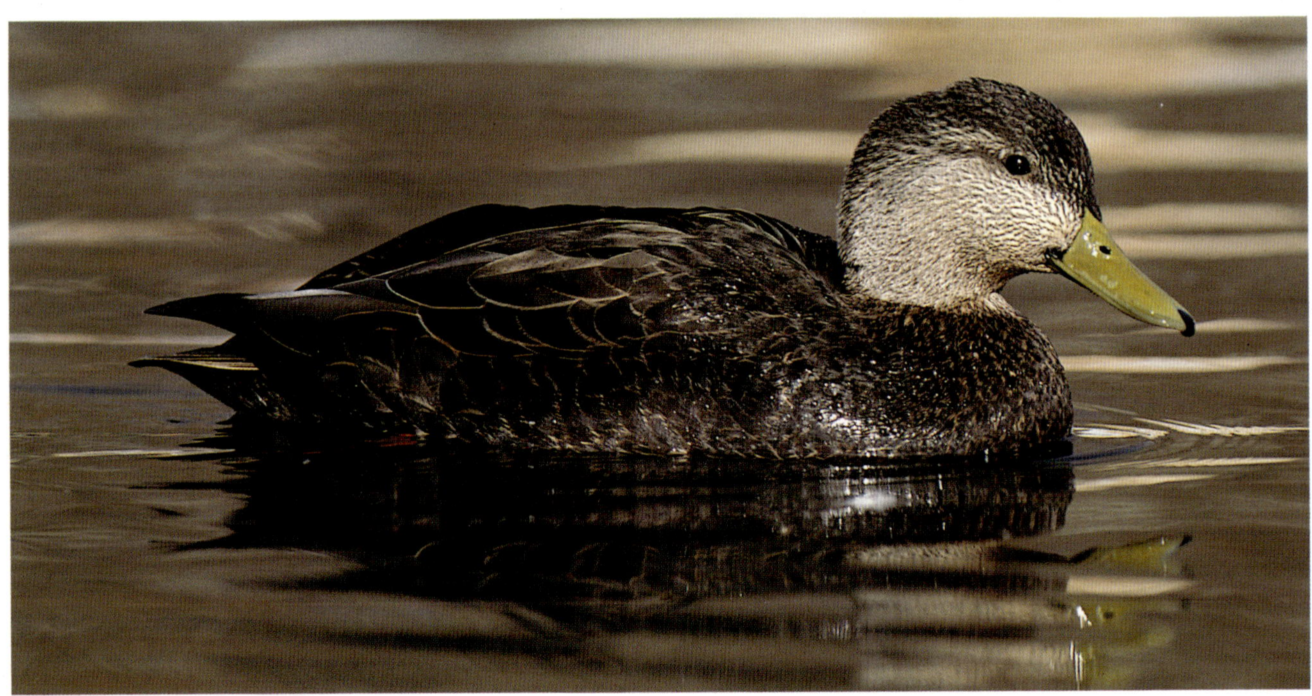

Black Duck (Rod Planck photo)

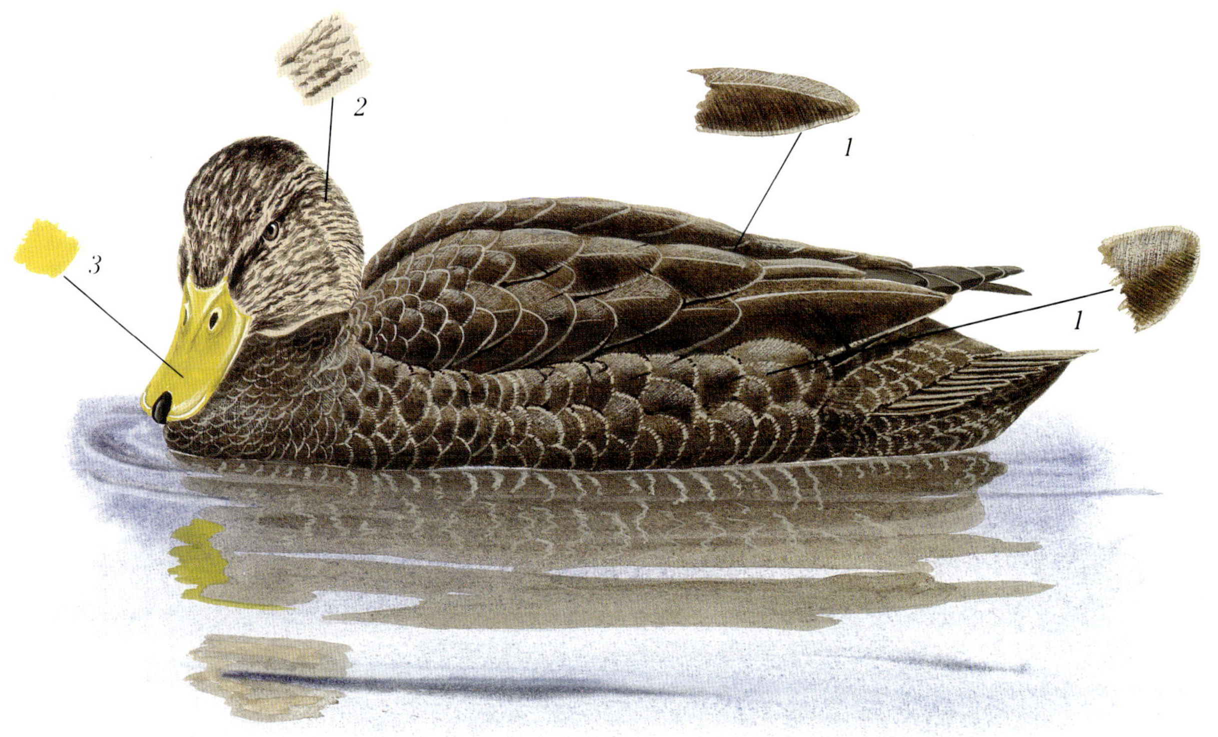

1. The base color of the duck's body is a thin wash of black and raw umber. Each section, such as the breast, flanks, scapulars and so on, should be painted separately until an even base coat is achieved. Each feather outline is detailed with a mixture of white and raw umber. This mixture is also used in the split-brush to highlight each feather. Thinned black is splitbrushed on the feathers to show shading. Feather breaks are added with opaque black.

2. The light head color is an opaque mixture of white, raw umber, and yellow ochre. The pattern is thinned black, splitbrushed with only the tip of the brush split to impart small irregular marks.

3. The bill is cadmium yellow pale mixed with a small amount of black.

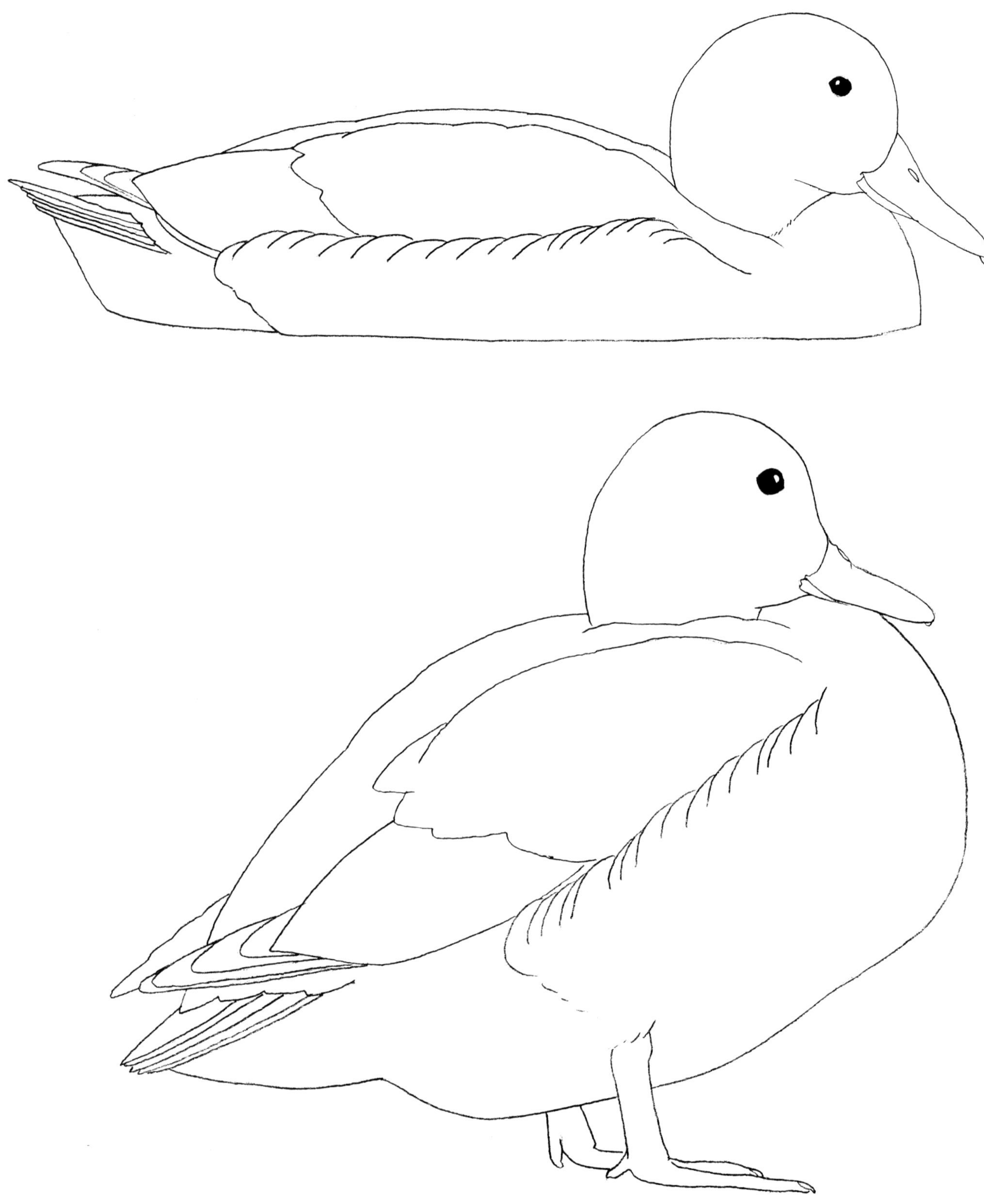

Black Duck

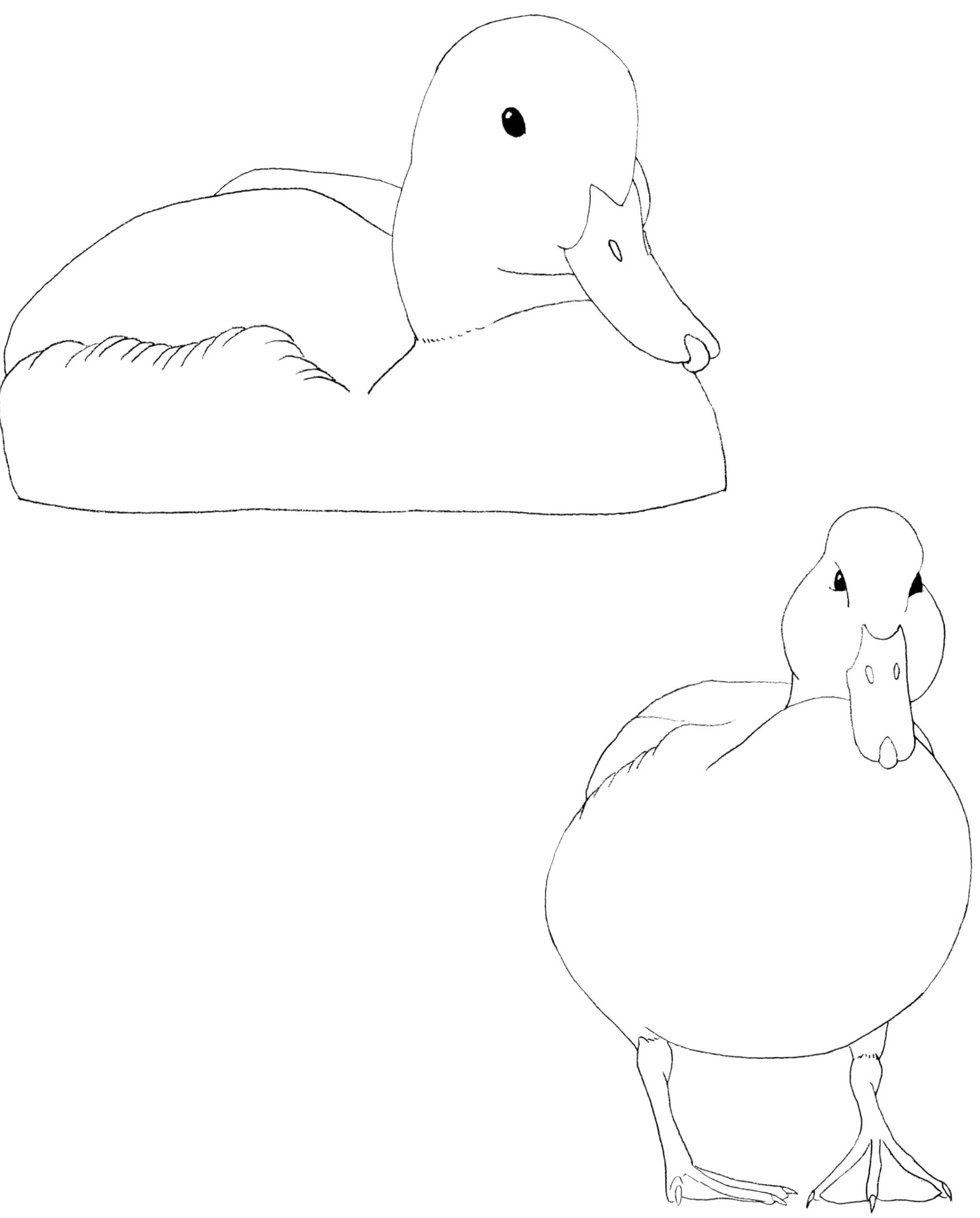

Black Duck

Wood Duck

Aix sponsa

Male and female wood ducks must be seen in nature for their full range of iridescent colors to be fully appreciated. The male is a myriad of patterns, vermiculation, and colors; they literally run from the tip of the bill to the tip of the tail. In addition to their distinctive patterning, wood ducks are the only North American ducks with two colors on the primaries. When relaxed, the head of the male tucks into the body with the crest expanded and the forehead feathers erect, which gives a squared-off look to the head. When agitated or excited, the neck stretches out, the forehead feathers compress to the head and the crest is pulled in. There is no mistaking the mood of a wood duck.

Wood ducks feed and nest in and around wooded bodies of water, such as swamps and river bottoms, so painting the correct habitat is essential. The male wood duck painted here is relaxed, resting on the water, head tucked, and tail pointing upward. The patterns of wood duck feathers usually remain constant. It is the intensity of the iridescence that varies, and its degree of depth will depend on the light striking the duck. The steps to painting a wood duck are broken into definite color groups related to the feather sections, so it is easiest to work on each area separately. For example, first paint the back and wing, then go on to the tail, and then the head—progress from one area to the next until the painting is finished.

Palette: Pelikan raw umber, red ochre, white, ivory black, yellow ochre, raw sienna, ultramarine blue pale, brilliant green, sap green yellowish, cadmium orange, cadmium red pale, cadmium yellow pale, and violet.

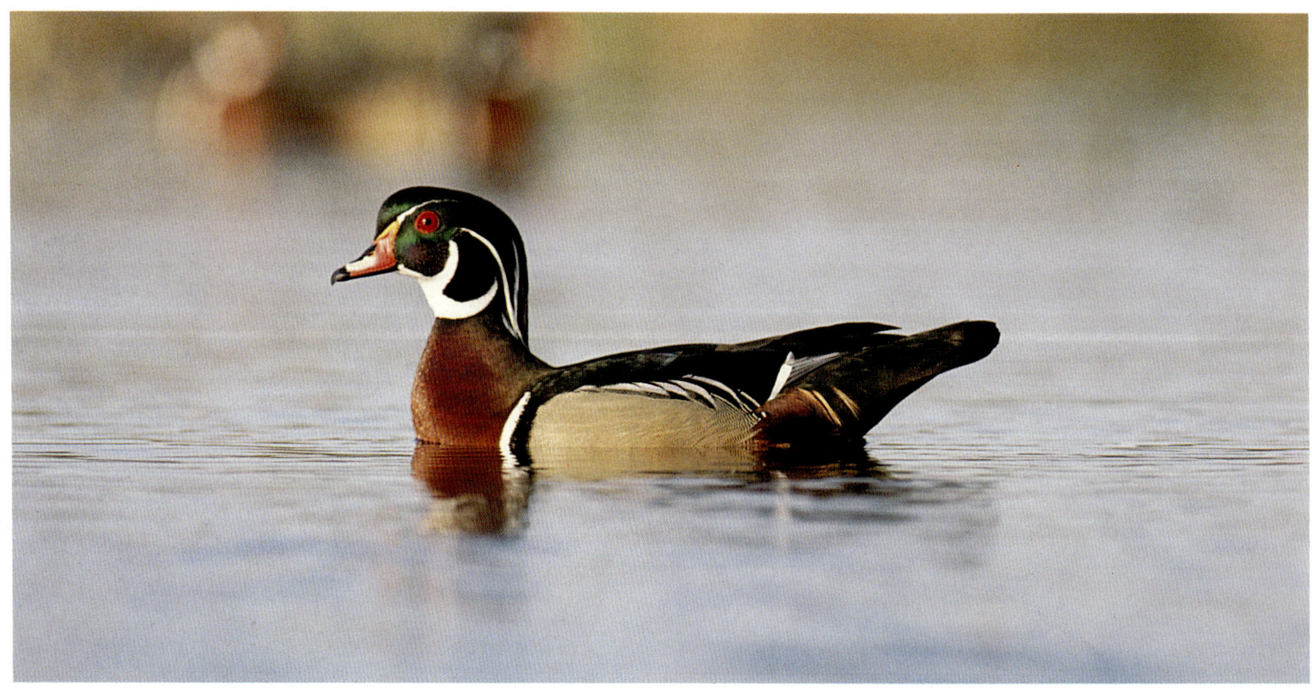

Wood Duck (Larry West photo)

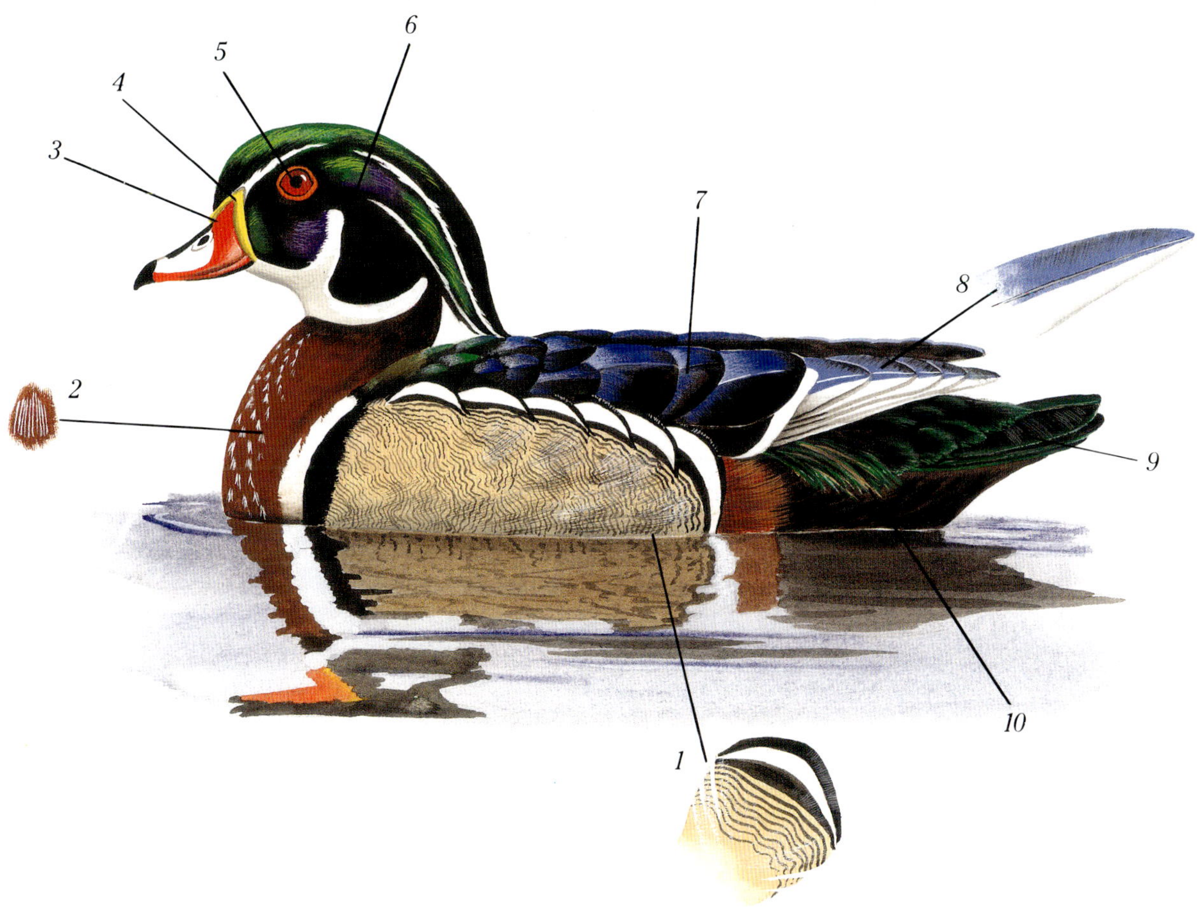

1. The base color of the side-pocket is an opaque mixture of yellow ochre and white. The vermiculation is detailed with opaque black. Splitbrushing opaque black and white adds feather shading and highlights.

2. Red ochre mixed with raw umber produces a mahogany color. Opaque white is used to detail on the pattern.

3. Opaque cadmium red pale, black, and white paint the bill.

4. The fleshy yellow area at the base of the bill is opaque cadmium yellow pale.

5. Thinned cadmium red pale is painted in the iris, while the fleshy eye ring is opaque cadmium orange.

6. The head is opaque black, except in areas where it iridesces (these areas may change depending on the amount of ambient light). The green iridescence is brilliant green highlighted with sap green yellow. The violet areas are opaque violet highlighted with a violet and white mixture.

7. The scapulars and tertials are a contrast of opaque black and ultramarine blue pale. The blue is shaded with splitbrushed opaque white. The degree and color of iridescence dramatically changes on these feathers depending on the ambient light present.

8. The blue of the primaries is a mixture of ultramarine blue pale and white.

9. Tail and upper tail coverts are black; the feather edges are detailed with brilliant green mixed with a very small amount of white.

10. These hairlike feathers are a mixture of red ochre and raw sienna. The dark shading is splitbrushed red ochre; the light shading is splitbrushed raw sienna.

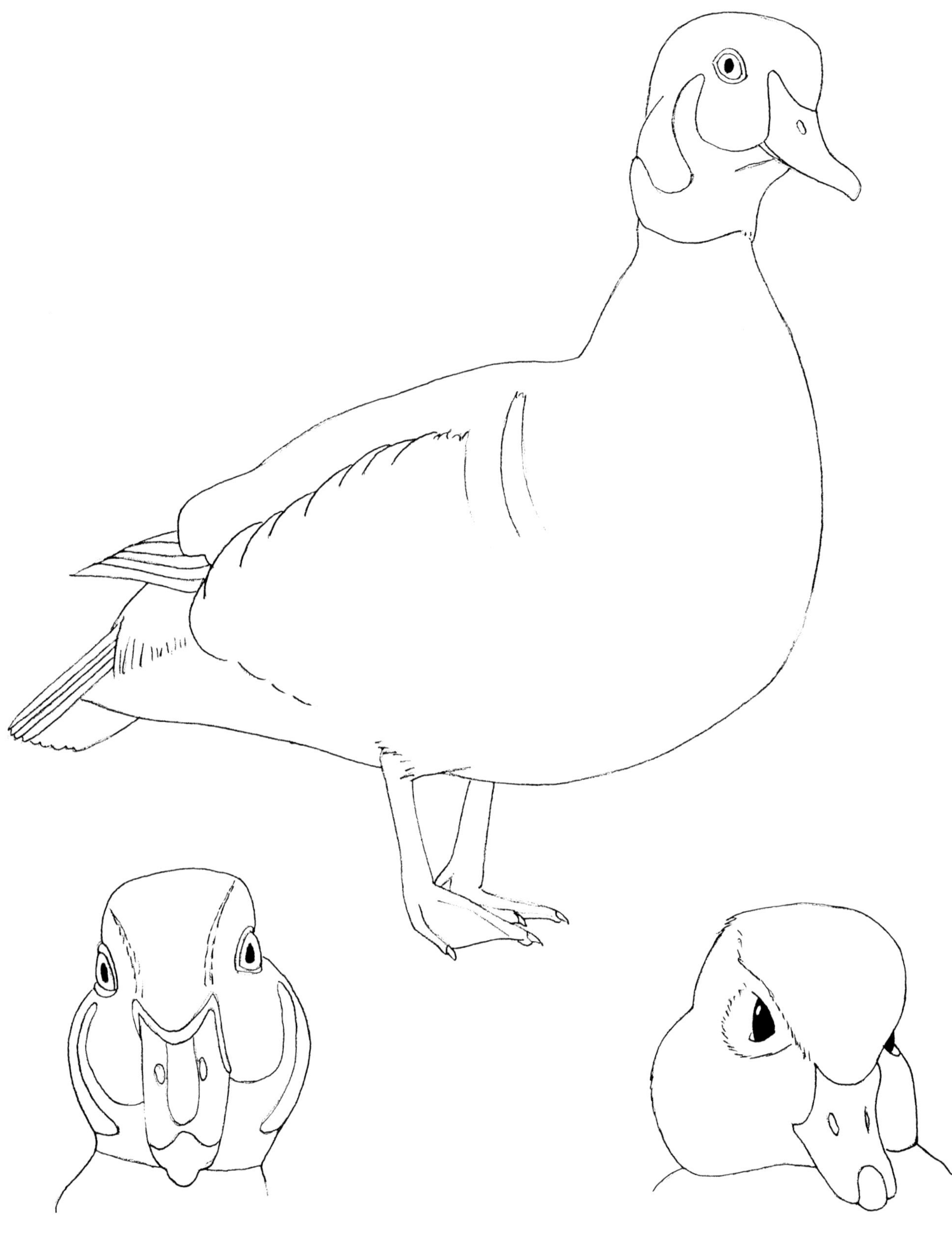

Wood Duck

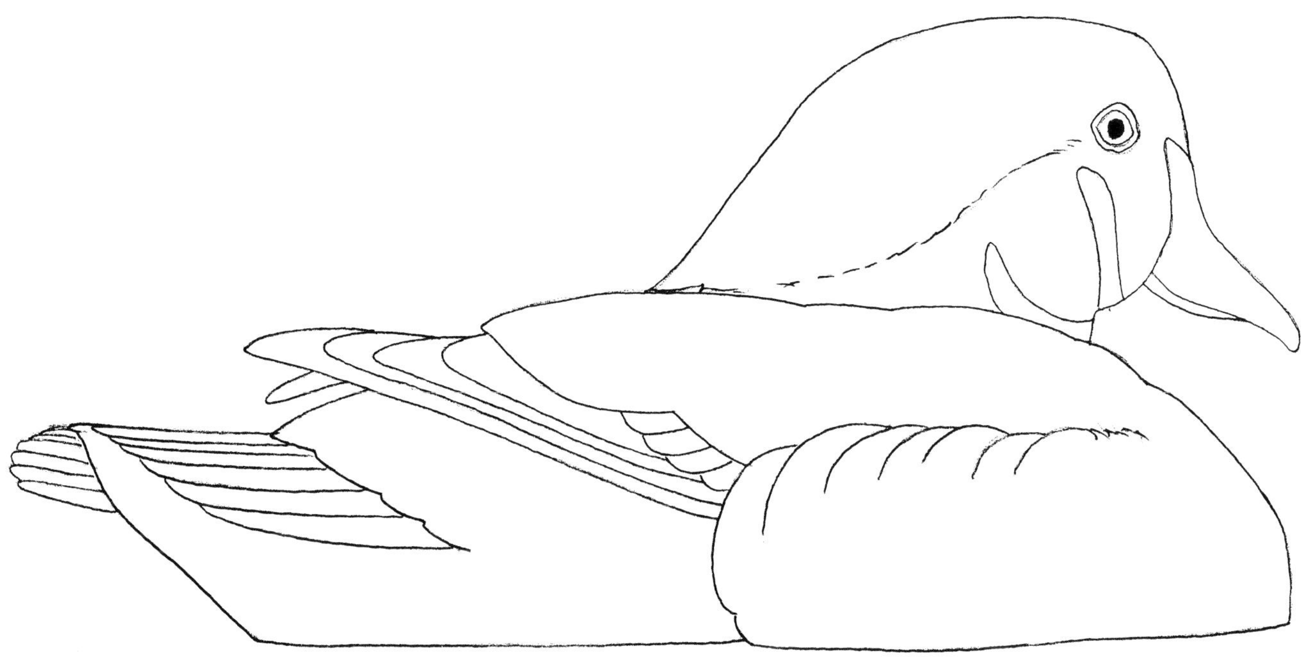

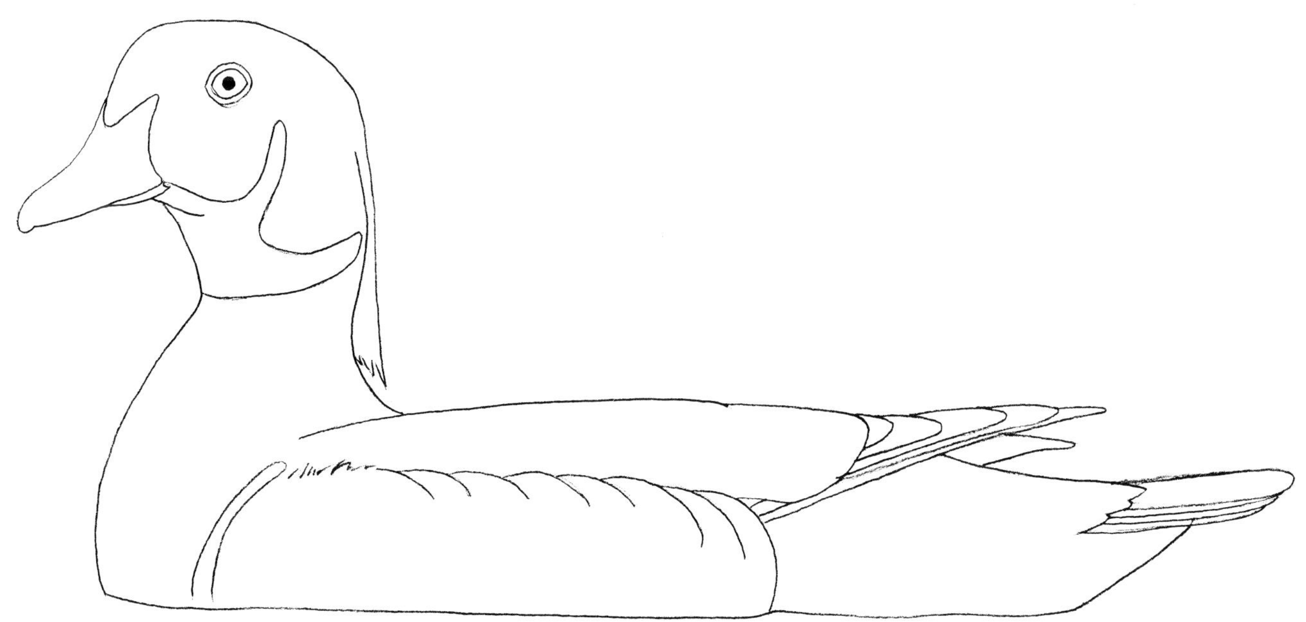

Wood Duck

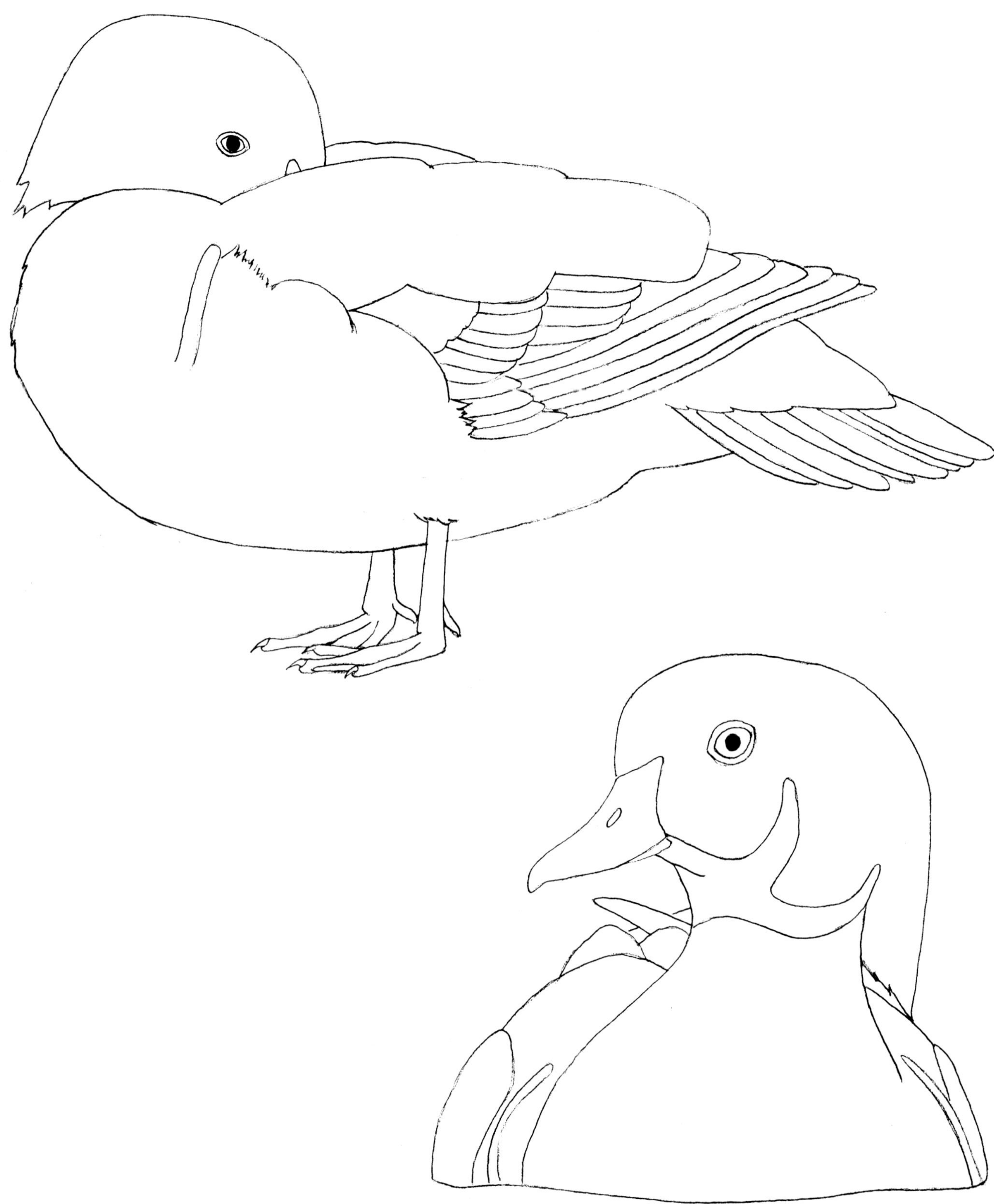

Wood Duck

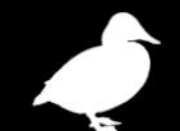

9 Reference Material

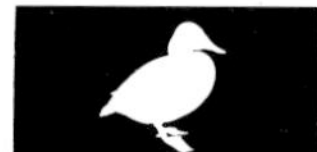

A frequent problem that bird artists have is obtaining adequate reference material. Ducks, however, are one of the few species of birds where this is not true; excellent reference sources are available to everyone. Although there is no substitute for observing the color, attitudes, postures, and habits of birds in the wild, other reference sources must be considered because few of us have the ability to remember the field marks, colors, and shape of a bird well enough to paint it accurately. When examining several reference sources, especially photographs and printed material, for a specific species of bird, you will notice wide variations in color for that bird in the different sources. These color variations are due to many factors, ranging from the time of day a photograph was taken (flat midday light or warm afternoon light) to the accuracy of the printer in reproducing a color. An artist must choose his reference material carefully so he can accurately portray the bird as he perceives it. The following are suggestions for sources of reference material.

Photographs. Most wildlife artists have a 35mm camera and telephoto lens with which to take their own reference photos of birds. Original photos are an excellent source of material; however, they should be used as an aid, not as a crutch. Unfortunately, many artists rely exclusively on photographs that they copy directly. Thus, their paintings are only renderings of photographs—a far cry from original art.

If you don't own or have access to a camera, there are professional photographs and videos of many duck species available (see Art and Carving Suppliers).

Nature Centers, Sanctuaries, and Zoos. All these provide the opportunity to watch live birds, caged and free. Be aware that some of the physical features may be affected by captivity. Caged birds may have tattered wings and broken bills from flying against the cage. Also, some of the birds, especially those at sanctuaries and nature centers, are brought in injured and could have broken wings or other disfigurements that should be taken into account. Some loose yet captive birds are pinioned (wing tip removed) to prevent flight; this means there is only one complete wing. Although this reads like a list of horrors, the birds are well cared for and give an artist the opportunity to closely observe some birds that are very difficult to see in the wild.

Books and Magazines. Both contain art and photographs that may be used for reference; most artists have files of material saved from magazines and other printed sources. There are scores of books on bird art, some of which are good sources of general reference. The rule here is: Don't use another artist's work as the *only* source of reference; if an error was made in the original art, you will just perpetuate it. Only use the art of others in conjunction with other reference material.

Preserved Specimens. Many museums and nature centers have collections of preserved birds, such as study skins, mounted in lifelike poses or frozen, awaiting preparation. If you can gain access to these collections, they are excellent sources of reference material. The anatomical accuracy of mounted specimens can vary greatly, depending on how long the bird has been mounted and the skill of the taxidermist. Again, there are things to remember. As soon as a bird dies, even if it's immediately frozen, it loses, for lack of a better term, its "life force." It becomes smaller as everything collapses, and colors begin to immediately fade, especially in the legs and bill. Most ducks may be hunted legally so they are one of the few bird species where actual specimens are readily available. If you do not hunt ducks, check with taxidermists or friends who hunt. They will probably allow you to sketch and photograph their trophies.

Carvers' Supply Sources. These stores sell feet, bills, and occasionally heads cast from actual duck specimens. Most also carry books, supplies, and photographs. An excellent reference source.

Reference Books

Audubon Society. *Field Guide to North American Birds, Eastern Region.* New York: Alfred A. Knopf, 1977.

———. *Field Guide to North American Birds, Western Region.* New York: Alfred A. Knopf, 1977.

———. *Master Guide to Birding,* 3 vols. New York: Alfred A. Knopf, 1983.

Austin, Oliver L. and Arthur Singer. *Birds of the World.* New York: Golden Press, 1961.

Bellrose, Frank C. *Ducks, Geese and Swans of North America.* Harrisburg, PA: Stackpole Books, 1980.

Burk, Bruce. *Complete Waterfowl Studies,* 3 vols. Exton, PA: Schiffer Publishing, 1984.

Burn, Barbara. *North American Birds.* The National Audubon Society Collection Series. New York: Bonanza Books, 1984.

Carlson, Kenneth L. and Laurence C. Binford. *Birds of Western North America.* New York: Macmillan Publishing, 1974.

Casey, Peter N. *Birds of Canada.* Ontario: Discovery Books, 1984.

Ede, Basil. *Basil Ede's Birds.* New York: Van Nostrand Reinhold, 1981.

Epping, Otto M. and Christine B. Epping. *Eye Size and Eye Color of North American Birds.* Winchester, VA: Privately printed, 1984.

Gromme, Owen J. *Birds of Wisconsin.* Madison: University of Wisconsin Press, 1974.

Holt, T. F. and S. Smith, eds. *The Artist's Manual.* New York: Mayflower Books, 1980.

Hosking, Eric. *Eric Hosking's Birds.* London: Pelham Books, 1979.

Jeklin, Isidor and Donald E. Waite. *The Art of Photographing North American Birds.* British Columbia: Whitecap Books, 1984.

Lansdowne, J. F. *Birds of the West Coast,* 2 vols. Boston: Houghton Mifflin, 1980.

Lansdowne, J. F. with J. A. Livingston. *Birds of the Northern Forest.* Boston: Houghton Mifflin, 1966.

———. *Birds of the Eastern Forest,* 2 vols. Boston: Houghton Mifflin, 1970.

LeMaster, Richard. *The Great Gallery of Ducks.* Chicago: Contemporary Books, 1985.

———. *Waterfowl, the Artist's Guide to Anatomy, Attitude and Color.* Chicago: Contemporary Books, 1983.

Madge, Steve and Hilary Burn. *Waterfowl.* Boston: Houghton Mifflin, 1988.

Perrins, Christopher M. and Alex L. A. Middleton. *The Encyclopedia of Birds.* New York: Facts on File Publications, 1985.

Porter, Eliot. *Birds of North America.* New York: A & W Visual Library by E. P. Dutton.

Robbins, Chandler S. et al. *A Guide to Field Identification—Birds of North America.* New York: Golden Press, 1966.

Saitzyk, Steven L. *Art Hardware.* New York: Watson–Guptill, 1987.

Scott, Shirley L., ed. *Field Guide to the Birds of North America.* Washington, D.C.: National Geographic Society, 1985.

Terres, John K. *The Audubon Society Encyclopedia of North American Birds.* New York: Alfred A. Knopf, 1980.

Tunnicliffe, C. F. *A Sketchbook of Birds.* New York: Holt, Rinehart and Winston, 1979.

———. *Sketches of Bird Life.* London: Victor Gollancz Ltd., 1981.

———. *Tunnicliffe's Birds.* Boston: Little, Brown and Company, 1984.

Art and Carving Suppliers

The list below includes only a few of the many general art suppliers. Most charge a small fee for their catalog.

Dick Blick
Box 1267
Galesburg, IL 61401

Arthur Brown & Bros., Inc.
P.O. Box 7820
Maspeth, NY 11378

Craft Cove
2315 West Glen Avenue
Peoria, IL 61614

Craftwoods
10921 York Road
Hunt Valley, MD 21030

Christian Hummul Co.
404 Brookletts Avenue
P.O. Box 1849
Easton, MD 21601

J. H. Kline
R. D. 2, Forge Hill Road
Manchester, PA 17345

Pearl
308 Canal Street
New York, NY 10013

Daniel Smith, Inc.
4130 1st Avenue South
Seattle, WA 98134

Wildlife Artist Supply Co.
P.O. Box 1330
Loganville, GA 30249

Woodcraft Supply
41 Atlantic Avenue
Woburn, MA 01888

Books: Old and New

Highwood Bookshop
P.O. Box 1246
Traverse City, MI 49685

Patricia Ledlie
P.O. Box 90, Bean Road
Buckfield, ME 04220

Videotapes and Photographs

The Duck Blind
8721-B Gull Road
Richland, MI 49083

Glossary

Acrylic Gesso. An acrylic polymer emulsion that can be either white or gray-black and serves as a ground for acrylic paints. This is not a true gesso as is used in oil painting.

Acrylic Paints. Pigments that are bound together with synthetic resins or polymer emulsions. Water-based, they dry fast and hard and are not water-soluble when dry.

Binder. A substance used to coat and hold pigment in suspension and to bind the pigment particles together when dry.

Blending. Bringing the edges of two colors together and mixing them to form a smooth transition rather than a hard line.

Blends. The combination of synthetic filaments and natural hair in the manufacture of brushes.

Boards. Paperboards of varying thickness that have a drawing, painting, or colored paper adhered to one side. Illustration, watercolor, and mat boards are all paperboards.

Bristle. Stiff, rigid hairs from hogs and pigs, characterized by split ends on each hair.

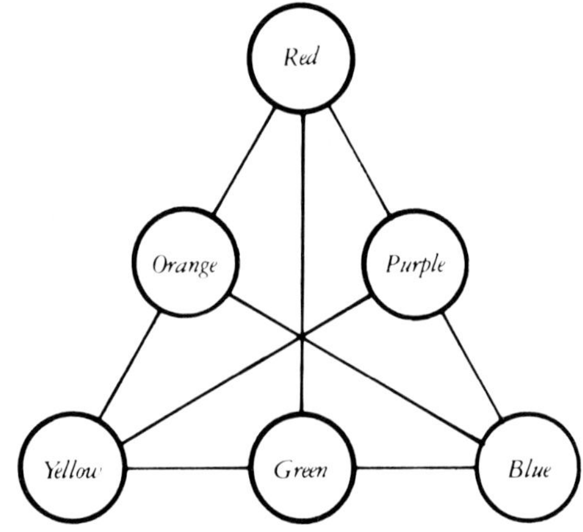

Canvas. A woven fabric used as a painting surface. The two most common fabrics are cotton and linen; they are classified by thread count and ounces per square yard. The finest canvas available is made from Belgian linen.

Complementary Colors. Colors opposite each other on the color wheel that, when mixed together, have a neutralizing or toning-down effect on each other; for example, to tone down a bright yellow add a very small amount of violet. The diagram shows a simple color wheel with the primary colors—red, yellow, blue—and their complementary colors. Orange is the complement of blue, green of red, and violet of yellow.

Consistency of Paint. Refers to the viscosity—the thickness or thinness—of paint.

Designers Colors. See Gouache.

Detailing. Painting fine-line details on a picture or carving.

Dimension. In painting, refers to shading that gives shape, separation, or roundness to a form.

Dry-brush. The technique of painting with very little paint in the brush to produce broken, irregular lines or shapes.

Earth Tones or Colors. Naturally occurring in organic pigments that contain clay or silica, they are processed and produce very permanent colors, such as raw umber, raw sienna.

Ferrule. The metal, plastic, or quill sheath that holds the hairs to the handle of a brush.

Filament. Any synthetic materials used in the manufacture of artificial brush hairs.

Filberts. Flat brushes that have rounded ends.

Finish. Describes the surface texture of a paper or board: hot press has a smooth finish; cold press has a medium finish; and rough has an irregular finish.

Flats. Flat brushes with squared ends.

Flow Release. Synthetic or natural (ox gall) wetting agents that reduce the surface tension of paints, increasing their ability to flow evenly.

Frisket. See Masking.

Fugitive Colors. Colors that are unstable and fade or disappear over time.

Gels. Thickening agents added to paints to increase their impasto effect.

Glazing. Painting a thinned color over a dry base color so that the two mix visually and some of the base color shows through.

Gouache (Opaque Watercolor, Designers Colors). A water-based opaque paint made with pigments, a gum binder, white, and other additives.

Grading. Creating a smooth transition from pure color to clear or no color.

Ground. A painting surface that serves as an absorbent stable base for the paint; for example, acrylic gesso is a ground for acrylic paint.

Gum Arabic. A natural gum from the acacia tree, used as a binder for gouache and transparent watercolor. It also may be added separately to give extra transparency.

Hair. Used in brushes, it is flexible and has a great degree of absorbency. The amount of spring, absorbency, and shape depends upon the type of animal hair used.

Hardboard. A composition wood-fiber board used in the construction industry. In its untempered form it provides a good painting surface when prepared with a ground.

Highlight. To emphasize an area on a painting surface that would catch and reflect intense light.

Impasto. Paint applied thickly to give a three-dimensional quality.

Lifting Off. A subtractive technique of moistening and removing dry paint.

Load. The amount of paint carried in the hairs of a brush. A full load is when the hairs are thoroughly saturated but not dripping.

Masking (Frisket). Blocking out an area with liquid masking or paper to form a barrier that does not allow paint to penetrate its surface.

Matte Finish. A flat, nonglossy finish.

Medium. The material with which an artist works or which, used as an additive, alters the materials.

Oil Paint. Pigments that use oils as binders and require solvents and oils as thinning agents.

Opaque. Refers to a paint able to cover a surface so that light cannot pass through it.

Opaque Watercolor. See Gouache.

Ox Gall. See Flow Release.

Ox Hair. Blunt hair from ox ears. Used in brushes it is dyed red and called sableline.

Palette. Any surface used to hold concentrated paint for paintings. Also the selection of colors used in a particular painting.

Permanence. The degree of light-fastness of a color, the longevity of which depends upon many factors, including ingredients used in manufacturing, light, humidity, pollutants, and so on.

Pigment. Coloring matter derived from natural or synthetic sources. Also used as a synonym for paint or color.

Premixed Colors. Shades of colors mixed by the manufacturer.

Retarder. An additive that slows the drying time of paints.

Round. The most commonly used watercolor-brush shape. The hairs are in a round ferrule and should come to a fine point.

Sable. Hairs in this category are from various members of the weasel family. They are generally characterized by having a fine point, great spring, and strength. Kolinskys are the finest hairs in this group and come from the Asian mink in Siberia.

Sableline. See Ox Hair.

Softening. Lightly brushing along the edge of a hard line to slightly blend it.

Soluble. Capable of being dissolved by a particular substance.

Splitbrush. Fanning the hairs of a brush until they split apart.

Tipping. Touching only the tip of a brush to a surface and lifting or dragging it to produce various marks.

Tone. General coloring of an area.

Tooth. The texture of a surface, whether paper or gesso, that influences how the paint will appear. A smooth surface has less tooth than does a rough surface.

Transfer. The act of transferring or duplicating a drawing from one surface to another.

Transparent. Refers to a paint that allows light to pass through it.

Transparent Watercolor. A water-based paint with a high concentration of finely ground pigments in a gum arabic binder.

Visual Weight. The perceived impact, brightness, and depth of a color.

Wash. The application of paint thinly or transparently; may be a continuous (even) tone, graded, or glazed.

Watercolor Paper. Handmade or machine-made, a variety of fibers are used in its manufacture, including wood pulp, bark, cotton, and combinations of these. The finest papers are made from 100 percent cotton fibers.